博雅 21世纪英语专业系列教材

International Business Correspondence (Fourth Edition)

国际商务英语函电（第四版）

主　编　◎吴　雯
副主编　◎王玮韦　戴浙闽

北京大学出版社
PEKING UNIVERSITY PRESS

图书在版编目(CIP)数据

国际商务英语函电 / 吴雯主编. —4版. —北京：北京大学出版社，2020.10
21世纪英语专业系列教材
ISBN 978-7-301-31657-3

Ⅰ.①国… Ⅱ.①吴… Ⅲ.①国际商务—英语—电报信函—写作—高等学校—教材 Ⅳ.①F740

中国版本图书馆CIP数据核字(2020)第182647号

书　　名	国际商务英语函电（第四版） GUOJI SHANGWU YINGYU HANDIAN (DI-SI BAN)
著作责任者	吴　雯　主编
组稿编辑	刘宗彦　张志国
责任编辑	初艳红
标准书号	ISBN 978-7-301-31657-3
出版发行	北京大学出版社
地　　址	北京市海淀区成府路205号　100871
网　　址	http://www.pup.cn　新浪微博：@北京大学出版社
电子信箱	alicechu2008@126.com
电　　话	邮购部 010-62752015　发行部 010-62750672　编辑部 010-62759634
印刷者	河北滦县鑫华书刊印刷厂
经销者	新华书店
	720毫米×1020毫米　16开本　18.5印张　480千字 2020年10月第4版　2022年4月第2次印刷
定　　价	53.00元

未经许可，不得以任何方式复制或抄袭本书之部分或全部内容。
版权所有，侵权必究
举报电话：010-62752024　电子信箱：fd@pup.pku.edu.cn
图书如有印装质量问题，请与出版部联系，电话：010-62756370

前 言

加入WTO后，随着全球经济的发展和市场化的运作，对商务人才的培养也提出了新的要求。一位优秀的商务人员不仅需要掌握国际上通行的贸易做法和商务程序，有一定的国际商务实际操作经验，而且要具备商务英语沟通能力和函电写作技巧，以适应充满机遇和挑战的时代，成为成功的复合型人才。

本教材的编写正是在上述前提下应运而生。本教材以培养学生商务英语信函写作能力为核心，在内容上将英语语言能力培养和商务知识学习有机地结合起来。在培养学生英语语言能力的同时，注重培养学生动手能力，使学习者在真实的场景下学习专业语言知识，掌握国际商务英语的交际和实战操作技能。

教材编排 本书主要以鞋子为主题商品，教学内容围绕一个案例展开，介绍了产品的分类、公司结构、报价细节等，覆盖了国际贸易一个完整的流程，如询盘、报盘、签订合同等，本书增加了样品与费用的环节，因为该环节是贸易流程中不可缺少的一部分。

全书采用模块教学，包含五大模块十三章。第一模块介绍商务英语信函和电子邮件的基本要素、格式和写作技巧，第二模块为开发客户，第三模块为业务磋商，包含询盘、样品、报盘与还盘，第四模块为合同的执行，包含合同、付款方式、审证、包装、装运、保险与索赔，第五模块为单证样本与实训。全书根据国际贸易进出口流程的主要环节逐一呈现知识点、相关实例与实训，每章由Objectives, Introduction, Writing Tips, Lessons, Exercises, Skill Training, Business Link 和 Useful Sentences 等几个部分组成。每章相互衔接又单独成一个教学环节，更加翔实与生动。

教材内容 教材内容采用公司信函实例，表格形式多，实用性强。(1) 词汇与专业术语：每个环节都收进了业务常用的最新术语与词汇，并分环节对国际贸易语言点进行介绍。例如：OEM, ODM, MOQ, leading time, HQ, TNT, PayPal 等，缩略语如 Pls, ASAP, yr 等。每个环节介绍了相关的专业知识，例如：retailer 境外零售商，包括百货公司、超级商场、商店类与特许经营组织等。（2）信函内容：采用公司业务实例，还原公司的商务操作，如 order inquiry 信函实例，与以往教材重复的内容不同，具备新颖性。单据图片特别是信头、询盘单、报价单与订购单等都是来自公司的实例，有别于以往教材只用几个表格表示的方式，也呈现了新颖性与实用性。

教材练习 本书的练习多样，练习题结合了托业考试的最新题型。此外根据每章的特点有针对性地设计了不同的练习形式。教材练习中的产品名称也以日常使用、学生喜欢的商品为主，如：背包、服装、工艺品和化妆品等。

实训环节 实训内容紧跟业务员的实际操作，形式尽可能多样化，注重单项技能训练与综合能力培养相结合。例如：现在建立业务关系主要是从网络与广交会获取信息，因此在实训中出现了网站建立公司、名片联系业务的练习，使场景更真实。此外合同、信用证也是采用实际案例，特别是按一笔交易展开，审核信用证就是根据前面签订成交的合同审核。

教材排版 以往函电教材一直是以冷冰冰的文字形式出现，与学生缺少互动，与其他教材相比少了趣味性与真实性。而本教材在介绍、课文、练习、实训等内容中穿插了不少图片，加进与商品有关的图片或者是公司的情景，传递重要信息，调动学生学习的积极性。

教学资源 同步提供与教材配套的教学参考书、教学课件。

本书由福建商学院外国语学院吴雯副教授任主编并负责全书的策划和统稿，集美大学王玮韦老师和福建师范大学戴浙闽老师担任副主编，全书共五个模块十三章，具体分工为：吴雯老师负责第一、二、三、五、六章和第十三章，第一至第十章实训及附录一、二的编写，福建工程学院陈宁教授与福建东方星进出口公司的吴伟经理负责第四章的编写，戴浙闽老师负责第七、八、九章的编写，王玮韦老师负责第十、十一、十二章及附录三的编写，吴伟经理提供了询盘单、报价单、估价单和发票等大量的原始单据与素材，并对业务环节进行指导，在此表示感谢。本书中提供的公司信头、询盘表格、包装图片和形式发票等皆为个人资料，不得据为他用，若有侵权，作者将依法追究。

本书可供高等院校商务英语专业和国际经济与贸易专业的学生、国际商务从业人员参考使用，也可作为从事国际贸易工作的专业人士、公司培训的自学参考书。

本教程在2011年8月出版第一版后，获得众多高等院校的青睐与支持，以其典型的电子邮件语言特点、新的教学内容和新的编排方式受到学校教学人员和外经贸从业人员的喜爱，多次重印。2018年随着电子商务和跨境电商的增长，作者意识到有必要体现这部分知识，在教材中增加了RFQ新的语言点和写作要求。从目前来看，本书还是能够满足对外贸易、电子商务和跨境电商这些工作环境的需求。作者将再接再厉，到外贸和跨境电商公司工作学习，有新的发现，也会体现在本书中。也希望广大相关工作人员能对本书提出宝贵的建议和意见，作者会根据这些建议和意见对本书进行相应修改。本书在编写过程中，参考了大量的相关书籍和资料，既有传统教材的优势，又有推陈出新的地方，在此也一并表示感谢。

编者

2020年1月

Contents

Module I Basics for International Business Correspondence

Chapter I Basics for International Business Correspondence 2

   I. An Introduction to the Course ·· 2

   II. Guidelines for Effective Business Correspondence ················· 3

   III. Layout of Business Letters & Emails ······································ 5

   Skill Training ·· 15

   Business Link ··· 16

Module II Establishing Business Relations

Chapter II Establishing Business Relations ···································· 19

   Lesson 1 About Us ·· 21

   Lesson 2 Self-introduction ·· 25

   Lesson 3 (A) A First Inquiry ·· 29

              (B) Reply to the Above ······································· 30

   Skill Training ·· 34

   Business Link ··· 35

   Useful Sentences ··· 36

Module III Business Negotiations

Chapter III Inquiry and Reply 40

   Lesson 4 (A) General Inquiry ·· 42

              (B) Reply to the Above ······································· 43

   Lesson 5 (A) An Order Inquiry ·· 48

              (B) Request for Quotation ··································· 49

   Lesson 6 (A) Status Inquiry ·· 53

              (B) Reply to the Above ······································· 54

   Skill Training ·· 57

Business Link	61
Useful Sentences	61

Chapter IV Samples and Charges … 63

Lesson 7 (A) Asking for Samples	65
(B) Reply to the Above	66
Lesson 8 (A) Refusing to Pay Sample Charges	71
(B) A Reply to the Above	72
Lesson 9 (A) Sending Samples	76
(B) Sending Duplicate Samples	77
Skill Training	80
Business Link	82
Useful Sentences	83

Chapter V Offers and Counter-Offers … 84

Lesson 10 A Firm Offer	86
Lesson 11 (A) A Counter-Offer	91
(B) Reply to the Above	92
Lesson 12 (A) New Price for Repeat Order	96
(B) Reply to the Above	97
Skill Training	100
Business Link	102
Useful Sentences	103

Module IV   Execution of Contracts

Chapter VI Order and Contracts … 106

Lesson 13 A Purchase Order	108
Lesson 14 (A) Partial Acceptance of an Order	113
(B) Reply to the Above	114
Lesson 15 (A) Sending a Sales Confirmation	118
(B) Counter-Signature Letter	119
Skill Training	126
Business Link	134
Useful Sentences	134

Chapter VII   Payment 136

    Lesson 16   (A) Asking for Payment by T/T 140

                   (B) Confirming Payment by T/T 141

    Lesson 17   Declining Payment by 60 Days' L/C 144

    Lesson 18   (A) Asking for Easier Payment 148

                   (B) Reply to the Above 149

    Skill Training 153

    Business Link 156

    Useful Sentences 157

Chapter VIII   Establishment of and Amendment to L/C 159

    Lesson 19   (A) Urging Establishment of L/C 162

                   (B) Confirming L/C Application 163

    Lesson 20   (A) Amendment to L/C 167

                   (B) Reply to the Above 170

    Lesson 21   (A) Asking for Extension of L/C 173

                   (B) Reply to the Above 174

    Skill Training 178

    Business Link 183

    Useful Sentences 184

Chapter IX   Packing & Marking 186

    Lesson 22   Inner Packing & Labeling 189

    Lesson 23   Outer Packing 194

    Lesson 24   Container Loading 200

    Skill Training 203

    Business Link 205

    Useful Sentences 207

Chapter X   Shipment 209

    Lesson 25   (A) Shipping Instructions 211

                   (B) Reply to the Above 212

    Lesson 26   (A) Requesting for Prompt Shipment 216

                   (B) Reply to the Above 217

    Lesson 27   Requesting for Partial Shipment and Transshipment 220

Skill Training ·· 223
Business Link ·· 225
Useful Sentences ·· 227

Chapter XI Insurance ·· 228
Lesson 28   Insurance Information ·· 230
Lesson 29   Asking for CIF Terms ··· 234
Lesson 30   (A) Inquiring for Insurance Rate ·· 238
             (B) Offering Insurance Rate ·· 239
Skill Training ·· 241
Business Link ·· 242
Useful Sentences ·· 244

Chapter XII Complaints, Claims and Settlement ································ 246
Lesson 31   Complaint about Inferior Quality ······································· 248
Lesson 32   Claim on Late Delivery ··· 251
Lesson 33   Settlement of Complaint ·· 255
Skill Training ·· 258
Business Link ·· 260
Useful Sentences ·· 261

Module V Documents

Chapter XIII Specimen of Documents ··· 263
Skill Training ·· 273

Appendix I   国际机构 ··· 283

Appendix II 海外展会 ··· 284

Appendix III 世界各大船公司名录 ··· 286

参考书目 ·· 287

Module I

Basics for International Business Correspondence

Chapter I
Basics for International Business Correspondence

Objectives:
After learning this chapter, hopefully you will have clear ideas about:
1. principles and approaches of writing business letters;
2. the usual structure of business letters and emails;
3. how to edit layouts and arrange the parts of a business letter in good order;
4. some knowledge about products and trade organizations.

❶ An Introduction to the Course

1. What Is Business English?

Business English focuses on vocabulary and topics used in the worlds of business, trade, finance, and international relations. It also refers to the communication skills used in the workplace, and focuses on the language and skills needed for typical business communication such as presentations, negotiations, meetings, small talks, socializing, correspondence, report writing, and so on. People study business English for very practical reasons: to improve their work performance, enhance their prospects for promotion, or in order to find a job.

2. Business English vs. General English

People study English for different purposes. Thus English learning falls into two categories: English for General Purposes (EGP) and English for Specific Purposes (ESP). Business English is a part of ESP and can be considered a specialism within English language learning and teaching. It implies the definition of a specific language corpus and emphasis on particular kinds of communication in specific context, while General English may encompass the broad vocabulary and varieties of styles found in literature and other general reading and in the world of entertainment and the media. Individuals may have interest in the culture; desire to travel or live abroad; a feeling that language skills will be useful or lead to better job prospects.

3. International Business Correspondence in English

International business consists of transactions that are devised and carried out across national borders to satisfy the objectives of individuals and organizations. Correspondence means communication. When people do business at the international level, they need to communicate with each other through letters, faxes, emails, telephones, online chatting tools and some other modern means. Letters have been the principle and traditional channels by business firms to exchange messages for a long time. Emails can be considered the electronic version of the letter. Today email has become a primary source of communication in the workplace. Therefore, this course focuses on writing good business letters in the context of international business. In international trade, a business letter not only serves as a business document, but also provides a permanent record. Successful business letters can facilitate positive and promising business dealings. This course is intended to develop skills of writing good business letter.

II Guidelines for Effective Business Correspondence

1. Writing Approaches for Business English Letters

A business letter is very short, brief and direct. The contents of a business letter usually consist of three or four paragraphs. The general rule is, one point for one paragraph.

The purpose of Business English letters is to deliver messages. Generally speaking, the messages conveyed in the letters can be divided into two categories: good news and bad news. Accordingly, there are two writing approaches for business English letters: direct approach and indirect approach. Direct approach is employed in delivering good news. Indirect approach is used in delivering bad news. In letters of establishing business relations, making inquiries and offer, placing orders and signing a contract, writers tend to adopt a direct approach. The writer will begin with the most important point and work downward. The direct approach gives the reader the sense of immediacy. Usually letters delivering good news contain three paragraphs or even less. The usual steps are opening, purpose and ending or only a paragraph stating the purpose. In business letters with bad news, you have to go through five steps. They are neutral statements as a buffer, reasons, refusal, alternative and an ending. Letters of making counter offer, declining terms of payment or repeat orders and lodging a claim fall into this category.

2. Writing Principles for Business English Letters

To make your writing effective, you may follow some generally accepted principles. Since all these principles begin with the letter "C", they can be summed up as 7Cs, i.e. Clarity, Consideration, Courtesy, Completeness, Conciseness, Concreteness and Correctness.

Clarity is the most important characteristic of good business writing. It means conveying your message to the recipient without being misunderstood. Avoid using ambiguous words or rarely used words. For example: As to the steamer sailing from Hong Kong to San Francisco, we have bimonthly direct services. The word "bimonthly" has two meanings. One is "twice a month", and another is "once every two months". Therefore, we can revise the sentence as follows:

We have a direct sailing from Hong Kong to San Francisco every two months.

We have a direct sailing from Hong Kong to San Francisco semimonthly.

We have two direct sailings from Hong Kong to San Francisco every month.

Consideration means sharing your reader's point of view and keeping your reader's needs in mind. Consideration mainly lies in "you-attitude". Compare the following sentences and you will find sentence b) is better and thoughtful.

  a) *We allow 2% discount for cash payment.*

  b) *You may earn 2% discount if you can pay us cash.*

Avoid using "you-attitude" when conveying bad news. In this situation, you have to handle it tactfully. Instead of saying, "Your letter is not clear at all. I cannot understand it." Just say: "If I understand your letter correctly…"

Courtesy is more than politeness. A good business letter should be positive, friendly, sincere and tactful. "Kindly please send me some pictures of your models." is courtesy and more effective than "We ask for some pictures of your models". Subjunctive mood is often used to give a polite request. Besides, respond to people and give an immediate response will improve courtesy in the communication process because people no longer get frustrated waiting for an answer.

Completeness implies sending complete information to the recipient. Be sure to include all the necessary information so as to avoid the trouble of busy exchange of correspondence which sometimes results in the loss of time and, what is worse, loss of opportunity. As in making an offer, the offer is incomplete if the seller does not include the price or important terms and conditions.

Conciseness is to make your point brief and clear. The message you convey is as short as possible while being complete. To achieve conciseness, the writer should avoid wordy statement and fancy language. Compare the following two pairs of sentences, you will find sentence b) in each pair is concise.

   1. a) *I wish to express my heartfelt gratitude to you for your kind cooperation.*
      b) *Thank you for your cooperation.*
   2. a) *We wish to acknowledge receipt of your letter of May 2 with the check for $200 enclosed and wish to thank you for the same.*
      b) *We appreciate your letter of May 2 and the check for $200 you sent with it.*

Concreteness is to make the message specific, definite and vivid. It is important especially when we write contracts, agreements, notices, advertisements and business letters like inquiries and offers. These materials should be written with specific facts, figures and time. Instead of writing, "This contract will come into effect from Oct. 1," you should say, "This contract will come into effect from and including October 1, 2009." This will avoid disputes and financial losses. Furthermore, expressions such as "prompt", "immediately", "as soon as possible", and the like should not be used in stipulations of time of shipment. If they are used, banks will disregard them.

Correctness refers not only to correct usage of grammar, punctuation and spelling, but also to standard language, proper statement, accurate figures and the correct understanding of commercial jargons. In terms of language, you should make sure that you make no grammatical mistakes. Pay attention to punctuation for it will affect the meaning of the sentence. For example:

Our shop, in Canada, was destroyed by fire.

From this sentence, we know that the writer has only one shop.

Our shop in Canada was destroyed by fire.

Here we know that the writer has more than one shop.

Layout of Business Letters & Emails

1. Layout of Business Letters
(1) The Structure of a Business Letter:

A formal business letter consists of fourteen parts in which seven parts are essential and seven parts are optional. Among all, nine parts are important.

A. Nine Important Parts

1) The letter head

Letter head is often printed on quality paper beforehand. It includes the essential particulars about the writer: the companies' name, postal address and zip-code, telephone and facsimile numbers, websites, etc. You can see examples below:

Sample 1

中国福建國際經濟技術合作公司
CHINA FUJIAN CORPORATION
FOR INTERNATIONAL TECHNO-ECONOMIC COOPERATION
中國福州華林路257號
257, HUALIN ROAD, FUZHOU, CHINA
http://fuzhou09841.114567.com

電話：（0591）87577815
傳真：（0591）87578240
郵編：350013
TEL：（0591）87577815
FAX：（0591）87578240
ZIP：（0591）87578240
Email：11359867@qq.com

Sample 2

Chinapack 中 国 包 装 进 出 口 福 建 公 司
CHINA PACKAGING IMPORT & EXPORT FUJIAN COMPANY
ATTN TO: Tel:（0591）87856078(EXT)
FAX NO.:   Fax:（0591）87856111

Generally, a company is a form of business organization but the precise definition may vary in different situations and in different countries. In China, state-owned enterprises, private companies, joint ventures and corporations are fairly common. In common law countries today, the most commonly addressed forms are corporations (Inc., Co., Corp.), limited companies, limited liability partnerships, limited partnerships, not-for-profit corporations, partnerships, sometimes called "general partnerships" and "sole proprietorships". Following are some examples of names of trade organizations in China:

 China National Cereals, oils & Foodstuffs Imp./Exp. Corp. 中国粮油食品进出口公司

 China National Construction Materials Imp./Exp. Corp. 中国建材进出口公司

 China National Arts & Crafts Imp./Exp. Corp. 中国工艺品进出口公司

 China National Metals & Minerals Imp./Exp. Corp. 中国五金矿产进出口公司

 China National Textiles Imp./Exp. Corp. 中国纺织品进出口公司

 China National Light Industrial Products Imp./Exp. Corp. 中国轻工产品进出口公司

 China National Garments & Costumes Imp./Exp. Corp. 中国服装进出口公司

 China National Petroleum Imp./Exp. Corp. 中国石油进出口公司

 China National Nonferrous Metals Imp./Exp. Corp. 中国有色金属进出口公司

 China National Electric Wires & Cables Imp./Exp. Corp. 中国电线电缆进出口公司

 China National Chemicals Imp./Exp. Corp. 中国化工进出口公司

 China National Complete Plant Imp./Exp. Corp. 中国成套设备进出口公司

 China National Agricultural Machinery Imp./Exp. Corp. 中国农业机械进出口公司

 China National Aero-Technology Imp./Exp. Corp. 中国航空技术进出口公司

 China National Medicines & Health Products Imp./Exp. Corp. 中国医药保健品进出口公司

China Metallurgical Imp./Exp. Corp. 中国冶金进出口公司
China National Foreign Trade Transportation Corporation 中国对外贸易运输公司
China Ocean Shipping Agency 中国外轮代理总公司
China Export Bases Development Corporation 中国出口商品基础建设公司
China Ocean Shipping Company 中国远洋运输公司

2) The date

The date should be placed two or four spaces below the letterhead to the right for indented style or the left for the blocked style. The date should be written in full and not abbreviated. Spell out the name of the month, and do not show the date in figure like 11/9/2007 to avoid confusion. This is because there are two ways in writing the date.

3) The inside address

The inside address usually consists of name of the person to whom the letter is sent, often with a social title and his or her company title, the name of the firms, and the mailing address of the firm. It appears exactly the same way as on the envelope, but not in all capital letters as on the envelope.

4) The salutation

The salutation is the polite greetings with which a letter begins. The customary formal greeting in a business letter is "Dear Sirs" or "Gentlemen". It should be placed two spaces below the inside address.

5) The subject line（optional）

Often useful as a time-saver is the practice of including at the head of a letter a short title announcing the subject-matter. It is often inserted between the salutation and the body of the letter to invite attention to the topic of the letter.

6) The body of the letter

This part carries the actual message of the letter.

7) The complimentary close

The complimentary close is merely a polite way of ending a letter. Just as the use of Dear Sir, etc., is purely conventional, so is the use of Yours faithfully, Yours truly, Cordially yours, and similar expressions. Nowadays, Best regards is customary formal ending.

8) The signature

A letter should be signed by hand, and in ink. Because many hand-written signature are illegible, the name of the signer is usually typed below the signature and followed by his job title or position.

9) The enclosure（optional）

Enclosure is important in a business letter as the recipient will know that samples or pricelists are sent as well. Two line-spacings between the carbon copy notation the writer may indicate one or more enclosures in the letter. Sometimes you may use the abbreviation "Enc."

B. The Optional Parts

10) The references

The references may include a file number, department code or the initial of the signer of the writer. They are marked "Our ref." and "Your ref." to avoid confusion. They may be placed immediately below the letterhead.

11) The attention line

The attention line is used to direct the letter to a specific individual or section of the firm. It generally followed the inside address.

12) The reference notation

The reference notations are made up of the initials of the person who dictates the letter and of the secretary or typist. The initials are usually typed two line-spacing below the signature against the left-hand margin. The two sets are separated by a colon or a slant, with the dictator's coming first. You may capitalize both, or neither, or only the first of the set.

Eg.　HW / JZ　　HW: JZ　　HW: jz　　HW / jz

13) The carbon copy notation

If the copy of the letter is to be sent to a third party, type cc or CC two line-spacing below the signature or immediately below the enclosure at the left-hand margin.

14) The postscript

Try to avoid the use of postscripts as far as possible, since it may suggest the writer failed to plan his letter before he wrote it or dictated it.

The following is designed in indented style to illustrate the position of each part mentioned above.

Chapter I Basics for International Business Correspondence

```
                    Letter head                                    (1)

                                        The references             (10)

                                        Date:_____              (2)


The inside address                                                 (3)


The attention line                                                 (11)


The salutation (Dear Sirs,)                                        (4)


                    Subject line                                   (5)

   Body of the letter (I'm sending you a copy of a letter by internal post that I
received this morning from Brian Rogers of Avalon Industries. He says that the
machine they received had a damaged case and that it did not work when turned
on. What's strange is that last week we received a fax confirming the arrival of the
machine in good condition.)                                        (6)


                                        Complimentary close        (7)
                                             Signature             (8)
                                        Your name and title


The reference notation                                             (12)
The enclosure                                                      (9)
The carbon copy notation                                           (13)
Postscript                                                         (14)
```

(2) Layout of a Business Letter

Basically, two main patterns of layout are in current use—the conventional indented style and the modern blocked style.

A. Indented Style

上海太平洋贸易有限公司
SHANGHAI PACIFIC TRADING CO., LTD.
Add: 108 LAOSHANG ROAD SHANGHAI, CHINA

Tel: 86-021-64875348   Your Ref: JH/nb
Fax: 86-021-64675346   Our Ref: SM/L02-0031
Email: heilight@public.bct.com

                                         Date: September 2, 2002

To:
S. M. Trading Co., Ltd.
403 Jalan Street, Toronto, Canada
ATTN: Mr M. Yasin Marlic

Dear Sirs,

<u>Re: New Design Brown Bear</u>

　　Thank you for your email expressing your interest in our products.

　　We also send a sample under separate cover and we are sure that you will be satisfied with their fine quality.

                          Yours faithfully,
                    SHANGHAI PACIFIC TRADING CO., LTD.
                               刘世元
                            Sales Manager

HW: jz
Encl.
C.C.: our branch office
P.S. The sample will be sent out tomorrow

B. Blocked Style

 中国包装进出口福建公司
CHINA PACKAGING IMPORT & EXPORT FUJIAN COMPANY

ATTN TO: Mr. Hudson   Tel: (0591)7856078(EXT)
FAX NO.: 74829402   Fax: 7856111

Date: September 2, 2002
Wongsheng & Co.
Rm509-511 Tongle Bldg
Shennan Rd, Shenzhen, China
Dear Sirs,

Re: Autumn-2002 Guangzhou Fair

We shall visit your Autumn-2002 Chinese Export Commodities Fair. Kindly let us have the following information:
1. Your Hall Number and Room Number at the fair.
2. Can you furnish us with some sample toys for free distribution?
3. The date on which we will visit your head office in Shanghai.

We await your reply with keen interest.

Yours faithfully,
China Packing Imp./Exp. Fujian Co.

EL/JA.
C.C.J.B. Anderson

(3) Addressing Envelopes

The three important requirements of envelope addressing are accuracy, clearness, and good appearance. Business stationery ordinarily has the return address printed in the upper left corner of the envelope. Name and address of the receiver should be typed above half way down the envelope, leaving enough space for the postmark and stamps. Post notations such as "Registered", "Certified", or "Confidential" should be placed in the bottom left-hand corner.

Example of Envelopes

```
SHANGHAI PACIFIC TRADING CO., LTD.
108 LAOSHANG ROAD
SHANGHAI, China
```

(Stamp)

```
                         Mr M. Yasin Marlic
                         S.M. Trading Co., Ltd.
                         403 Jalan Street,
                         Toronto, Canada
(Registered)
```

2. Layout of Emails

Although in the past people could not even imagine the wonders made by modern electronic and computer technology, these tools are now nearly indispensable in modern offices. The full name of email is "electronic mail". Emails are widely used in modern business circles, refers to computer-based whereby one computer sends a message to another via the Internet. Sending email is relatively cheap, quick and messages can be sent or picked up anywhere in the world and stored in the mailbox until they are retrieved. Emails had become by far the most popular means of communication in business.

(1) Structure of an email

Since an email is an electronic version of letter, it consists of most parts of a letter but in a simpler form. An email usually includes:

Chapter I Basics for International Business Correspondence

Heading The heading is usually made up of the following parts:

To: email address of the recipient

From: email address of the sender (usually automatically filled in)

Subject: main idea of the message

Date: (usually automatically filled in)

Cc: (carbon copy) recipients whom the writer wishes to publicly inform of the message.

Attachment: refers to documents or photos sent with emails

Body The body part is the message of the email. Paragraphs can be blocked or indented. Regardless of format, skip a line between paragraphs.

(2) Example

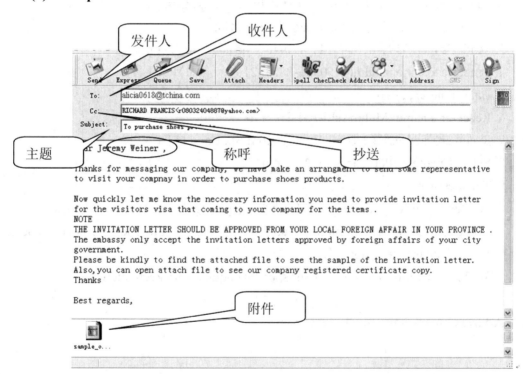

Exercises

I. Write out the following in English.

1. 中国服装进出口公司
2. 中国建材进出口公司
3. ABC 橡胶与塑料产品有限公司
4. 纺织品和皮革制品
5. 礼品及工艺品

II. Arrange the following in proper form as they should be set out in a letter.

1. Sender's name: China National Textile Imp. & Exp. Company
2. Sender's address: 123 Hubin Road, Fuzhou, China
3. Sender's Fax: 0591-87654321, Email: senda@hotmail.com
4. Sender's telephone number: 0591-87543210
5. Date: June 23, 2010
6. Receiver's name: Muhib ULLAH Co., Ltd.
7. Receiver's address: 63 Tunis Hse, Harford St., London E1, 4PR
8. Subject-matter: 5000 dozen Table Cloth
9. The message:

   We thank you for your letter of March 16 enquiring for the captioned goods.

   The enclosed booklet contains details of the Table Cloth and will enable you to make a suitable selection.

   We look forward to receiving your specific enquiry with keen interest.

III. Address an envelope for the above letter.

Chapter I Basics for International Business Correspondence

Skill Training

Exercise I. Establish a company and organize the company.

Divide your class into several groups. Each group forms a company and names the company. Following the Company Organization chart, appoint each member a position responsible for a department. Prepare a presentation about the company and your responsibility.

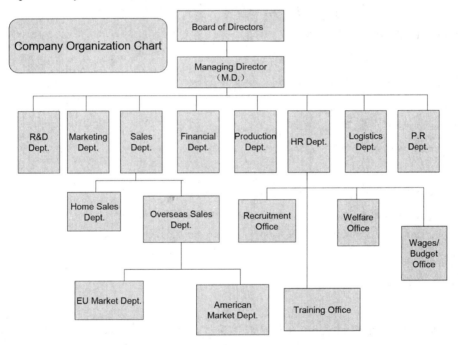

Exercise II. Search alibaba.com and find the categories of products. Click a category and find its related products. Study one of the products and take it as the product of the above formed company.

Business Link

Categories of Products

Apparel 服装
Automobiles & Motorcycles 汽摩及配件
Beauty & Personal Care 美容及个人护理
Chemicals 化学产品
Computer Hardware & Software 计算机硬件和软件
Construction & Real Estate 建筑与房地产
Consumer Electronics 消费类电子产品
Electrical Equipment & Supplies 电气设备及用品
Energy 能源
Fashion Accessories 时尚配饰
Food & Beverage 食品及饮料
Furniture 家具
Gifts & Crafts 礼品及工艺品
Health & Medical 健康与医疗
Home Appliances 家电
Home & Garden 家居与园艺
Lights & Lighting 照明灯
Machinery 机械
Mechanical Parts & Fabrication Services 机械部件及制造服务
Minerals & Metallurgy 冶金矿产
Office & School Supplies 办公室及学校用品
Packaging & Printing 包装印刷
Shoes & Accessories 鞋类及配件
Sports & Entertainment 体育和娱乐
Textiles & Leather Products 纺织品和皮革制品
Toys & Hobbies 玩具及嗜好
Transportation 交通运输
Business Services 商业服务
Electronic Components & Supplies 电子元件及系统
Environment 环境

Excess Inventory 库存过剩
Luggage, Bags & Cases 行李，箱包
Measurement & Analysis Instruments 测量与分析仪器
Rubber & Plastics 橡胶及塑料
Security & Protection 安全和保护
Service Equipment 服务设备
Telecommunications 电讯
Timepieces, Jewelry & Eyewear 钟表、珠宝及眼镜

Module II

Establishing Business Relations

Chapter II
Establishing Business Relations

Objectives:

After learning this chapter, you will

1. be able to get information of foreign firms through different channels;
2. be able to write letters on establishing business relations;
3. be familiar with some business types and trade workers;
4. be familiar with some useful expressions in establishing business relations.

Introduction

As we know, no customers, no business. Therefore, we must try to seek for new connections while consolidating the old ones from time to time. We should, from any sources, get information on foreign firms. Among the usual channels through which we secure necessary information are:

1) Internet
2) Attendance at trade fairs and exhibitions held at home and abroad
3) Banks
4) Commercial Counselor's Office
5) Chambers of Commerce both at home and abroad
6) Trade Directory
7) Advertisements
8) Mutual visits by trade delegations and groups, etc.

Computer and Internet technology change the ways of doing business. People get to know each other from the Internet. Some important websites for doing E-commerce business are listed in Appendix 34. Among them, alibaba.com becomes one of the world's largest marketplaces for global trade. Attendance at trade fairs and exhibitions held at home and abroad are traditional but the most constantly used channels for merchants to approach each other. In Appendix II you may have a general idea of some important fairs and exhibitions. Some companies have fixed booth in Spring Canton Fair, Autumn

Canton Fair and Frankfurt Fair held every year. Commercial Counselor's Office and Chambers of Commerce both at home and abroad aims to operate and promote foreign trade, to introduce advanced foreign technologies, to conduct activities of Sino-foreign economic and technological cooperation in various forms and to promote the development of economic and trade relations between China and other countries and regions around the world. There are some other channels you can get information of a new businessman like middlemen, business houses of the same trade, etc.

Writing Tips

A letter aiming at establishing business relations often consists of the following parts:

1) the source of your information;
2) your intention for export or import;
3) a brief introduction to your business scope, experience and products;
4) the reference as to your firm's credit standing;
5) expectation for cooperation and an early reply.

Lesson 1 About Us

See Our Company Profile

Established in 1995, Fujian Oriental Footwear Imp. & Exp. Co., Ltd. is a professional mould manufacturer and exporter with a registered capital of USD500,000. Covering an area of 20,000 square meters and the display room, we now have more than 500 employees and 10 QC inspectors. We specialize in producing all sorts of EVA sandals and slippers. We accept OEM and  ODM orders. We have acquired ISO9001, SGS, TUV and SEDEX certification. Featuring high quality, novel style and competitive price, our products are selling well in USA, Japan, Europe and Middle East.

Our company integrates research, manufacturing and marketing together and owns first-class equipment. We have set up a Sales Department in our company mainly engaged in establishing business relationships with customers all over the world. Many customers choose to cooperate with us due to our excellent capability of meeting their special requirements.

Our company practices Corporate Social Responsibility and we focus on training our staff with the right corporate values. Over the past seven years, we have taken "Credit first, quality first" as our principle, continuously improving management capacity and productivity. Thus, we have earned our customers' high praise and trust.

We look forward to cooperating with your company. Your detailed inquiries will receive our full attention and rapid replies.

Notes

1. **About us** 公司介绍，常见于网页上，现在公司简介多数是发布在商务网站上，双方可通过简介互相了解公司的整体情况，或者使用搜索引擎搜索。公司简介一般包括以下几个方面：
   1) 公司概况
   2) 公司主要产品
   3) 销售业绩及网络
   4) 公司发展状况
   5) 公司文化

2. **establish** *v.* 创建（业务）等，开立（信用证）等
   Established /Founded in… 成立于……，公司介绍常使用的句型。
   establish business relations 建立业务关系，establish an L/C 开立信用证

3. **manufacturer** *n.* 生产商
   目前按照业务类型（business types）主要分为五种：代理商(agent)、采购办事处(buying office)、分销商/批发商(distributor/wholesaler)、生产商(manufacturer)和贸易公司(trading company)

4. **registered capital** 注册资金

5. **QC: quality controller** QC人员，相当于一般企业中的产品检验员，包括进货检验员（IQC）、制程检验员（IPQC）和最终检验员（FQC）。平常人们也称他们为跟单员。

6. **specialize/expert in** 专营
   We have been specializing in the export of leather products for many years.
   我们已经专营皮革产品出口好多年了。

7. **footwear** 鞋类产品
   种类有：dress shoes 礼服鞋，时装鞋；sports shoes 运动鞋；casual shoes 休闲鞋；sandals 凉鞋；boots 靴子；slippers 拖鞋；flip flop 人字拖；leather shoes 皮鞋等。

8. **OEM and ODM orders** 贴牌加工与设计代工
   OEM（即ORIGINAL EQUIPMENT MANUFACTURER）意为"原始设备制造商"，即贴牌加工。ODM（即ORIGINAL DESIGN MANUFACTURER）意为"原始设计制造商"，即设计代工，代理商或经销商生产自己的品牌。出口商品

中，90%属于代工生产或贴牌生产。
OBM（即ORIGINAL BRAND MANUFACTURER）意为"原始品牌制造商"

9. **certification** *n.* 证明，证明书，保证书

quality certification 质量认证 quality certification system 质量认证制度
certification body 认证机构 certification mark 证明商标；商品标志
professional certification 专业资证 conformity certification 合格认证 china compulsory certification 中国强制认证（3C认证）

10. **be engaged in** 经营

类似的有：handle, trade in, be in the line of, deal in 等
Our company is mainly engaged in the design, production and export of various kinds of shoes.
我公司经营各种鞋的设计、生产与出口。

11. **competitive price** 具有竞争性的价格

attractive price 有吸引力的价格，reasonable price 合理的价格，favorable price 优惠价格

12. **sell well** 畅销

类似的还有：enjoy popularity, find a ready market, meet with a warm reception, be popular, be well received, command a good sale等。

13. **meet one's requirements/needs** 满足……的需求

14. **Corporate Social Responsibility** 企业社会责任

15. **look forward to** 盼望 (结尾常用句)

We look forward to seeing you in the near future.
我们盼望在不久的将来见到你。

I. Translate the following expressions.

A. From English into Chinese.

1. engage in
2. mould manufacturer
3. import and export
4. OEM order
5. establish business relations
6. sell well

B. From Chinese into English.

1. 满足某人的需求
2. 盼望

3. 公司宗旨　　　　　　　　　4. 注册资金

II. Guided translation from Chinese into English.

1. We are informed that _____ (你们是一家雨衣制造商).
2. _____ (成立于1999年), we focus on men's jacket.
3. We are _____ (专营纺织品出口业务).
4. _____ (这些产品在……畅销) in Europe, Japan and South Africa.
5. We are a Sino-US joint venture _____ (注册资金1,000,000美元).
6. We _____ (盼望你们的询盘).

III. Fill in the basic information according to the lesson above.

Company profile	Basic information
Company Name:	
Business Type:	
Product/Service(We Sell):	
Number of Employees:	
Year Established:	
Main Markets:	
Export Percentage:	71%—80%
Factory Size:	
Factory Location:	9/F Minfa, Building No. 88, Dongshui Road, Fuzhou
No. of R&D Staff:	7
No. of QC Staff:	
Contract Manufacturing:	

IV. Search alibaba.com and find out the certificates required for the products transacted.

Products Transacted	Certificates Required	Agencies Recommended
machine tools		
green tea		

Lesson 2　Self-introduction

From: alicia0618@tchina.com
To: jdeal@paemaesales.com
Date: 15 Aug., 2018 9:30
Subject: establishing business relations
Attachment: catalogue

Dear Sirs,

We obtain your name and address from the Chamber of Commerce in Beijing and learn that you are in the market for Footwear. We are seeking the possibilities to build business relations with you.

We are an experienced joint venture specializing in producing a wide range of slippers under Dizzy brand. Most of our products are exported to American and European markets. Being in this line for more than 25 years, we are proud that we can comfortably meet our customers' demand.

In order to acquaint you with our business lines, we are enclosing a copy of our latest electronic catalog, in which we list the fast sale items with best price for your examination. The fashion slippers on Page 2-3 combine Western fashion elements with our design concepts to develop simple, beautiful, graceful shoes to enhance wearers' charm. We have a good variety of colors and sizes to meet different needs. For more information, please view our website as below.

We are looking forward to your inquiries.

Best regards,
Alicia Wu
Fujian Oriental Footwear Imp. & Exp. Co., Ltd.
Tel:86-0591-12345678
Fax:86-0591- 12345678
Email:alicia0618@tchina.com
Website:http://www.orientalfootwear.com

1. Self-introduction letter
这是写给进口商的一封建交函，信函的公司介绍与About us略有不同。除了介绍一些基本的情况，还应选取一些对客户有意义的优势，如介绍经营范围、新产品等。

2. obtain from 从……获悉
这是建交函中常见的开头句，指明信息来源，目的是为了避免唐突和冒昧。
类似的表达法有：
We are indebted to…for your name and address.
We come to know the name and address of your firm through…
Through the courtesy of … we come to know your name and address.
We owe your name and address to…

3. Chamber of Commerce 商会

4. be in the market 要买或卖
We are in the market for Groundnuts. 我们想要购买花生仁。
　Pls advise us when you are in the market. 需要购买(出售)请通知我们。

5. joint venture 合资企业
公司类型有：私营企业（private company），国有企业（state-owned corporation），股份公司（stock corporation），上市公司（public/listed company）等。

6. acquaint … with 使熟悉，使了解
You will have to acquaint us with the details. 你们必须让我们了解详情。
We are well acquainted with the market conditions in Southeast Asia.
我们对东南亚市场很了解。

7. enclose *v.* 附上
　under separate cover 另邮；另函
也可以说by separate mail，如附在信里则用enclose（随函）。

8. latest catalogue 最新的目录

9. combine…with 与……结合
We mainly supply Chinese clothing which combines tradition with modern fashion.
我们生产的中国服装将传统与现代融为一体。
Chanel models combine elegant style with sublime designs.
香奈儿模特展示了优雅的款式与高级设计。

Chapter II Establishing Business Relations

10. as below/as follows/as attached 如下

Referring to your inquiry of November 20, we have quoted as below.

依据您11月20日的询问函，我们报价如下。

I. Translate the following expressions.

A. From English into Chinese.

1. be in the market for
2. private company
3. under separate cover
4. ODM order
5. fast sale items
6. latest catalogue

B. From Chinese into English.

1. 国有公司
2. 多种多样
3. 商会
4. 供你们参考

II. Fill in the blanks in their proper forms.

Dear Sirs,

We get your name and address from internet. We _____

               1. (A) deal

                 (B) specialize in

                 (C) trade

                 (D) handle in

exporting arts and crafts and have satisfied customers and friends throughout the world. We shall be very much _____ to become your good partner in the near

             2. (A) pleasing

                 (B) pleased

                 (C) pleasant

                 (D) pleasure

future.

We would like to send you some latest models and new offers for your reference. Please find the details as _____.

        3. (A) belowing

            (B) followed

            (C) attaching

            (D) attached.

We welcome your inquiries. Please visit our official website at http://www.orientfootwear.com. cn.

If you need more information, please feel free to _____ us.

        4. (A) contact with

            (B) contact

            (C) contacting

            (D) contacting with

We appreciate your comments and looking forward to _____ together with

        5. (A) work

            (B) worked

            (C) being worked

            (D) working

you soon.

Best regards,

Jessy

III. Put the following into English.

1. 现借此机会向贵公司介绍，我们是外资企业，专门经营工艺品。

2. 我们想熟悉一下钢材的供应情况。

3. 我们随函附上一份价目表。

4. 我们公司在全球有28个分销商。

5. 我们是中国轻工产品的主要出口商之一，愿与你公司建立业务关系。

IV. Translate the self-introduction sentences in Useful Sentences in Chapter II.

Lesson 3

(A) A First Inquiry

From: 9768523137@hotmail.com
To: alicia0618@tchina.com
Date: 20 Aug., 2018
Subject: inquire about slippers

Gentlemen:

We understand from your information posted on Alibaba.com that you are a leading supplier of footwear.

We are a large retailer in Italy, having many years' experience and extensive connections. Actually we are JCP Penny traders. Now we are interested in indoor slippers, axidos and sport sandals and hope you would kindly send us a detailed pricelist and pictures of the latest models we can choose from. They have to be in size 36/45 as Europe is our main market.

Hoping to hear from you soon.

Best regards,
Jeremy Weiner
Purchasing Corporate Development Manager
AL ABRA SUB TRADING EST.
Mobile No: 12345678910
Jeremy Weiner@hotmail.com

(B) Reply to the Above

From: alicia0618@tchina.com
To: 9768523137@hotmail.com
Sent: 22 Aug., 2018 10:07 AM
Subject: Reply & Canton Fair
Attachment: pricelist & booth location

Dear Jeremy Weiner,

Thank you very much for your kind inquiry to us. This is Alicia, sales representative of Fujian Oriental Footwear Imp. & Exp. Corp. Thanks to Michael's assignment, I am pleased to have the opportunity to contact you and take charge of our cases directly. From now on, I will help to follow up your orders and offer best sales service with my professional experience.

I hereby send you some photos of our products for your reference. The pictures of models and the pricelist are all in the attachment. Should any of the items be of interest to you, please let us know.

Meanwhile, we will also exhibit in Canton Fair. We sincerely invite you to attend the coming 124th Canton Fair, the booth No. is 7.4H03. Full collections for all the latest styles will be presented on our booth.

  Exhibitor Name: Fujian Oriental Footwear Imp. & Exp. Corp.
  Address: Pazhou Exhibition Centre, Guangzhou
  Time: Oct. 15th—Oct. 20th, 2018
  Booth No: 7.4H03.

We look forward to your visiting and dissussing business in detail.

Best regards,
Alicia Wu
Fujian Oriental Footwear Imp. & Exp. Company
Tel:86-0591-12345678   Fax:86-0591-12345678
Email:alicia0618@tchina.com   Website:http://www.orientalfootwear.com

Chapter II Establishing Business Relations

1. **inquiry** (英：enquiry) *n.* 询价，询购，询盘

   They sent us an enquiry for our "Cool" Brand Air Conditioner.

   他们来信询购我"凉爽"牌空调。

   inquire (或enquire) *v.* 询购，询问

   We are writing you to inquire the current price of gloves of high quality.

   我们特写信询问有关高质量手套的时价。

2. **retailer** *n.* 零售商，包括百货公司、超级市场、商店类、购物中心、会员制营销等。

   境外贸易商主要有中间商broker，批发商wholesaler，零售商retailer和分销商distributor等

   类似的词汇还有： supplier 供货商， dealer 经销商

3. **connections** 业务联系，客户，生意合伙人

   The company has wide connections in North America. 该公司在北美有着广泛的业务联系。

4. **JC Penny** 彭尼公司

   JC Penney Company, Inc. (known as JC Penney) is an American department store chain with 1095 locations in 49 U.S. states and Puerto Rico. In addition to selling conventional merchandise, JC Penney stores often house several leased departments such as Sephora, Seattle's Best Coffee, salons, optical centers, portrait studios, and jewelry repair.

5. **axido** *n.* 沙滩鞋

6. **kindly** *adv.* 商业信函中表示请求的礼貌用词

   Kindly contact us for details of our requirement.

   请联系我们了解我们所需。（买方询盘中用语）

   Kindly inform me so that all necessary arrangements can be made.

   请通知我以便能做好一切必要的安排。

7. **Canton Fair** The Canton Fair is a trade fair held in the spring and autumn seasons each year since the spring of 1957 in Guangzhou, China. Its full name since 2007 has been China Import and Export Commodities Fair (中国进出口商品交易会), renamed from Chinese Export Commodities Fair (中国出口商品交易会), also known as The Canton Fair (广交会). Regarded as the largest scale, the highest level, Canton Fair presents the most comprehensive exhibition covering the widest range of industries and sectors, as well

as the richest products and commodities. Usually Canton Fair will be divided into three phases according to different industries and sectors, There are many similarly themed trade shows held in the world, which gather a large number of buyers for sourcing products, such as ISPO, GDS, etc.

8. attachment *n.* 附件

attach *v.* 附上

Attached is the label for your translation.

附上标签请翻译。

9. be of interest to 使感兴趣（主语为商品）

This article is of special interest to us.

我们对这个商品特别感兴趣。

10. exhibit *v.* 参展

exhibitor *n.* 参展商，相对应的是采购商：buyer

11. assignment *n.* 分配；任务 (公司领导把获得的客户资料分给业务员，业务员运用自己的方式联系客户)

12. follow up this case/ order 跟单

order follow up 跟单，sample follow up 跟样

I. Translate the following expressions.

　　A. From English into Chinese.

　　1. distributor　　　　　　2. exhibitor

　　3. APEC　　　　　　　　4. broker

　　5. wholesaler　　　　　　6. booth No.

　　B. From Chinese into English.

　　1. 商品交易会　　　　　　2. 单证员

　　3. 销售代表　　　　　　　4. 货代员

II. Put the following into English.

　　1. 我们是从企业同业名录里得知你方公司的名称和地址。

　　2. 我有两年以上跟单和船务经验。

　　3. 我们有在英国热销的运动鞋款式的图片。

4. 已另邮一些样品和小册子供你方参考。

5. 我们对你方目录里的电器用品感兴趣，请寄报价表来。

6. 我们特此通知你们，我们的新产品在16号展台展出。

III. Writing practice.

Directions: Read the email
From: The Splenia International Co. To: Fujian Oriental Footwear Imp. & Exp. Co., Ltd. Subject: Product Information Sent: July 23, 4:32 P.M. Dear Water, We are currently looking to expand our product line including memory foam mattresses and pillows. I will come to China next month. In the meantime, I would like to collect as much information as possible on prices and specifications. Please advise us at your earliest convenience. Best regards, Michael

Directions: Respond to the email above. Respond as if you were the salesman from Fujian Oriental Footwear Imp. & Exp. Co., Ltd.
(Type your response here)

Skill Training

Exercise I. Draft a letter to a company asking for establishing business relations.

On April 4, 2013 at the Canton Fair, Chen Xiuqin, the sales representative from Fujian Hengde Co., Ltd. met Thomas Sturm, a senior buyer from a German company and learned he was interested in RUCKSACK (CANVAS & NYLON BAGS). They got name cards exchanged at the Fair and agreed to contact each other later. Following are the name cards:

> 福建恒德进出口股份有限公司
> Fujian Hengde Co., Ltd.
>   陈秀琴 Chen Xiu Qin
>
> 福建省福州市五四路119号福祥大厦18楼
> F.18 FuXiang DaSha, No.119 Wusi Road, Fuzhou
> Tel: 0591-87218878 Fax: 0591-87218888
> Email: hengde@hotmail.com

> STURM HANDELS GMBH
> THOMAS STURM
> Address: D-72108 ROTTENBURG. GARTENSTR. 88 GERMANY
> Tel: 07472-16088
> Fax: (49) 7472-160809
> Email: Wendy@STURM.com

Suppose you are Chen Xiuqin, the sales representative from Fujian Hengde Co., Ltd., write an email attaching a pricelist to Thomas Sturm to establish business relations after returning home from the Fair.

Exercise II. Write an email to introduce your factory or your company and your products according to the following information.

Company Name: Qingdao Fengyue Textiles Co., Ltd.

Business Type: Manufacture & Trade
Main Category: Apparel, Dresses
Main Products: Apparel, fabric, uniform, children's garments, beach shorts
Year Established: 2001

Business Link

I. E-commerce Websites

中国商品网	http://ccn.mofcom.gov.cn	阿里巴巴网	www.alibaba.com
全球资源网	www.globalsources.com	欧洲黄页	www.europages.com
美国进出口网	www.usaexportimport.com	美国出口登记	www.aernet.com
阿根廷贸易线索在线	www.tradeline.com.ar	比利时及卢森堡出口网	www.belgiumexports.com
巴西商务网	www.brazilbiz.com.br	加拿大出口网	www.exportingcanadaonline.com
捷克经济网	www.economy.ez	邓白氏商业资料查询	http://www.dnb.com
埃及贸易指南	www.egtrade.com	托马斯美国厂商名录	www.thomasregional.com
德国商业链接网	www.businesslink.com	科法斯企业评估网	http://www.cofacerating.com
印度市场	www.indiamart.com	前往希腊	www.gogreece.com
美国—以色列商务网络	www.std.com	意大利买主	http://anibo.com
意大利工业贸易世界	www.italyindustry.com	中华人民共和国商务部	http://www.mofcom.gov.cn
韩国商业广场	www.bizkorea.com	墨西哥信息中心	www.mexico-trade.com
马来西亚产品	www.malaysiaproduct.com	网上俄罗斯	www.citilink.ru
葡萄牙商务网	www.portugaloffer.com	西班牙产业网	www.spaindustry.com
瑞士信息网	www.swissinfo.com	泰国贸易网	www.thaitrading.com
土耳其出口网	www.turkex.com	到迪拜去	www.godubai.com

II. Types of Traders and Foreign Trade Workers

importer 进口商

exporter 出口商

traders 贸易商，境外贸易商主要有中间商、批发商、零售商和分销商等

import middlemen 进口中间商，可分为进口商、佣金商、进口经销商与进口代理商

wholesalers 进口批发商，可分为综合批发商与专业批发商

retailer 境外零售商，包括百货公司、超级商场、商店类与特许经营组织等

distributor 分销商

senior buyer 高级采购商

exhibitor 参展商

documentary handler /merchandiser /documentary clerk 跟单员

deal officer, merchant, sales coordinator, businessperson 外贸业务员

documentation officer 单证员

forwarding agent, forwarder 货运代理、承运商、货代员

customs declarer 报关员

customs broker 报关代理

sales assistant 销售助理

sales supervisor 销售监管

general company, head office, national corporation 总公司

board of directors, the board 董事会

finance department, general accounting department 财务部

products development department 产品开发部

sales department, marketing department 销售部

human resources department 人事部

research and development department, R&D department 研发部

Useful Sentences

I. Opening sentences

1. Having had your name and address from the Commercial Counselor's office of the Embassy of the People's Republic of China in…, we now avail ourselves of this opportunity to write to you and see if we can establish business relations by a start of

some practical transactions.
2. As your name and address were listed in the *International Business Daily*, we are writing in the hope of opening an account with your company.
3. Your name has been recommended to us by the Chinese Consul stationed in your city as large exporters of … goods produced in…
4. We have seen the introduction of your products in the local newspaper.
5. We learn from… that your firm specializes in…, and would like to establish business relationship with you.
6. Through the courtesy of…we have learned that you are one of the representative importers of…
7. Your name and address has been given to us by Messrs. J. Smith & Co., Inc., in New York, who have informed us that your firm has been recommended to us by the Chamber of Commerce in Tokyo, Japan.
8. We are given to understand that you are potential buyers of Chinese…, which comes within the frame of our business activities.

II. Self introduction

1. Founded in 1995, ABC Co., Ltd. is a national Hi-tech enterprise in aerosol industry.
2. We are the renowned Exporters based in Kerala, India, specializing in manufacturing and supplying all kinds of textile floor coverings. Being in this trade more than 20 years we are proud that we can comfortably meet any customers' demand. We listed below the categories we are mainly dealing: PRODUCT INFORMATIONS1. Coir DOOR MAT / HOLLANDER MAT-Fancy Designs (100% Coir material available in different designs and sizes, std. Size 45×75, 40×70, 40×60 cms.).
3. Multi-Grace Projects and Services Limited is a proudly Nigerian company registered to carry out business in importation, trading and supplies of consumer home appliances. With active trading in the last one year, our business has been able to achieve a great feat in the little time of operation.
4. Every year, we develop more than 2500 new designs by professional designers. With novel design, reasonable price, good quality, prompt delivery, all products are exported to America, Europe, Southeast Asia, Middle East and some countries such as Australia, Japan, and have enjoyed great reputation from customers.
5. Located in Longqiao Industrial Zone, Longmen, Anxi, Fujian Province of China, Anxi Lifeng Handicrafts Co., Ltd. Quanzhou is a leading manufacturer specialized in

producing small K/D wooden furniture, products, gift items and wooden crafts.

6. With an area of over 200,000 square meters, beautiful environment, standard plants, advanced manufacturing equipment, and a group of senior engineers, Nanxing has established a complete system of scientific research, design, manufacture, sale and service.

7. We are one of the leading importers and wholesalers of various light industrial products in London, having a business background of some 40 years, and are now particularly interested in Industrial Products of all types.

Module III

Business Negotiations

Chapter III
Inquiry and Reply

Objectives:

After learning this chapter, you will

1. be familiar with some useful expressions in making inquiries;
2. be familiar with writing steps in making inquires;
3. be able to know basic points of inquiries;
4. be able to write letters on business inquiries and status inquiries.

Introduction

In international business, inquiries fall into two categories: business inquiries and status inquiries.

Business inquiries are usually made by buyers without engagement to obtain information about the goods to be ordered. They could be divided into general inquiries and specific inquiries in terms of the contents. In a general enquiry, the importer may only ask for the basic information, such as a price and conditions of sales, and asks for a catalogue, a pricelist, a sample, or some other reference materials from the exporter. If both parties have never dealt with each other before, then the importer will inform the exporter of the source of his information at the beginning of his letter. Details of his own company and / or business will also be included. The letter as such is known as a "First Enquiry". The importer who sends a specific enquiry may require information as to price, specifications, discount, quantity, terms of payment, date of shipment, etc. regarding some definite goods in addition to reference materials. But in practice, a specific inquiry is often referred to as an order inquiry

Status inquiries are usually conducted at the beginning of establishing business relations. They are letters at the beginning of establishing business relations or executing orders, and letters asking for information about the financial position, credit, reputation, and business methods of the prospective business partners. The main sources from which such information could be obtained are as follows:

Chapter III Inquiry and Reply

1. Bank
2. The Economic and Commercial Counsellor's office of our Embassy in Foreign Countries
3. Chambers of Commerce
4. Professional inquiry agencies such as SINOSURE (中信保)
5. Another company that has business with the new company

Writing Tips

A general inquiry usually includes products interested, asking for general information, catalogue and pricelist, wishes for relationships, etc.

A specific inquiry should include the following: specific products interested, asking for such details as quantities, color, size, price, package, leading time, and terms of payment. Also wishes for relationships are put at the end of letters.

Letters of status inquiries are more or less stereotyped. They usually begin with the request or inquiry, followed by a brief clarification, and then end with a promise to keep the information provided secret. Some large firms even make their status inquiries on specially printed forms containing the questions they would like to have answered. They are generally headed "Confidential" or "Private and Confidential", which is also written on the envelope.

Lesson 4

(A) General Inquiry

From: Jeremy Weiner @hotmail.com
To: alicia0618@tchina.com
Date: 5 November, 2018 11:49
Subject: Slipper & Flip Flop

Dear Alicia,

I am the purchasing manager from AL ABRA SUB TRADING EST. We have met each other in last Canton Fair. Thank you very much for your hospitality in your booth at the Canton Fair 2018.

We are looking to produce for Spring 2019 for our European market. We would be interested in producing flip flop slippers similar to the "Men Slipper" TRF081142 (focusing on smaller boys' sizes). However, I do not like the "frills" on the strap. Do you have a model that is simpler? We would add our brand to the foot strap. We should not have a problem meeting minimums. Can you give me an estimate on how much 5,000 units would cost (US$)? I estimate that our first order will run about 5,000 pairs and future orders will be significantly larger. Can you send samples to our Catania offices?

If you need more objective information concerning our credit, please refer to the Banca Monte Dei Paschi Di Siena S.P.A.

We are looking forward to your reply.

Best regards,
Jeremy Weiner
Corporate Development Manager
AL ABRA SUB TRADING EST.
Jeremy Weiner @hotmail.com

(B) Reply to the Above

From: alicia0618@tchina.com
To: Jeremy Weiner @hotmail.com
Sent: November 8, 2018 10:07 AM
Subject: Flip Flop

Dear Jeremy Weiner,

Thank you very much for your kind inquiry to us.

Regarding flip flop similar to "Men Slipper", the price for you is as below:

"Men Slipper" TRF081142   USD0.80 /pair FOB Fuzhou

And the packing charges are not included in the above price.

The price we give you is on the basis of MOQ 7000pcs for each color. If your order reaches a certain amount, the cost of making molds can be offset. We can give you a special discount of 2% for quantities over 1,4000 pairs.

We can change the "frills" on the strap. We have rich experience in making OEM slippers. You can send your logo and detailed requirements to us. All sizes and different designs are welcome.

The price can be various if the quality is different. If you have different opinions or target price, please don't hesitate to contact me. I sincerely hope we can have a chance to open an account soon.

Regarding samples, we are arranging now. I will confirm you when we send out. Normally we need 5 days to send out a new sample.

Best regards,
Alicia
China Oriental Footwear Import & Export Corp.

Notes

1. hospitality *n.* 盛情，热情款待

2. look for/to 找寻……（询盘常用句子）
We look to buy alarm clock. 我们要购买闹钟。
I am looking for a supplier for solar energy products. 我在寻找太阳能产品的供应商。

3. estimate *n./v.* 估计；估价
I will give you an estimate on the amount of time it will take to complete this job.
我会告诉你完成这份工作预计所需的时间。

4. order *n./v.* 订单；订购
regular order 定期订单, trial order 试订单, first/initial order 首次订单
place an order with sb. 向某人订购

5. significantly *adv.* 显著地，大大地

6. Banca Monte Dei Paschi Di Siena S.p.A. 意大利西雅那银行
Founded in 1472, it is the oldest surviving bank in the world and the third largest Italian commercial and retail bank by total assets. According to the announcements of BMPS and Banco BPM, Banco BPM overtook BMPS as the third largest bank in terms of total assets on 31 December, 2016.

7. refer to *vt.* 咨询，提交，查阅，参阅，转给 *vi.* 谈到，谈谈，提到
We refer you to our bank for our financial standing.
请你们向我们的银行了解我们的资信状况。
We refer you to our letter of March 15.
请你们参阅我方3月15日信函。
The matter of difference shall be referred to arbitration.
不同意见将提交仲裁。
Your enquiry for watches has been referred to us for attention.
你方对手表的询价已经转交给我们办理。

8. regarding *prep.* 关于
商品是商务英语信函传递的信息，是主要话题。因此突出商品功能的这类连词比其他不同类型语篇的明显要多，其他的还有 as regards, with reference to, covering 和 concerning 等。
We have already written to you regarding this matter.
关于此事我们已写信答复。

Chapter III Inquiry and Reply

9. charge *n.* 费用

10. on the basis of 在……基础上

It is our foreign trade policy to trade with foreign countries on the basis of equality and mutual benefit.

我们的外贸政策是在平等互利的基础上与各国人民做贸易。

11. MOQ =minimum order quantity 即最小订购量，起订量（最小订单量）

后面跟具体的数量，一般公司都会规定最小订单量，达到这个量才可以卖。

12. offset *vt.* 补偿；抵消

He has to offset his small salary by living economically.

他薪水微薄，不得不节俭度日。

13. discount *n.* 折扣

We may offer 2% trade discount only for the order this week.

我们仅对本周订单提供2%的折扣。

14. brand *n.* 品牌

15. logo *n.* 徽标；商标

16. open an account 开立账户

公司之间开立账户，意味着双方建立贸易关系，即 enter into business relations/ establish relations。

17. confirm *v.* 证实，确认

His letter confirmed everything. 他的信证实了一切。

We confirm having agreed on the following points. 兹确认双方就下列各点达成协议。

I. Translate the following expressions.

   A. From English into Chinese.

    1. special discount   2. objective information

    3. logo   4. MOQ

    5. open an account   6. on the basis of

   B. From Chinese into English.

    1. 数量折扣   2. 订购

    3. 查阅   4. 首次订单

II. Choose the best answer.

1. If you can supply this article, kindly _____ me a detailed price list.
   A. sending   B. sent   C. to send   D. send

2. We are a corporation, _____ both the import and export of textiles.
   A. handling in B. trading   C. specializing D. dealing in

3. If your price is reasonable, we shall _____ an order _____ you.
   A. place/with   B. make/from   C. have/with   D. take/for

4. We confirm _____ your inquiry of June 15.
   A. to receive   B. received   C. having received D. receive

5. We have been importers _____ foodstuffs for many years.
   A. to   B. of   C. for   D. on

6. One of our clients _____ Chinese black tea.
   A. in the market for   B. are in the market for
   C. is in the market for   D. be in the market for

7. Please refer _____ the pricelist enclosed.
   A. to   B. with   C. for   D. on

8. Please let us have a copy of your pricelist so that we may acquaint ourselves _____ your products.
   A. to   B. with   C. for   D. in

9. We are a Germany (Berlin) _____ company looking for a long term partner.
   A. based in   B. on the basis of C. based   D. based on

10. _____ your information, we are giving the details you ask for.
    A. To   B. With   C. For   D. On

11. The email we received yesterday is an inquiry _____ discounts.
    A. for   B. after   C. before   D. unless

12. Our products are displayed in Stand B22, _____ you will find me during office hours.
    A. when   B. which   C. that   D. where

III. Put the following into English.

1. 我们在寻找能够供应手提电脑的可靠厂家。
2. 我们想购买电脑配件，请寄最小订单量的详细价目表并告知运费。
3. 关于所附的这种型号，我们的目标价位是每台 9.5 美元。
4. 订购量超过 1000 件，可允许给予 3% 的折扣。
5. 至于我们的信用情况，请向中国银行上海分行咨询。

IV. An inquiry exercise.

You work for a German company that sells laptops—Kurt Schiller Gmbh, Freidenstrasse 44, Hamburg, Germany. You are interested in importing computer parts & laptops from China. After examining the catalog sent by Moly (the seller), you find some products interesting. Write an inquiry for Mr. Johann Schmidt, the sales manager. Inquire for price, time of delivery, etc.

V. Translate sentences 1—10 in Useful Sentences in Chapter III.

Lesson 5

(A) An Order Inquiry

From: Jeremy Weiner @hotmail.com
To: alicia0618@tchina.com
Sent: November 12, 2018
Subject: Flip Flop
Attachment: sketch+size spec

Dear Alicia,

Attached sketch+size spec (4 pages) for yr price quotation, details as below (no sample can be sent at this moment):
 -Style: Flip Flops
 -Material: EVA
 -Upper Material: EVA
 -Outsole Material: EVA
 -Model Number: HC13097, HC808B301
 -Color: navy blue, black
 -Size range: 35/41

Other details pls refer to sketch details sheet.
 -Quantity: HC13097: 950CTNS/22800PRS
 HC808B301: 350CTNS/8400PRS
 -Delivery date: before Jan.15, 2019 ETD
 -Payment terms: L/C 60 days
 -Final inspection will be taken by our customer and must be using OOCL shipping agent in Xiamen.

Pls urgently quote your best price in USD FOB + Commission 2% Fuzhou, flat packed in carton, Azo free and Nickel Free.

Need your reply by tomorrow morning, thanks.

B. rgds / Jeremy

(B) Request for Quotation

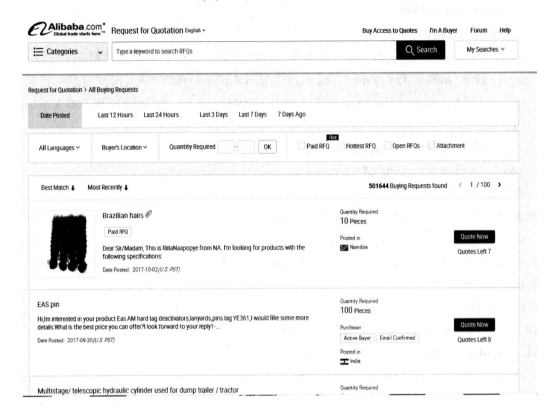

1. **Order Inquiry** 客户询盘，买方详细地说明订购产品所要求的材料、型号、颜色、尺寸等，要求卖方综合细节进行报价。一般在客户下 Purchase Order 之前，都会有相关的 Order Inquiry 给业务部，以便做一些细节上的了解。
2. **sketch** 草图
3. **spec** 为 specification 的缩写， **Size Spec/Spec sheet** 尺寸表
   在电子邮件中还流行使用一些由首字母或读音组成的缩略词，如：yr: your; pls: please; ASAP: as soon as possible; PCS: pieces; CTN: carton; ETD: estimated time of delivery; PRS: pairs。
4. **quote** v. 报价

Please quote us the lowest price for Printed Shirting.
请报印花细布的最低价。

quotation *n.* 报价

quotation 后可接 for 或 on; 若买方提到卖方已对某货作出的报价时，可用 of。

send / give / make / fax / email sb. a quotation for / on sth. 向某人报某商品的价格

We should be obliged if you would give us a quotation for the supply of 200 Kitchen Cupboards.
如能向我方报200个橱柜的价格，我们将不胜感激。

Your quotation of Sewing Machines is too high to be acceptable.
你方缝纫机的报价太高，不能接受。

5. **sample** *n.* 样品，这里指买方提供的样品。

6. **upper material** 鞋帮材料 outsole material 大底材料

7. **navy blue** 海军蓝，其他颜色还有：beige 米色，bone 骨色，camel 驼色等。

8. **delivery date** 交货期

9. **payment terms** 付款方式，分三种：信用证、托收和汇付。

10. **L/C 60 days** 60天的远期信用证，即期信用证为 L/C at sight。

11. **Orient Overseas Container Line (OOCL)** 东方海外

Orient Overseas Container Line Limited ("OOCLL") and OOCL (Europe) Limited are wholly-owned subsidiaries of Orient Overseas (International) Limited, a public company (0316) listed on the Hong Kong Stock Exchange. OOCL is one of the world's largest integrated international container transportation, logistics and terminal companies. As one of Hong Kong's most recognized global brands, OOCL provides customers with fully-integrated logistics and containerized transportation services.

12. **shipping agent** 海运代理，货代

13. **FOB** 全文是 Free On Board，即船上交货(指定装运港)，习惯称为装运港船上交货。
    另两个常用的是 CIF: Cost, Insurance and Freight 与 CFR: Cost and Freight。

14. **commission** *n.* 佣金，指买卖中付给中间人的报酬。

The above price includes your commission of 2%.
以上价格包括了你方百分之二的佣金。

There are three items of commission left unpaid.
还有三笔佣金未付。

This amount includes all commissions.
此数包括一切佣金在内。

Chapter III　Inquiry and Reply

15. AZO 偶氮化合物，主要存在于纺织品、皮革等染料中，具有致癌的危险，所以欧美国家对其强制限量使用。

　　AZO free 不含偶氮化合物　　nickel free 不含镍

16. Need your reply by tomorrow morning. 电子邮件经常使用省略句与非完整句子。在简单句中，主语被省略，体现现代人快捷迅速的特点。后面课文中还会出现类似结构的句子。

17. RFQ (request for quotation) RFQ 是由买方发起的，目前在互联网及电子邮件的主题中经常出现。与客户询盘一样，买方给出产品的综合信息，要求卖方报价。在电子贸易中，买卖成交都是从 RFQ 开始逐渐谈成的，外贸业务员针对 RFQ 不仅仅简单报价的问题，要善于使用各种技巧，引导客户，从而把每个 RFQ 促成实盘，最后签订合同和订单。

Did you receive the RFQ for the new program?
你收到新项目的询价单了吗？

I. Translate the following expressions.

　　A. From English into Chinese.

　　1. order inquiry　　　　　　　　2. FOB
　　3. payment terms　　　　　　　 4. ASAP
　　5. Model Number　　　　　　　 6. ETD

　　B. From Chinese into English.

　　1. 装运代理人　　　　　　　　　2. 以美元报价
　　3. 尺寸范围　　　　　　　　　　4. 交货期

II. Fill in the blanks with the proper forms of the given expressions.

consideration   manufacturers   cooperation   mention   turnover   price

Dear Sirs,

We are a large trading company in India having a group _____ of over USD16 million.

We are looking for _____ who can give good quality and price to meet India's competitive market.

We therefore would like you to send your valued offer together with comprehensive technical specification for our _____ and to proceed with purchase. Kindly email yr best lowest CIF C10% Mumbai _____ by Sea.

Your offer should _____ usual terms of price validity, delivery, terms of payment, warranty period and so on.

In view of existing close _____ between us and future prospects, we are confident that you will provide us with your best quotation without fail.

We look forward to your favorable reply at an early date.

Yours faithfully,

×××

III. Put the following into English.

1. 请按美元报 1000 套床单 CIF 伦敦价。
2. 所附价格单将提供有关你方最感兴趣的型号的具体情况。
3. 请告知你方能按什么价格及什么付款方式供应下列商品。
4. 本公司想询问贵公司型号 277 洗衣机 500 台的价格。
5. 如果你们价格具有竞争性的话，我们将向你们大量订购。

Chapter III Inquiry and Reply

Lesson 6

(A) Status Inquiry

From: alicia0618@tchina.com
To: water123@hotmail.com
Sent: November 20, 2018
Subject: Status Inquiry

CHINA CITIC BANK
BEIJING, CHINA
Private & Confidential

Dear Sirs,

We have received an order for goods for US$11,520 from a new customer, AL ABRA SUB TRADING EST. We should highly appreciate it if you would inform us, in confidence, of the financial and business standing of the above firm.

The reference they have given us is Banca Monte Dei Paschi Di Siena S.P.A. Please approach the said bank for all possible information we require.

Any information you may give will be treated as strictly confidential and without any responsibility on your part.

Yours faithfully,
Alicia
Sales Manager
Fujian Oriental Footwear Imp. & Exp. Co., Ltd.

(B) Reply to the Above

From: water123@hotmail.com
To: alicia0618@tchina.com
Sent: November 25, 2018
Subject: Status Inquiry

Fujian Oriental Footwear Imp. & Exp. Co., Ltd.
Private & Confidential

Dear Sirs,

We have received your letter of 20 Nov. asking us to obtain the information concerning the financial and credit status of AL ABRA SUB TRADING EST. We now have the information you required.

AL ABRA SUB TRADING EST. is a chain of American mid-range department stores registered to carry out business in trading and supplies of shoes, jewelry, bedding, windows and furniture. The information we have indicates that it enjoys a good reputation and meets its commitment promptly. The credit amount mentioned in your letter seems to be safe.

The information above is confidential without any liability on our part.

Yours faithfully,
CHINA CITIC BANK
BEIJING, CHINA

1. **CHINA CITIC BANK** 中信银行，原名中信实业银行，成立于1987年，是中国最早参与国内外金融市场融资的商业银行，并以屡创中国现代金融史上多个第一而蜚声海内外。
2. **status enquiry** 资信调查，资信征询
   credit investigation 信用调查
3. **inform** v. 告知；通知；报告；提供资料

Chapter III　Inquiry and Reply

We shall inform you of the market situation later.

我们以后向你提供市场信息。

We wish to inform you that business has been done at USD110 per ton.

兹告知这笔生意已按每吨 110 美元成交。

Please be informed that we have already sent the samples requested.

兹告知我们已寄所需样品。

4. **financial position** = financial standing 财务状况

5. **reference** *n*. 资信证明人

   trade reference 商行备资

6. **We should highly appreciate it if** … 如蒙……我们将不胜感激。

   appreciate *n./v.* 欣赏；感激，理解。商业信函中常用此词表示客气。如：

   We appreciate your kindness. 感谢你方好意。

   We shall appreciate your giving this matter your serious consideration.

   若贵方对此事能给予认真考虑，我们将不胜感激。

   It would be appreciated if you could send us your catalogue and samples.

   如能给我方寄目录和价目单，我们将不胜感激。

   We shall appreciate it if you will make us an offer for 800 bicycles.

   如能给我方报 800 辆自行车，我们将不胜感激。

7. **in confidence** 机密

8. **approach…for…** 与……联系某事

   We have been approached by several buyers for the supply of walnuts.

   许多买主与我方联系核桃供应事宜。

9. **on sb.'s part** (on the part of) 在……方面，就……而言

   The fault is on the part of the shipping company.

   责任由船运公司负责。

   On our part, we always keep our promise.

   我方历来遵守诺言。

10. **in advance** 预先

11. **enjoy/gain a good reputation** 享有较高的声誉

12. **meet one's commitment** 履行承诺

Exercises

I. Translate the following expressions.

A. From English into Chinese.

1. status inquiry
2. general inquiry
3. reference
4. financial standing
5. make quotations
6. CIF

B. From Chinese into English.

1. 预先
2. 规格
3. 合资企业
4. 机密

II. Fill in the blanks in their proper form with the words or phrase given below.

| Inform | advise | buy | handle | appreciate | appreciate it |
| confidence | fall | under | be in the market for | | |

1. As the items _____ within the scope of our business activities, we shall be pleased to enter into direct business relations with you.
2. _____ separate cover, we are sending you a pattern book.
3. Will you _____ a fountain pen this coming Sunday?
4. If you send us a catalogue by air, we shall _____ very much.
5. Please _____ at what price your clients will place orders with us.
6. We _____ your sending us a special offer for walnutmeat.
7. We would like to _____ you that a number of our clients _____ Chinese walnut-meats.
8. Our corporation _____ exclusively the import and export business of light industrial products.
9. This information is given in _____.

III. Translate the following sentences into English.

1. 我们是为了出口化工产品的事与你方联系的。
2. 关于罐头食品，我们建议你们与天津食品进出口公司直接联系。
3. 如能提供有关上述公司的资信状况，我们将不胜感激。

Chapter III Inquiry and Reply

4. 有关本公司业务概况的资料，请向中国银行北京分行及中国国际商业银行查询。
5. 对你方提供的任何资料，我们都予以保密。

Skill Training

Exercise I. You get product details and company profile via alibaba.com. You are interested in TV stand ACT036. Send your message to this supplier. Your message must be at least 50 characters.

View Product Details: Acrylic TV stand

FOB Price: Get Latest Price
Port: Shenzhen Port
Minimum Order Quantity: 50 Piece/Pieces
Supply Ability: 10000 Piece/Pieces per Month
Payment Terms: T/T

Ms. Alice Sun

Specifications

Item No.	ACT036
Color	clear
Material	Clear high-quality acrylic
Size	customized
Appearance	fashionable, elegant, exquisite, faddish
Characteristics	durable, easy to clean & maintain, eco-friendly
Package	seaworthy packing
MOQ	50PCS or can be discussed
payment terns	30% deposit and the balance 70% before shipment
Logo	customer's logo is welcome
OEM&ODM	welcome
Port	Shenzhen Port
Delivery Time	3-5 days for samples and 15-20 days for lead time, or according to your order

Exercise II. Fill in the inquiry sheet with the hints from your teacher.

发件人： frenchas || Mathias Eylers

发送时间：2010-11-12 21:08:28

收件人：christina@terafundchina.com

抄送：

主题： Flip Flop straps

Dear Mr. Christina Chen,

Thank you for your company information on alibaba.com via private message. We are a Germany (Berlin) based company looking for a long term partner for the following product:

Product requirements:
1. flip flop straps sizing 38 to 44 (European sizing)
2. each size must come in 8 color possibilities
3. material: TPU or rubber
4. OEM design
5. please provide sample designs via picture or mail
6. amount: 264000 pairs p.a.

NOTE: We are ONLY looking for Flip Flop straps! No soles or entire Flip Flops are needed.

Would you please complete the attached inquiry-sheet (required for new cooperation partners) and send samples in different colors sizing 38—45 (only rubber or TPU and at least each size one sample 0.12min.) to our partner address in Shanghai. There is no need to send them via express to GERMANY.

Please only get in touch if you can match above mentioned product specifications. Thank you!

For further information contact me via email/pm or cell.

I'm looking forward to hearing from you!

Kind regards,
Mathias Eylers

ship samples to:

short name:	DBC Office
contact name:	Feng Chen
company name:	Shanghai Baoshan Shangmao Youxian Gongsi
c/o	frenchas shoe GmbH
address line 1:	No.550 Lu Jia Bang Road
address line 2:	Room 1516
city:	Shanghai
postal code:	200011
country:	China

your company:	
company name:	
contact name:	
address line 1:	
address line 2:	
city:	
postal code:	
country:	
others:	
email:	
cell:	
website:	
color code (RAL; CMYK...):	
packaging:	
shipping:	
price per pair (USD/EUR):	
material (rubber/TPU only):	
OEM design:	

strap designs

product requirements	European sizing (38 to 44)							
amount per size/sizes	38	39	40	41	40	42	43	44	TOTAL
color 1 # (black)	200	400	550	600	400	450	400	300	**3300**
color 2 # (white)	200	400	550	600	400	450	400	300	**3300**
color 3 # (pls see note)	200	400	550	600	400	450	400	300	**3300**
color 4 # (pls see note)	200	400	550	600	400	450	400	300	**3300**
color 5 # (pls see note)	200	400	550	600	400	450	400	300	**3300**
color 6 # (pls see note)	200	400	550	600	400	450	400	300	**3300**
color 7 # (pls see note)	200	400	550	600	400	450	400	300	**3300**
color 8 # (pls see note)	200	400	550	600	400	450	400	300	**3300**
TOTAL	1600	3200	4400	4800	3200	3600	3200	2400	**26400**

!!! NOTE: colors will be defined in cooperation with your company after receiving the information on which color codes you use (e.g. RGB_HEX; RAL; Pantone; CMYK…)

（注：RGB_HEX; RAL; Pantone; CMYK 等为色卡。）

Chapter III Inquiry and Reply

Business Link

Terms and Terminologies

general inquiry 一般询盘
specific inquiry 具体询盘
quotation in Renminbi 以人民币开价
bottom price 最低价
bedrock price 最低价
ceiling price 最高价
cost price 成本价
prevailing price 通行价格
original price 原价
maximum quantity 最大数量
minimum quantity 最小数量
total quantity 总量
sufficient quantity 足够的数量
moderate quantity 中等的数量
quantity discount 为扩大销售而使用的数量折扣
price discount 价格折扣
special discount 为了实现某种特殊目的（如开发新客户）而给予的特别折扣
trade discount 商业折扣
wholesale discount 批发折扣
hidden discount 暗扣

Useful Sentences

1. Thank you for your email of Mar. 15.
2. I wish to extend my appreciation for your kind offer.
3. If your prices come up to our expectations, we would expect to place regular orders.
4. We have seen your cotton garments displayed at Shanghai Trade Fair and have pleasure to ask you to send us details of goods with lowest CIF Vancouver price.

5. Please send us your brochure and wholesale pricelist with terms of payment.
6. Please quote us your best price FOB Tianjin for 1,000 m/t Portland cement for shipment in June, 2002.
7. We shall appreciate your lowest quotation CIF New York for 2,500 dz. bed-sheets of the following specifications, inclusive of our 5% commission.
8. We are looking at ordering initially a mix of the above to fill a 40-footer container. Please send us your quote, other specification, pictures and warranty with you company profile and contact details. It would also be helpful for you to provide us info on the present distribution of said tires specifically in North America.
9. Please send us some of your samples to acquaint us with the quality and workmanship of your supplies.
10. Should your price and delivery date be found acceptable, we will place a large order with you.
11. Full particulars as to prices, quality, quantity available and other relative information would be appreciated.
12. We shall be pleased to receive your order, which have our prompt and careful attention.
13. We are quite interested in your products. Please let us know what quantities you are able to deliver at regular intervals. And please quote your best terms of CIF Guangzhou.
14. We are happy to introduce our new branch office to you in the United Kingdom. We are opening a new big fashion shop and interested in the following products of yours, kindly let us have the sample collection, delivery time and total cost for small and large quantity.
15. We are interested in buying in bulk qty Plastic Magic Cube (5.5cm size) customised with our logo printing, pls send photo-quotation with all the packing details, individual packing OPP/box packing, no of PCS/CTN, weight/CTN, cbm/CTN, delay time, competitive price, pls quote for qty of 5,000pcs, 10,000pcs, 25,000pcs and 50,000pcs.

Chapter IV
Samples and Charges

Objectives:
After learning this chapter, you will
1. understand the function of sending samples;
2. grasp useful expressions and key language points in samples and charges;
3. be familiar with writing skills in requiring samples and charges;
4. be able to write letters on samples and charges.

Introduction

Qualities of goods are indispensable to international trade. In international trade, there are two ways to indicate the quality of the goods: either by description or by sample. Sale by sample refers to the transaction method which is done by the sample agreed by both the buyer and the seller. The sample refers to the article which can be used to represent the quality of the whole lot. In merchandising, a sample is a small quantity of a product, often taken out from a whole lot or specially designed and processed, that is given to encourage prospective customers to buy the product. The transaction that is concluded on the basis of the sample representing the quality of the whole lot can be called sales by sample. This method is used when the transaction is hard to conclude by standard, grade or words, such as some certain arts and crafts products, garmenture, local specialty, light industrial products, etc. Sale by sample includes three cases, i.e., sale by the seller's sample, sale by the buyer's sample and the counter sample.

In many cases, the customers may feel constrained for the payment for the samples or delivery of samples. In practice, it is impossible to send samples to all customers since it will present a heavy burden to the sellers. Samples of latest styles can be sent to old customers free of charge if they are small articles. But for valuable goods you should manage to win the customers' cooperation and ask them to pay the charge. You should be cautious because some new customers are not real traders but cheaters for samples only. It is a sticking point that sellers and buyers come to the solution through the communication by business letter.

Writing Tips

A letter sending samples usually covers the following points:

1) Thanks for the inquiry and interests in the products.

2) Sending samples and confirming tracking numbers.

3) Options for offering samples.

There are mainly four options for offering samples:

1) Upon the request of old clients, or if the values of samples and the shipping charges are not dear, the sellers would send free samples.

2) The sellers may ask new customers or others to pay for all samples and courier.

3) The sellers may send free samples and ask the customers to pay the costly courier fee themselves.

4) The suppliers may ask for charges but they will refund the charges when the buyers confirm the order.

Lesson 7

(A) Asking for Samples

From: Arne Jense @hotmail.com
To: alicia@hotmail.com
Sent: October 10, 2018
Subject: Flip Flops

Dear Alicia,

We are interested in Flip Flops from you. We would much appreciate it if you could email us the photo quotation of the items which we have selected from your booth using our attached standard photo quotation sheet. Please also email us the individual pictures of those selected items in JPEG file.

Please quote us for: 10,000/50,000/100,000 pairs.

Can we have 2 pairs for testing? If so, we would like to receive two pairs in Size 45 by SF Express on freight prepaid basis.

TRF081174, TRF081175, TRF081150, TRF081142, TRF081180

Please confirm details.

Regards,
Arne Jense
Hong Kong ABC Com., Ltd.
Purchasing
Shenzhen Office:
5th Floor, Block C, F 3.8 Building Tianjing
Tianan Cyber Park, Jiansha District
Shenzhen, China
TEL: 0086-987654321

(B) Reply to the Above

From: alicia@hotmail.com
To: Arne Jense @hotmail.com
Sent: Monday, October 12, 2018
Subject: Flip Flops

Dear Arne Jense,

How are you?

The attached files are the price offering. This price is valid in 30 days. If the exchange rate or raw material cost changes in export tax rebates or other force majeure.

As to terms of payment, we accept T/T (30% deposit balance against copy B/L) or L/C at sight.

It is OK to send you a sample for test first. I will check the samples' availability again, as I was told that there were no samples since last week. But we can provide the similar slippers for you, you can evaluate the quality. If you accept, please tell us your express account and the detailed address so that we can send the sample asap.

It will cost USD200 but we will refund the charge if you confirm the order.

We are awaiting your early reply.

Best regards,
Alicia
China Oriental Footwear Import & Export Corp.

Attachment:

Flip Flops Quotation
FUJIAN ORIENTAL FOOTWEAR IMP. AND EXP. CO., LTD.

Add: 9/F MINFA BUILDING NO. 88, DONGSHUI ROAD, FUZHOU, CHINA

Tel: 0086-0591-345678   Mobile: 86-12345678

Web: www.orientalfootwear.com   Email: alicia0618@tchina.com

Price Term: FOB FUZHOU   Quotation No: FP12245

Art No.	Unit Price (Quantity 10,000)	Unit Price (Quantity 50,000)	Unit Price (Quantity 100,000)
TRF081174	USD0.88/pair	USD0.76/pair	USD0.68/pair
TRF081150	USD1.80/pair	USD1.60/pair	USD1.53/pair
TRF081180	USD0.90/pair	USD0.88/pair	USD0.86/pair
TRF081175	USD1.30/pair	USD1.10/pair	USD1.08/pair
TRF081142	USD2.60/pair	USD2.45pair	USD2.20/pair

Remarks:

1. MOQ: 7000PRS
2. PAYMENT TERMS: 30% deposit, 70% T/T or L/C
3. DELIVERY TIME: after receiving deposit within 30-40days
4. Price is valid in 30 days. If the exchange rate or material cost or export tax rebates changes a lot, or other force majeure
5. Packing: 1) inner packing: one pair/box. 2) outer packing: 24 pairs/carton
6. Sample Fee: USD200; we will refund after you place an order

TRF081174　　TRF081150　　TRF081180　　TRF081175　　TRF081142

  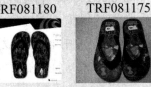

1. **sample** *n.* 样品

   通常需要技术部确认的样品有:初样(头样) initial sample，proto sample; 尺寸样 measurement sample/size sample; 确认样 confirmation sample; 产前样 pre-production sample; 大货船样 production sample

   此外还有试穿样 testing sample, fit trial sample; 回样 counter sample 等。

2. **SF Express** 顺丰速运公司 (sf-express.com): 民营区域性快递企业，主要经营国际、国内快递业务及报关、报检等业务。

3. **freight prepaid** 运费预付，寄件人缴纳所需邮寄费用

   on collect basis 运费到付，收件人缴纳所需邮寄费用

   on a basis of 以……为基础，on a barter basis 以易货方式

4. **valid** *adj.* 有效的，确定的

   类似的词还有：good, open 等。

   This offer remains valid/firm until the end of this month.

   该报盘保留至月底有效。

   We are prepared to keep our offer open until the end of this month.

   我们准备保留报盘到月底有效。

5. **exchange rate** 兑换率，汇率

6. **material cost** 材料费，原料费

7. **force majeure** 不可抗力

8. **export tax rebates** 出口退税，export rebates 出口退(减)税

   rebate *n./v.* 折扣，回扣，打折扣

   price rebate 价格折扣，insurance rebate 保险回扣

9. **T/T** 汇付的一种，业务中常用的付款方式之一，分前T/T与后T/T。

   电汇是汇出行应汇款人的申请，采用电讯手段为另一个国家的分行或代理行解付一定金额给收款人的一种汇款方式。优点在于收款人可迅速收到货款。

10. **deposit** *n.* 押金,保证金,存款 *v.* 存放

    We hope that your company confirms the deposit soon.

    我方希望贵公司尽快确认押金。

11. **balance** *n.* 收支差额，结余，余额；天平，平衡 *v.* 结算，平衡，称，权衡

12. **copy B/L** 提单副本，Original B/L 提单正本

13. **evaluate** *v.* 评估，评价

It is hard to evaluate the possible results of negotiation in advance.
很难事先评价谈判的结果。

14. **refund** *v.* 退还，归还；偿还 *n.* 退款；偿还金额

If the shoes do not wear well the shop will refund the money.
如果鞋不经穿，商店将退给你钱。

She took the faulty radio back to the shop and demanded a refund.
她将有毛病的收音机拿回商店去要求退款。

I. Translate the following expressions.

A. From English into Chinese.

1. proto sample
2. measurement sample
3. exchange rate
4. confirmation sample
5. material cost
6. freight prepaid

B. From Chinese into English.

1. 复制样品
2. 提单副本
3. 供我方参考
4. 押金

II. Fill in the blanks with appropriate propositions.

1. Our quotation _____ 30 tons of Shandong groundnuts is valid _____ 10 days.
2. You can rest assured that the sample will prove _____ your entire satisfaction.
3. We would like to receive two pairs _____ Size 45 by SF Express _____ collect basis.
4. I am completely satisfied _____ your sample.
5. Kindly send us samples _____ airmail.
6. We'd like to place a trial order _____ you _____ 2,000pcs cotton pillow cases.
7. Our clients are interested _____ your sample.
8. Most products at the fair are _____ no interest _____ us.

III. Put the following into English.

1. 确认样有效期为2年。
2. 我公司有意从贵公司进口银制品，请寄样品和价格单。
3. 已收到你方的样品，非常感谢。
4. 一旦收到你们的订单，我们会把费用退还给你们。
5. 随函附寄我们的样本书，请确认。

Chapter IV   Samples and Charges

Lesson 8

(A) Refusing to Pay Sample Charges

From: Arne Jense @hotmail.com
To: alicia@hotmail.com
Sent: Monday, October 13, 2018 10:07 AM
Subject: Sandals/Flip Flops

Dear Alicia,

I am sorry but I can not pay samples according to my company policy. Pls note that we do not want this sample to get profits, only for testing purpose, so it is necessary to test it to start working.

Anyhow I will tell you that I will pay transportation fee by TNT. Our courier number is 123456.

Please send it to this address:

*** System S.L.

Poligono Inudstrial de Cabanillas

Best regards,
Arne Jense

(B) A Reply to the Above

From: Arne Jense @hotmail.com
To: alicia@hotmail.com
Sent: October 17, 2018
Subject: Flip Flops

Dear Arne Jense,

Thanks for your kind support to me first.

Regarding sample charges, I really hope we can find a way to move forward to the project. It is honored for me and our company to work with you and your company, and we feel sure that we can start the initial order soon.

Concerning charges, I really hope you can do me the favor. Basically, we are so pleased to be of this service to our customers. However, we have to send out lots of samples at customers' requirements every day. Frankly speaking, it will be no doubt a heavy burden for us to process every case on the basis of free charge. We are forced to ask you to share the cost with us. We understand yours is a big company, and you have your own rules for samples. And I know the sample charge is small money. But we are a factory; it is not small amount of money for us if we offer free samples and postage charges to all customers. We believe it is fair for every customer to buy samples. And we got the support from other customers too. Please help us on this point. We promise to give you a better price in return.

Mr. Jense, when we start the cooperation and work better and better, we definitely hope we can do more for customers and always do our best. But now we hope you do your part to pay the charges for samples. Could we get your understanding and support?

Looking forward to hearing from you soon.

Best regards,
Alicia

Chapter IV　Samples and Charges

1. **company policy** 公司规定
2. **note** *v.* 注意
   Please make 4 different models, each model 2pcs samples. Please note the Ref No. is 3011 / 3012 / 3013 / 3014 accordingly.
   请做四个型号，每种两个样品。请注意相应参考文号是3011 / 3012 / 3013 / 3014
3. **TNT** 快递，世界上有四大著名快递公司，分别是 DHL, TNT, FedEx, UPS。
   TNT Express: TNT集团是全球领先的快递和邮政服务，总部设在荷兰阿姆斯特丹。
   DHL: DHL国际快递，总部设在比利时布鲁塞尔，现由德国邮政全球网络100%所拥有。
   UPS=Universal Postal Service 联合包裹服务公司，总部位于美国。
   FedEx=Federal Express 联邦快递，总部位于美国。
4. **courier number** 快件单号
5. **honor** *n./vt.* 荣幸，尊敬，荣誉，光荣；兑现，履行
   honor a check 兑现支票
   It is a great honor for me to attend the international business conference.
   我荣幸地参加国际商务会议。
   dishonor *n./vt.* 不名誉，玷辱，使蒙羞；不兑现
   dishonor a bill 拒付
6. **heavy burden** 巨大的压力
7. **initial order** 初次订单

I. Translate the following expressions.
   A. From English into Chinese.
   1. Express account   2. heavy burden
   3. sales by sample   4. company policy
   5. force majeure   6. on the basis of

B. From Chinese into English.

1. 数量折扣
2. 快件单号
3. 抽样
4. 联合包裹服务公司

II. Choose the best answer.

1. We shall be glad to send you our samples _____ receipt of your detailed requirements.
   A. at   B. on   C. as soon as   D. in

2. If you are interested, we will be pleased to send you a sample lot _____ charge.
   A. with   B. without   C. free of   D. free

3. Necessary information can be _____ from Commercial Counselor's Office stationed abroad and advertisement in the newspapers and magazines.
   A. have   B. obtained   C. gain   D. won

4. We are looking forward to _____.
   A. hear from your samples soon   B. receive your samples soon
   C. get your samples soon   D. your samples soon

5. We should be so glad to send you a sample _____ our own expense.
   A. in   B. at   C. against   D. on

6. Please get in touch with us _____ your sample request.
   A. for   B. in   C. against   D. with

7. Your letter of sample requirement has _____ to us for attention and reply.
   A. passed on   B. been passed on
   C. passed   D. been past through

8. The buyer shall open through a bank acceptable before July 1, 2011 _____ for negotiation in China until the 15th day after the date of shipment.
   A. testing   B. deposit   C. valid   D. refunding

9. We usually do business _____ equality and mutual benefits.
   A. based in   B. on collect basis
   C. based   D. on the basis of

10. The advantage of sending samples in this method will save 10% of the cost, because we have price _____ agreement with SF Express.
    A. rebate   B. balance   C. valid   D. evaluate

III. Put the following into English.

1. 带图解的目录和样品已由DHL快递寄出，查询号为QD1234。
2. 样品是免费的，但是根据公司规定，客户必须支付运费。
3. 你方生产的产品应与我方随函附照片完全一致。
4. 当标准运费70美元转至我们在汇丰银行的账户，或提供你们的DHL，UPS账号后，我们会立即发送样品。
5. 由于大量寄送样品对我们工厂是沉重的负担，我们不得不请求贵公司与我们分担费用。

Lesson 9

(A) Sending Samples

From: Jeremy Weiner @hotmail.com
To: alicia0618@tchina.com
Sent: November 20, 2018
Subject: Flip Flop
Attachment: samples

Dear Alicia,

We are pleased to send our samples to you including Art. HC13097, HC808B301 by DHL on Nov. 17 and its Tracking No. is QH12345.

Pls duplicate the samples accordingly and return them for our approval asap.

No need logo on mock-up samples this time but may need logo in further approval samples / mass production.

Attached please find the pictures, which could indicate our requirements in details.

We await your early reply.

B. rgds/ Jeremy

Chapter IV Samples and Charges

(B) Sending Duplicate Samples

From: alicia0618@tchina.com
To: Jeremy Weiner @hotmail.com
Sent: November 22, 2018
Subject: Flip Flop
Attachment: samples

Dear Jeremy Weiner,

We have pleasure in informing you that our duplicate samples including Art. HC13097 and HC808B301 were dispatched by FedEx this morning with its Tracking No. 061000.

It is our usual practice to make 4pcs for each model, 2 of which have been forwarded to you for your confirmation, and the remaining 2pcs will be kept by us.

Please confirm the above samples as soon as possible, thus enabling us to arrange production accordingly.

We look forward to your orders.

Best regards,
Alicia

1. **Tracking No.** 查询号
2. **duplicate** *n.* 复制品，副本 *adj.* 复制的，副本的 *v.* 复制，复印
   duplicate sample 复制样品
   duplicate order 重复订单
   in duplicate 一式两份
   As the carpets sell well in our market, we are glad to place a duplicate order.
   由于地毯在我处畅销，我方很高兴下一个重复订单。
   As our clients are quite satisfied with your products, we will duplicate our last order.
   由于我方客户对贵方产品非常满意，我方打算重复订购上一批货。

3. usual practice 惯例

4. accordingly *adv.* 相应地

5. for one's approval 供某人批准

6. mock-up 实体模型，实物的原尺寸模型

　　samples 样品; mock-up 大模型; prototypes 原型; initial samples 最初样品

7. forward *v.* 运送，寄送

　　Samples and the books you required have been forwarded to you.
　　你所要的样品与书已寄送给你。

8. confirm *v.* 确认

　　confirm sample 确认样品
　　confirmation sample 确认样

9. arrange production 安排生产

　　production sample 大货样，船样
　　大货样是生产完大货以后从大货中拿出的样子，其实也就是大货。
　　mass production 大量生产

I. Translate the following expressions.

　　A. From English into Chinese.

　　1. color sample　　　　　　　2. sample for reference

　　3. prototypes　　　　　　　　4. arrange production

　　5. in duplicate　　　　　　　　6. confirmation sample

　　B. From Chinese into English.

　　1. 最初样品　　　　　　　　　2. 一式两份

　　3. 产前样　　　　　　　　　　4. 供我方同意

II. Fill in the blanks in their proper form with the words or phrase given below.

> interest　be connected with　introduce　feel sure　honor　testing
> appreciate　look forward to　be engaged in　on the basis of
> place an initial order　generally speaking

Dear Sirs,

We take the liberty to _____ ourselves to you. Our company _____ import business for a long time and _____ all the major dealers in African market. We always keep the promise and _____ the contract and do business _____ mutual benefit.

We _____ in your Sandals/Flip Flops and _____ the color and the design of your products. Therefore, we _____ that we can start our trade by _____ if your quality is good. We would like you to send us some samples of the goods for _____.

_____, if the quality and price of your products are satisfactory, we will have large and regular orders from you. We hope this would be a good start of a long-term business relationship.

_____ your favorable reply.

Yours sincerely,
×××

III. Writing practice.

以买方的名义给卖方写一封信，确认收到卖方所寄来的复制样品。

1. 确认收到复制样品，并表示感谢。
2. 向卖方下订单订购3000件圣诞蜡烛。
3. 为了赶上销售季节，要求卖方立即安排生产。
4. 对双方贸易前景的展望。

International Business Correspondence (Fourth Edition)
国际商务英语函电（第四版）

Skill Training

Exercise I. Type your response here.

Directions: Read the email.
From: The Splenia International Co. To: Fujian Oriental Footwear Imp. & Exp. Co., Ltd. Subject Sent: July 23, 4:32 PM Hi, Grace, Regarding free samples, we have confirmed 3pcs during our meeting. Now you changed to 2pcs. Please check and confirm. We would like to get your good support and work on more orders. Best regards, Michael

Directions: Respond to the email. Respond as if you were the salesman from Fujian Oriental Footwear Imp. & Exp. Co., Ltd.
(Type your response here)

80

Chapter IV   Samples and Charges

Exercise II. Fill in the table with the information given below.

Sample Requirement

confirmation sample 确认样

The confirmation sample must be constructed as detailed in the approved Product Package Specification Sheet. Confirmation samples are to be submitted to the buyer no later than 45 days prior to production.

Fit trial 试穿样

One pair each of size 6 and 9 per style need to be sent to Steve Grave's attention at least 45 days prior to the XF date. ABS does not require Fit trial sample for Children's patterns. JCP will only have fitting sessions every 2nd and 4th Friday of each month.

Testing sample 测试样

Two pairs of shoes, any size, darkest color; 12"×12" swatches all colors of upper material, lining material and sock lining need to be sent to HKMTC at the following address. Testing must be done as early as possible. The test report can be available at the following website 5 working days after shipment be received by HKMTC.

TYPE OF SAMPLE	QUANTITY	ETA
confirmation sample	4 pairs in size 11 and 3 pairs in size 3 per color	
Fit trial		45 days prior to the XF date.
Testing sample		

Business Link

一般服装样板分为三个阶段:

1. 下单前

   proto/Initial/first spl 初/头样

   counter spl 覆样(根据初版改良过的,也可以是根据客人原样做的)

   buying spl 定货样(下不下单就看这件)

   salesmen spl 大样,顾名思义就是给营业员的,少则一件,多则过百。

2. 下单后

   fit spl 试穿样(试裁剪,尺寸)

   wear trial spl 试布料

   grade/Size set spl 放码/尺寸样

   photo/Press spl 照像样(因模特身材比常人高,通常尺寸会加长5cm左右。)

3. 生产期(全部大货物料)

   pre production spl 产前样

   test spl 测试样

   mock shop/presentation spl(试商品成列)

   production/seal/shipment spl 生产/封/船样

   proto/outcome/first approval/outturn sample 报样/初样/头样(用于一开始接到款式资料后做的第一次样品/样衣,可以代用,即用手头现有的面料、颜色、辅料做。)

   pre-production sample (PP sample) 产前样(产前样,即在大生产之前用正确的面料、辅料和包装做给客户确认的最后一次样衣,必须全部正确,意思是:"我们大货将按照这样生产,请确认。"客户确认了产前样之后才可以进行大货生产。)

   approval sample 确认样(用来确认的样品,可以是为了大货做的确认样,也可以是为了销售样等做的确认样等。)

   shipment sample 大货样/船样(船样是大生产结束后,从大货中抽出来的成衣样品寄给客户看的,意思是:"我们的大货就是和这个船样一样的,没有问题,请您放心。"数量和什么时候寄一般是由客户决定的。当然,大货中有时会有些瑕疵,有些工厂会特别挑好的或特别做件船样给客户看。)

   sample provided by customers/customer's sample/original sample 客人来样(即客户提供的样品)

   modified sample 修改样

Chapter IV Samples and Charges

Useful Sentences

1. We've received the sample which you sent us last Sunday.
2. We've got here our sales samples Type 1 and Type 2.
3. Our quality is based solely on our sales samples.
4. We sell goods as per the sales sample, not the quality of any previous supplies.
5. You know we sell our tea according to our samples.
6. You can see the difference between these grades.
7. The color of the shipment is much darker than that of your previous consignment.
8. No doubt you've received the outturn samples of the inferior quality goods.
9. I must advise you of the specification of the goods.
10. Have you received the specification as shown in our catalog?
11. We found the goods didn't agree with the original pattern.
12. The "Double Fish" brand is not so bad, the design is fresh and vivid.
13. The new varieties have very vivid design and beautiful colors.
14. We're here to discuss the trade marks of your products.
15. It is OK to send us the sample invoice. But please consider the bank charges of TT transfer.
16. We are willing to pay the sample fees. But again there is payment problem! How can I pay you a small amount of just a few dozen dollars? If TT by bank it may charge you / me both handling fees more than our TT amount.
17. We will charge sample fee for 5 times of quotation sheet for each sample.

Chapter V
Offers and Counter-Offers

> **Objectives:**
> After learning this chapter, you will
> 1. understand the difference between firm offer and non-firm offer and their relative expressions;
> 2. be familiar with the terms & conditions involved in an offer and be able to write them independently;
> 3. be able to make an offer in the form of quotation;
> 4. be able to make concessions and attacks politely and reasonably when writing counter-offers.

Introduction

Replies to inquiries concerning the prices of products or services are often called offers. An offer is an expression of will from the exporter to sell particular goods under the terms and conditions stated. It not only quotes the price of products you want to sell but also makes clear all the necessary terms of sales for the buyer's consideration and acceptance. The person making the offer is called the offeror. The person to whom the offer is made is called the offeree.

An offer is a proposal made by sellers to buyers in order to enter into a contract. In other words, an offer refers to trading terms put forward by offerors to offerees, on which the offers are willing to conclude business with the offerees. There are two kinds of offers. One is firm offer and the other is non-firm offer. A firm offer is made when a seller promises to sell goods at a stated price within a stated period of time. Once it has been accepted it cannot be withdrawn. A non-firm offer is usually made by means of sending catalogues, pricelist, pro forma invoices and quotations. It can be considered as an inducement to business.

If the buyer finds any terms or conditions in the offer unacceptable, he can make a counter-offer to renew the terms, negotiating with the seller. A counter-offer is virtually

Chapter V Offers and Counter-Offers

a partial rejection of the original offer and also a counter proposal initiated by the buyer or the offeree. The buyer may show disagreement to the price, or packing, or shipment and state his/her own terms instead. The effect of a counter-offer is that the original offer is no loner valid, and the offeree now becomes the offeror as the counter-offer is that the original offer is no longer valid, and the offeree now becomes the offeror as the counter-offer becomes the new offer. This process can go on for many rounds until business is finalized or called off.

Writing Tips

A satisfactory offer will include the following:

1) an expression of thanks for the inquiry, if any;
2) details of commodities, price terms, terms of payment, packing and date of deliver;
3) the validity period of the offer;
4) an expression of encouraging business.

A counter-offer letter usually covers the following points:

1) express thanks to the offer;
2) express regret at inability to accept and state reasons for non-acceptance;
3) make a counter-offer if, in the circumstances, it is appropriate;
4) suggest other opportunities to do business together.

A reply to the counter-offer usually covers the following points:

1) tell the reader that you have known his interest and show your regret;
2) express your acceptance or regret that counter-offer is not acceptable;
3) explain the reasons for accepting or declining the counter-offer;
4) wish to establish long business relations.

Lesson 10 A Firm Offer

From: alicia0618@tchina.com
To: Jeremy Weiner @hotmail.com
Sent: November 13, 2018 10:07 AM
Subject: Flip Flop
Attachment: PI

Dear Jeremy,

Thank you very much for your order inquiry.

At your request, we are pleased to make you an offer, subject to your reply reaching us by November 20, 2018 as follows:

"Fail Fascia" Brand Flip Flops (EVA style)
Unit price: HC13097   USD0.75/piece FOB C2 Fuzhou
            HC808B301 USD0.85/piece FOB C2 Fuzhou

Size range: 35/41
Color: navy blue, black
Quantity: 31,200 pairs
Packaging: Each pair in a poly bag, 24 pairs/CTN
Leading time: within 45 days upon receipt of L/C or 30% deposit payment
Payment: Western Union, MoneyGram, PayPal.
               Or 30% deposit T/T in advance, 70% balance by irrevocable L/C at sight.

Pls check our attached PI for your reference.

As there has been a large demand for the items, such a growing demand can result in an increase in price. We advise you to place an order ASAP.

We look forward to your feedback.

Best regards,
Alicia
China Oriental Footwear Import & Export Corp.

Attachment:

Issuer FUJIAN ORIENTAL FOOTWEAR IMP. AND EXP. CO., LTD. 9/F MINFA BUILDING NO. 88, DONGSHUI ROAD FUZHOU		福建东方鞋业进出口贸易有限公司 形式发票 **PROFORMA INVOICE**	
TO AL ABRA SUB TRADING EST. 94017 REGALBUTO CATANIA, ITALY		**No.** WW0803015A	**Date** Nov. 7, 2018
		Terms of payment 30% deposit T/T in advance, 70% balance by irrevocable L/C at sight	
Transport details From Fuzhou, China to Catania, Italy		**Contract No.**	
Marks and numbers	**Number and kind of packages; description of goods**	**Unit price**	**Quantity**	**Amount**
N/M	SLIPPERS ART. NO. HC13097: 950CTNS/22800PRS SIZE: 35 36 37 38 39 40 41 navy blue 1 2 3 3 2 1 0 black 0 1 2 3 3 2 1 ART. NO. HC808B301: 350CTNS/8400PRS SIZE: 35 36 37 38 39 40 41 navy blue 1 2 3 3 2 1 0 black 0 1 2 3 3 2 1	FOB FUZHOU USD0.75 USD0.85	22800 8400	USD17,100.00 USD7,140.00
TOTAL:	1300CTNS/31200PRS	—	—	USD24,240.00
	Authorized Signature			
Packing: Each pair in a poly bag, 24PRS/CTN				
PORT OF LOADING: FUZHOU				
DESTINATION PORT CATANIA				
Insurance:				
Time of delivery: before Jan.15, 2019ETD				
BANK NAME: CHINA CITIC BANK FUZHOU BRANCH				
SWIFT: CIBKCNBJ350, A/C NO: 7341010182300010769				
BANK ADDRESS: NO. 99 HUDONG RD., FUZHOU, FUJIAN, CHINA				

Notes

1. non-firm offer /offer without engagement 虚盘。虚盘是发盘人有保留地表示愿意按一定条件达成交易，不受发盘内容的约束，也不做任何承诺，任何时候都可以改变、修改甚至取消。因此，虚盘是不受约束的、试探性的报价，其目的在于了解顾客、了解市场。虚盘表示方法如下：

subject to change without notice 如有变更，不做预先通知

subject to our final confirmation 以我方最后确认为条件

subject to goods being unsold 以货物未售出为条件

subject to prior sale 以先售为条件

without engagement 无约束力

2. firm offer 实盘或确盘。实盘主要特点是：对发盘人具有约束力，在实盘规定的有效期内，发盘人不得随意撤回或修改实盘的内容。实盘一经受盘人在有效期内无条件地接受，即无须再经过发盘人的确认，就可以达成交易，构成对双方都有约束力的合同。实盘表示方法如下：

subject to your reply reaching here before October 2

以我方10月2日前收到你方答复为有效

offer firm the following on the same terms and conditions

按照同样的条件报盘如下

offer valid until Thursday our time

发盘至我方当地时间星期四有效

offer open three days 发盘3天有效

offer reply in ten days 发盘10天内回复

3. offer n./v. 报盘

作为名词时与动词make, send, give, email 等连用，后接介词 for, on 或of, 接for最普遍，接on较少见。买方提及卖方的报盘时，接of为好。

We are working on your offer of 2000 kilos Black Tea.

动词offer可以作及物动词，也可以作不及物动词，作及物动词时宾语可以是人也可以是物，还可以是双宾语。

We offer firm the following on the same terms and conditions.

We will offer asap.

4. at your request 按照要求（或请求）

商业书信按对方要求办某事后在通知对方时，常用于句首。类似的还有 as

Chapter V Offers and Counter-Offers

requested, 或in compliance with your request, 或complying with your request 等。

5. **subject to** 以……为准，以……为条件/有效的

    Each list is flexible and subject to review at the end of the day.

    每张单子都要灵活掌握，每天下班前要重新检查一下。

    This offer is subject to our final confirmation.

    本报价以我方最后确认为准。

    We make you the following offer, subject to our receiving your reply before Oct. 2.

    我们做出如下报盘，以我方在10月2日前收到你方答复为准。

6. **Unit price:** USD0.77 /piece FOB Fuzhou

    单价： 货币单位+公制单位+贸易术语+港口

    计量单位还有：piece, dozen, pair, keg, set, yard, bale, metric ton, gross 等。

7. **Leading time**订货到交货的周期，是客户下单到交货的时间，交货时间以合同签订的贸易术语规定的风险和货物转移时间计，严格意义上是这么算的，但实际操作中往往都会把在途运输时间也计算在内。

8. **Western Union**西联汇款，是西联国际汇款公司的简称，迄今已有150年的历史，是美国财富五百强之一的第一数据公司（FDC）的子公司。

    MoneyGram速汇金业务，是一种个人间的环球快速汇款业务，可在十几分钟内完成由汇款人到收款人的汇款过程，具有快捷便利的特点。

    PayPal贝宝，1998年12月由 Peter Thiel 及 Max Levchin 建立，是总部在美国加利福尼亚州圣荷西市的因特网服务商，允许在使用电子邮件来标识身份的用户之间转移资金，避免了传统的邮寄支票或者汇款的麻烦。

9. **PI**: proforma invoice形式发票，估价单，是出口商应进口商的要求发出的，有出售货物的名称、规格、单价等内容的非正式参考性发票，供进口商向贸易或外汇管理当局申请进口许可证或外汇等时用，另外还可作为报价单使用。

10. **feedback** *n.* 反馈

I. Translate the following expressions into Chinese.

   1. "联想"牌电脑
   2. 永久牌自行车
   3. 每桶净重……美元CFR Lagos

4. 每打人民币10元CIF 香港

5. 每床15英镑伦敦成本保险加运费含5%佣金

II. Categorize the following expressions. "F" for firm offer and "N" for non-firm offer.

(   ) a) subject to change without notice

(   ) b) offer valid until Thursday our time

(   ) c) subject to our final confirmation

(   ) d) subject to goods being unsold

(   ) e) offer firm the following on the same terms and conditions

(   ) f) subject to prior sale

(   ) g) offer open three days

(   ) h) subject to your reply reaching here before October 2

(   ) i) without engagement

(   ) j) offer reply in ten days

III. Put the following into English.

1. 根据你方要求，我公司就如下货物向贵方报价，以我方最后确认为准。

2. 我们了解到你方市场对EVA行李箱需求强劲，随函附上第555号报价单，供你方考虑。

3. 兹报盘，茉莉花茶每千克价格为1125元人民币，神户（Kobe）CIF价，下周交货。

4. 感谢贵公司对电镀铁板（Galvanized Iron Sheet）的询盘，现报价如下，敬请惠顾订货为盼。

5. 此报盘以我货未售出前、收到你方接受的回函为准。

IV. Writing practice.

You receive the inquiry made in Exercise I of Skill Training in Chapter III. You know the buyer is interested in TV stand ACT036. Give a reply to the inquiry.

Lesson 11

(A) A Counter-Offer

From: Jeremy Weiner @hotmail.com
To: alicia0618@tchina.com
Sent: November 15, 2018
Subject: counter-offer

Dear Alicia,

Thank you for your email and your samples.

For your information, our customers are quite satisfied with the test result of your samples but they are still holding back.

After careful examining and comparison with similar products of other makes, we find your quotation on the high side. I contacted another company in China, whose sales person Ms. Lynne Feng mailed me the price USD0.65/piece for ART. NO. HC13097. Please check my attached file. Also a large number of slippers of similar design from Hong Kong are now commanding ready sales here and these sell at prices 10% below those that you have quoted.

Unless the prices could match the market level, it is difficult to persuade our customers to purchase from you. If your product price is set with my budget, I will give you an order.

Actually, competitive prices for a trial order can often lead to a high market share with enormous profits in future. We hope you will take this factor into account and wait for your early reply.

B. rgds/ Jeremy
Corporate Development Manager
AL ABRA SUB TRADING EST.
Jeremy Weiner @hotmail.com

(B) Reply to the Above

From: alicia 0618@tchina.com
To: Jeremy Weiner @ hotmail.com
Sent: November 16, 2018
Subject: counter-offer

Dear Jeremy Weiner,

Thank you for your email.

The price USD0.75 FOB FUZHOU really is most favorable if you take the quality into consideration. There are many cheaper products. But if you get our products, you may see the difference. Our products are made of EVA instead of EVA recycle. EVA recycle saves your cost 10% to 15% according to mixing but they are easily broken. We use only the finest materials and employ only the most skilled craftsmen. Furthermore, you may have seen from our samples that our packages are excellently designed and printed, which also cost us a lot, so we can hardly make any price reduction.

However, in order to start business, we are prepared to reduce the price to USD0.71/piece for ART. NO. HC13097 and USD0.81/piece for HC808B301. Other conditions remain unchanged.

If you still doubt my words, how about placing a 20GP for trial order and compare? We are confident that a trial order would convince you that our products are excellent value for money.

Best regards,
Alicia
China Oriental Footwear Import & Export Corp.

Chapter V　Offers and Counter-Offers

1. **counter-offer** *n.* 还盘，还价　*vt. / vi.* 还盘，还价

   Your counter-offer on walnutmeat is under our serious consideration.
   我们正在认真考虑你有关核桃仁的还盘。
   If you cannot accept, please make a best possible counter-offer.
   若无法接受，请尽力给一个最好的还盘。
   We counter-offer as follows, subject to your acceptance here before the end of this month.
   现还盘如下，以你方接受的回复于本月底前到达此地为有效。
   The price you counter-offered is not in line with the current market.
   你方还盘价格与市场价格不符。

2. **hold back** 犹豫

3. **on the high / low side**（价格等）偏高 / 偏低

   It seems that your price is on the high side, which prohibits us from placing an order with you.
   你方价格似乎偏高，使我们无法向你们订购。
   We regret being unable to accept your bid as it is on the low side.
   抱歉因你方递价偏低而无法接受。
   类似的表达有：
   Your price is a bit high. / Your price is too high. / Your price is excessive.
   你方价格过高。
   Your price is prohibitive.
   你方价格令人望而却步。

4. **reduce** *vt.* 减少，降低

   reduce a price by… 将价格降低多少
   reduce a price to… 将价格降低到多少
   To meet your request, we are prepared to reduce our freight by 3%.
   为满足你方要求，我们准备将运费降低百分之三。
   To be more competitive, you should try to reduce your price to the bottom without sacrificing the quality.
   为了更有竞争力，你们应尽量在不影响质量的前提下将价格降至最低。
   reduction *n.* 减少，降低
   make a reduction of … % in price 把价格降低百分之……

93

You are requested to make a reduction of 5% in your price to attract more customers.

为吸引更多的客户，请你们降价百分之五。

5. EVA recycle 用EVA或PE发泡过的边角料造的再生粒子产品

6. convinced *adj.* 相信的

We are convinced of the commercial integrity of the supplier.

我们相信该供应商的商业信誉。

We are convinced that he is innocent.

我们相信他是无辜的。

Exercises

I. Translate the following expressions.

A. From English into Chinese.

1. make a reduction of
2. on the high / low side
3. counter-offer
4. OBM order
5. sell well
6. be convinced of

B. From Chinese into English.

1. 类似产品
2. 竞争力的价格
3. 试订
4. 测试结果

II. Fill in the blanks in their proper forms.

Dear Mr. Prentice,

Thank you for your _____ about our T-shirts for men and women.

    1. (A) offer

       (B) counter-offer

       (C) inquiry

       (D) quotation

We have pleasure in _____ our latest pricelist which come into effect the end of this

    2. (A) receiving

       (B) enclosing

       (C) asking for

       (D) obtaining

Chapter V Offers and Counter-Offers

month. You will see that we have increased our prices on most models. We have, however, refrained _____ doing so on some models of which we hold large stocks.

  3. (A) on
   (B) in
   (C) from
   (D) to

The explanation for our increased for stems from the fact _____ we are now paying 10%

            4. (A) why
             (B) what
             (C) that
             (D) which

more for our raw materials than we were paying last year, along with some of our subcontractors having _____ their prices as much as 15%.

  5. (A) reduced
   (B) raised
   (C) lost
   (D) saved

We hope you will understand our position and look forward to your cooperation.

Best regards,

×××

III. Put the following into English.

1. 虽然我方非常愿意与贵方开展贸易往来，但遗憾的是我们不能将价格降到你方所求，因为我方经准确计算成本后，已将价格降到最低点。

2. 我们对市场条件仔细研究后认为，为应付激烈竞争，你们必须降价10%，否则，生意成交无望。

3. 我们遗憾地告诉你方，你方所报塑料手提包价格与我地市场行情完全不一致。

4. 我们对标题商品还实盘125美元，以本地时间星期三中午前答复有效。

5. 我们高兴地随函附上下列规格的自行车1000辆的形式发票，一式三份。获得进口许可证后，请即电告以便备货。

Lesson 12

(A) New Price for Repeat Order

From: Arne Jense @hotmail.com
To: alicia@hotmail.com
Sent: Nov. 22, 2018
Subject: Sandals/Flip Flops

Dear Alicia,

I'm pleased to tell you that the 24,000 pairs of slippers ex S.S. "Dongfeng" have arrived in good condition and are selling well. We would like to place a repeat order for 50,000pcs.

By "Fail Fascia" they will buy 2×40HQ, the same as last time and the target price has to be USD0.78. Please send the PI with this price and also for the new Animal Slipper order.

For the big order, today I talked to the manager and they said that in this period, he will place an order IF GIVEN A BETTER PRICE.

Regards,
Arne Jense

(B) Reply to the Above

From: alicia@hotmail.com
To: Arne Jense @hotmail.com
Sent: Nov. 25, 2018
Subject: Sandals/Flip Flops

Dear Arne Jense,

Please don't push us too hard. As you know, owing to the rising cost of materials and the appreciation of Renminbi Yuan, prices have gone up a lot and the price I offer you is quite competitive. Let's compromise to USD0.82 per pair for both Fail Fascia and Animal Order. That's the best we can do. But you'd place these two orders together. I need these quantities added to convince financial department to accept such a low price.

Attached the PI for your confirmation.

For JCP Penny order, I need your detailed information, and then will offer you the final price. But frankly speaking, it's near the cost of production, and difficult for us to make any concession.

Best regards,
Alicia
China Oriental Footwear Import & Export Corp.

1. **repeat order** 或 re-order 续订单，俗称翻单或返单。客人下了一份订单，觉得销路不错，就再下一个与上一单要求差不多的订单。这种形式就是翻单。有的订单因为质量好连续翻单。
   repeat *n.* 续订订单，复数为：repeats, repeat orders, further orders。
   repeat order 与原订单除装运期不同外，价格与数量甚至详细规格亦未必相同。假定除装运期不同外，其他一些条件都相同则称为 duplicate order。

2. **ex** *prep.* 从；在……交货

ex. S.S. "Peace" 由和平轮卸下（主要用于进口业务中）

per S.S. "Victory" 由胜利轮装运（主要用于出口业务中）

3. **in good condition** 状况良好

4. **HQ: High Cube (containers),** CUBE发音为Q，所以HIGH CUBE也简写为HQ **GP: General Purpose (Containers)**

   GP和HQ是集装箱规格的简称，HQ是高箱。还有OT是开顶柜，FR是框架柜，HT是挂衣柜，RF或RH是冷藏柜，RH是指40高的冷藏柜，GP/DC是指干货柜。

   理论上，各船舶公司集装箱的箱内尺寸有细微差别，一般在3mm之内。

   一般理论标准尺寸是以下规格：

   20'GP的精确箱内尺寸：5898mm (长) × 2352mm (宽) × 2393mm (高)。

   40'GP的精确箱内尺寸：12032mm (长) × 2352mm (宽) × 2393mm (高)。

   40'HC的精确箱内尺寸：12032mm (长) × 2352mm (宽) × 2698mm (高)。

5. **target price** 目标价格

6. **make some concession**

   Can we each make some concession?

   我们能不能双方都做些让步？

7. **compromise** *v.* 妥协；折中；和解

   He refused to compromise his principles. 他拒绝放弃原则。

8. **Animal Slipper** 动物拖鞋

I. Translate the following expressions.

   A. From English into Chinese.

   1. offer without engagement   2. target price
   3. make a reduction of   4. HQ
   5. repeat order   6. latest catalogue

   B. From Chinese into English.

   1. 按照要求   2. 重复订单
   3. 还盘   4. 由胜利轮装运

Chapter V Offers and Counter-Offers

II. Read the statements and pick out the expression which doesn't match with each complete sentence.

1. To our regret, you feel that _____ (我们的价格与现行市价不一致).

   A. our offered prices are not in line with the ruling market level

   B. the prices in our offer can't match the current market level

   C. our quoted prices can't match up to the prevailing market level

   D. our inquired prices are out of line with the prevailing market level

2. The best we can do is _____ (给你们5月底以前来的订单打8%的折扣) as a special concession.

   A. to give you a discount of 8% on all orders coming to us before the end of May

   B. to allow you a 8% discount on all orders if they come to us by the end of May

   C. to grant you a discount by 8% on all orders that are reaching us by the end of May

   D. give you an allowance of 8% on all orders that are reaching us by the end of May

3. To encourage the promotion of our products, we are prepared to _____ (给你们降价10%，这种降价只能持续很短的时间).

   A. reduce your price by 10%, which can only be maintained for a short time

   B. give you a 10% reduction in our price we can maintain only for a short time

   C. reduce 10% of the price, which is kept open only for a short time

   D. cut our price by 10% that is valid only for a short time

4. We would like to point out that the price is our lowest level _____ (所获利润微薄).

   A. which makes the margin of profit very thin

   B. that leaves you with very little profit margin

   C. so that we can earn a very narrow margin of profit

   D. which includes very small profit

5. Because there is a ready market here _____ (急需) additional quantities of the goods, kindly arrange early shipment of our repeats.

   A. badly in need of   B. in urgent need of

   C. in bad need of   D. in great need of

III. Translate the following letter.

> 敬启者：
>
> 　　感谢你们9月13日发来的电子邮件。很遗憾地获悉你们认为我们的报价过高。实际上，为了促进我们之间的贸易，我们已报最低价，致使我们获利甚微。我们必须指出，其他供应商不可能以低于我们的价格供给同样质量的拖鞋，我们已以现价收到了许多国家寄来的订单。请你们再次考虑我们的报盘，及时订货。
>
> 　　盼早复。
>
> 　　　　　　　　　　　　　　　　　　　　　　　　　　　　　　谨启

Skill Training

Exercise I. Practice.

1) There are two forms in making an offer. One is tabulated form, in which the offer is made in Lesson 10. The other is letter form using linking method, in which the terms and conditions are given at the same time linked together by prepositions. This offer is used when there is one single item or making a counter-offer. Now look at the following examples and fill in appropriate prepositions.

Following pls find the detailed info for yr inquiry _____ Dobby Table cloth: 5000pcs _____ Type AP303 _____ $6.80 per piece CIF New York against L/C at sight _____ shipment _____ July/August equally divided.

2) Practice: Make the following offer in the two above-mentioned forms.

> 敬启者：
>
> 　　感谢您5月21日的询盘。我方现报盘如下，此报盘须经本公司最后确认为准。
> 　　300把黑色转椅，每把100美金CIF旧金山价，规格见附页，船期2017年8月、9月。要求以保兑的、不可撤销的信用证凭即期汇票支付。
> 　　请注意，我方不提供佣金，但对超过1000把转椅的订货给予5%的折扣。
> 　　另函附寄各型号样本、商品目录和价格表。
> 　　我们相信上述条款是您可以接受的并期待您早日订货。
>
> 　　　　　　　　　　　　　　　　　　　　　　　　　　　　　　谨启

Chapter V   Offers and Counter-Offers

Exercise II. Fill in the Proforma Invoice with the given information.

埃及公司James Brown & Sons打算向ST Trading Co., Ltd.公司购买5000个化妆包（Model No.: A156）。按他们的要求，ST Trading Co., Ltd.公司于7月22日为该公司开具了号码为PI20110407的形式发票：每个化妆包单价为USD2.80 FOB Xiamen, 包装：12 units per master carton., 付款方式：保兑的、不可撤销的信用证。

Cosmetic Bag

Model No.: A156 Size: 24×16×6cm Material: Cowherd Material

Issuer:		形式发票 PROFORMA INVOICE	
To:		No.:	Date:
		Terms of payment:	
Transport details: From Xiamen, China to		Contract No.:	

Marks and numbers	Number and kind of packages; description of goods	Unit price	Quantity	Amount
N/M	Size: Packing: ********************* FOB Xiamen			
TOTAL:				
	Authorized Signature			

Insurance:
Time of delivery:
BANK NAME: AGRICULTURAL BANK OF CHINA, XIAMEN BRANCH KEJIYUAN SUB-BRANCH
SWIFT: ABOCCNBJ800, A/C NO: 40352014040003753
BANK ADDRESS: 1/F HENGSHENG BUILDING YUEHUA ROAD, HULI DISTRICT, XIAMEN, P.R. CHINA

Business Link

Currency in Different Countries

货币名称	英文与旧符号	ISO 货币符号	货币名称	英文与旧符号	ISO 货币符号
人民币元	Yuan, ¥	CNY	俄罗斯卢布	Russian Rubble (or Rouble)	RUB
日元	Yen, Yen	JPY	瑞士法郎	Swiss France SF	CHF
港元	Dollar, HK $	HKD	波兰兹罗提	Polish Zloty	PLN
新加坡元	Dollar, S $	SGD	加拿大元	Canadian Dollar, Can $	CAD
韩元	Won, W	KRW	美元	United states Dollar, US $	USD
印尼盾（卢比）	Rupiah, Rp	IDR	墨西哥比索	Mexican Peso, MEX	MXP
马来西亚林吉特	Malaysia Dollar, M $, Mal $	MYR	古巴比索	Cuban Peso, Cub $	CUP
菲律宾比索	Peso, P	PHP	埃及镑	Egyptian Pound, LE	EGP
泰铢	Thai, Baht, B	THB	澳大利亚元	Australian Dollars, $ A	AUD
印度卢比	Rupee Rs/Re	INR	新西兰元	New Zealand Dollar, $ NZ	NZD
越南盾	Dong, D	VND	中非金融合作法郎	Central African Finan-Coop Franc	XAF
欧元	Euro €	EUR	朝鲜圆	Korean Won	KPW
英镑	Pound Sterling, £, £ stg	GBP	瑞典克朗	Swedish Krona/Kronor, SKr	SEK

资料来源：《世界货币手册（1990年版）》（中国金融出版社，1991年）。

Chapter V　Offers and Counter-Offers

Useful Sentences

1. Our quotations are open for acceptance within the period stated therein, or, when no period is stated, within 30 days only after the date of such quotations.
2. Further to our letter dated June 24, 19—, we now have pleasure in enclosing our new price list which is operative from August 1, 19—.
3. We state that said offer remains firm only for a period of twenty days and there after it will be subject to further confirmation.
4. In consideration of the situation at your end, we would exceptionally extend the offer until you have heard any definite information about the import license.
5. We very much regret that your clients find our price on the high side. We, however, would work further if you could let us know your counter-offer.
6. We have received your offer but regret that your price is too high to be acceptable. Unless you reduce your price in line with the market conditions here, we do not think any business can be done.
7. We are much interested in your watches but because your minimum limit for order is too big for this market, we have difficulty in inducing buyers to place trial orders for your products.
8. After carefully studied the market conditions here, we are of the opinion that you have to cut your price by 3% in order to cope with heavy competition, otherwise there will be no hope of business.
9. We regret having to inform that a certain Japanese supplier has underquoted you for the same kind of products as you offered. So, if you fail to take this matter into consideration seriously, your products may probably be squeezed out of the market.
10. In spite of our efforts we have not been able to find a buyer for your products. We, therefore, would suggest that you reconsider you price and send us a suitable quotation.
11. We are much favourably impressed with both the appearance and specifications of your Alternator, but only consider its price a little higher. We, therefore, ask for your indulgence for another three weeks for us to have sufficient time to complete a thorough comparison with other makes and thereupon to make a counter-offer.
12. Your counter-offer is still far from being acceptable to our user, we have no choice but to give you a negative reply again with great reluctance.
13. I admit your black tea is of good quality, but the price is still on the high side even

if we take quality into consideration. To be frank with you, it's easy for us to select a similar quality of black tea from other countries at a level about 10% lower than yours.

14. In reply, we regret to inform you that our buyers in Rotterdam find your price much too high. Information indicates that some parcels of Indian origin have been sold here at a level about 10% lower than yours.

15. We do not deny that the quality of Chinese kernels is slightly better, but the difference in price should, in no case, be as big as ten per cent. To step up the trade, we counter-offer as follows, subject to your reply received by us on or before 14th September.

Module IV

Execution of Contracts

Chapter VI
Order and Contracts

Objectives:
After learning this chapter, you will
1. learn how to place and confirm an order;
2. be familiar with the contents of a sales contract or sales confirmation;
3. be able to fill in a contract in English;
4. understand the obligations of buyer and seller.

Introduction

Orders are usually written on a company's official order form, which has a date, and reference number that should be quoted in any correspondence which refers to the order. Even if the order is telephoned, it must be confirmed in writing, and an order form should always be accompanied by either a compliment slip or a covering letter. A covering letter is preferable as it allows you the opportunity to make any necessary points and confirm the terms that have been agreed upon.

Writing Tips

Usually, the covering letter should:
1) explain there is an order accompanying the letter;
2) confirm the terms of payment;
3) confirm the agreed discounts, if any;
4) confirm the delivery dates;
5) state the methods of delivery;
6) advise your supplier how you want the goods packed.

As soon as a supplier receives an order, it should be acknowledged. This letter should:
1) express thanks for the order received;
2) enclose a sales confirmation if necessary;
3) restate the terms of trade;

4) assure the buyer of your prompt delivery and careful attention to the goods ordered;

5) express your desire for further orders.

However, the seller can not accept an order for some reasons, such as goods ordered out of stock, unfavorable terms your customer has asked for, etc. In this case, you should be very careful when writing such rejecting letters. Otherwise, you may affect your potential business with your client. The following are some tips for your benefits:

1) Express thanks for the order received;

2) Give the reasons why you can not accept the order while showing your appreciation of the buyer's interest in your company and express your regret of inability to entertain the order;

3) Offer alternative suggestions for the transaction and express your concern for future contacts.

Lesson 13 A Purchase Order

From: Jeremy Weiner @hotmail.com
To: alicia0618@tchina.com
Sent: Nov. 22, 2018 10:07 AM
Subject: A Purchase Order
Attachment: A Purchase Order

Dear Alicia,

We are glad to confirm receipt of your duplicate samples and feel satisfied with them. Attached is our PO No. 03.05.GB24.

Pls note that confirmation samples are to be in our possession latest Nov. 27, 2018 and production samples to be in our possession latest Dec. 20, 2018.

These items will have to be dispatched freight prepaid. Please advise dispatch details to us immediately.

As we are in urgent need of the ordered goods, please arrange production without any delay. We believe it will mark a good beginning between us.

Best regards,
Jeremy Weiner

Attachment:

Purchase Order No. 03.05.GB24. Page 1 of 2	Order Date: 21 October, 2018 Print Date
Buyer: AL ABRA SUB TRADING EST. 94017 REGALBUTO CATANIA, ITALY	**Supplier: FUJIAN ORIENTAL FOOTWEAR IMP. AND EXP. CO., LTD.** Add: 9/F MINFA BUILDING NO. 88, DONGSHUI ROAD, FUZHOU, CHINA Tel: 0086-0591-345678 Mobile:86-12345678

Shipping No: 03.05.GB24	Latest ETD: 30 Dec., 2018	Payment: L/C at sight
Port of Departure: Fuzhou	Country of Dest: ITALY	
Country of Origin: China	Port of Arrival: CATANIA	Forwarding Agent: NHK

Chapter VI Order and Contracts

(Continued)

Conditions: FOB C2 FUZHOU	Currency: USD	For assortments and confirmation and production samples: See Page 2	
CBM Art. Supplier Art. Sizes Pairs Price Total Amount Article Description			
HC13097　AK12-0029　35/41　22,800　0.71　USD16188.00　sandal with main material			
808B301　AK12-0029　35/41　8,400　0.81　USD6804.00　EVA style			
USD22,992.00			
Please return the copy stamped and signed	Accepted & Confirmed by	Amount summary: Sub Total: 22,992.00 No Claim: 2% Order Amount: 22,532.16	
Important: This order is not valid until the confirmation. Samples are confirmed in writing and signed by Fujian Oriental Footwear Company. By acceptance of our order the supplier is unconditionally committed to deliver our orders in accordance with our purchase and other details in our order sheets. Supplier needs to supply to the buyer an official report which proofs that the goods are free of AZO, Cadmium, Nickel, PCB etc. This report is required by European Law.			

注：Page 2 of 2 are requirements for samples, labeling and packing of the goods, etc.（内容可见有关章节）

1. purchase order 购货订单

订购函可以是表格形式，如订单、购货确认书，或者购货合同，也可以是商务信函。订货时，内容必须准确、清楚，讲究礼貌，对于重要的交易条款必须做出明确规定。其他还有：

order for custom-made 定制的订单，outstanding/pending order 未完成订单

substantial order 可观的订单，fresh order 新订单

routine orders 日常订货，following up the order 订货追踪

confirmation of order 确认订单，standing order 长期订单

to execute/fulfill/fill/carry out an order 执行订单

to decline/turn down/refuse an order 拒接订单

to close/confirm/take on an order/entertain an order 接受订单

to cancel/withdraw/revok an order 取消订单

to hold up/suspend an order 暂停执行订单

2. in one's possession 为某人所有（或占有）

Anyone who has in his possession the property of the decedent shall take good care of such property

存有遗产的人，应当妥善保管遗产。

3. satisfy *v.* 使……满意

Your explanation cannot satisfy us.

你的解释不能令人信服。

satisfactory *adj.* 令人满意的

We find the price and quality satisfactory.

我们认为价格和质量是令人满意的。

4. be in urgent/great need of 或 **be badly in need of** 急需

We are in urge need of raw materials.

我们急需原材料。

5. without any delay 迅速

Please rush documents without any delay.

请速寄交单证。

6. mark a good beginning 标志良好的开端

We hope this will mark a good beginning of our long, friendly and mutually beneficially business relations.

我们希望这标志着我们双方长久、友好、互利的良好关系的开端。

7. unconditionally *adv.* 无条件地；无限制地；绝对地

He accepted the offer unconditionally.

他无条件地接受了提议。

8. be committed to 委身于……，被交给……，答应承担……义务

To be honest, since you are not in a position to make any decision, you shouldn't have committed yourself.

老实说，既然你不是处于决策者的位置，你就不应该作承诺。

commit *vt.* 承诺，约束；使负有责任（商业上常指订货）

owing to heavy commitments=as they are heavily committed 由于订单太多

We are too heavily committed to be able to entertain fresh orders.

由于订单太多，无法接受新的订单。

We shall try our best to do as requested but cannot commit ourselves.

我们将尽力按照你方要求去做，但不作任何承诺。

Our manufacturers have committed themselves to substantial orders for a few months ahead.

生产厂家在未来几个月有许多大笔订单要完成。

9. **in accordance with** 与……相一致；按照，根据

   in exact/full accordance with 与……完全一致

   in strict/precise accordance with 与……严格一致

   The quality of the goods must be in strict accordance with that of the sample.

   货物的质量必须与样品质量严格一致。

   In accordance with faxes exchanged, we are glad to have purchased from you 100 dozen cotton bed-sheets.

   根据往来电传，很高兴向你方购买了100打棉质床单。

I. **Translate the following expressions.**

  A. From English into Chinese.

   1. routine orders   2. standing order

   3. entertain an order   4. pending order

   5. in duplicate   6. substantial order

  B. From Chinese into English.

   1. 订货追踪   2. 定制的订单

   3. 迅速   4. 急需

II. **Fill in the blanks with correct forms of the words given below.**

  A. satisfy

   1. The quality of your new product _____ us in every respect.

   2. We assure you that the goods will turn out to the _____ of your end-users.

   3. We are not quite _____ with the shipment.

   4. We are confident that this order will be _____ to you.

  B. regard

   1. In _____ to S/C No. 1360, please ship the goods without delay.

   2. As _____ the balance, we'll advise you the position in a few days.

3. We _____ this as a good beginning
4. We know nothing _____ the market condition there.

C. regret
1. We find it _____ that you failed to book the shipping space on s/s "Asia".
2. We expressed _____ at the delay.
3. We are _____ that we cannot supply the entire quantity required.
4. It is _____ that the matter should still be hanging unsettled.

III. Write a letter ordering the items listed below, specifying quantity, unit price, total amount and terms of payment, shipment, etc.

品名	数量	货号	价格	价格条件
不粘锅	3500	26"	USD121 per set	CFRD3 Chicago
	1400	30"	USD164 per set	CFRD3 Chicago

付款方式：即期汇票信用证
装运时间：12月25日之前及时抵达

Chapter VI Order and Contracts

Lesson 14

(A) Partial Acceptance of an Order

From: alicia0618@tchina.com
To: Jeremy Weiner @hotmail.com
Sent: Nov. 22, 2018
Subject: Purchase Order

Dear Jeremy Weiner,

Thank you for your kind email.

Upon receipt of your order, we contacted our manufacturers but they cannot entertain your order owing to heavy commitments and shortage of raw materials. However, after our repeated efforts at persuasion, they agreed to accept your order but the maximum is 29,472 pairs and to deliver the half of order starting from December this year. The remaining are to be shipped in January. If you agree, it is a deal.

We are aware that you are badly in need of these goods and we are approaching other manufacturers for possible supply of earlier deliveries. If we succeed, we will let you know. Regarding the goods in stock, we are enclosing a list for your perusal. In case you are interested, please do not hesitate to let us know.

At the same time, attached please find the logo and barcode for your approval.

Could you send the packing pictures to us, such as the color-printed paper picture?

Best regards,
Alicia
China Oriental Footwear Import & Export Corp.

(B) Reply to the Above

From: Jeremy Weiner @hotmail.com
To: alicia0618@tchina.com
Sent: Nov. 24, 2018
Subject: Purchase Order
Attachment: 1. Revised PO No. 03.05.GB24
               2. Packing PDF, label sample and preferred label placement

Dear Alicia,

I understand your situation and thanks for all your efforts done for us. Pls make up and ship the order asap. Attached is the revised PO No. 03.05.GB24.

The logo is OK. But as discussed we need Serial No. with barcode not the barcode sticker.

As in Serial No. you will have to print the Serial No. with barcode bar in a series.

Attached please find the packing PDF, label sample and preferred label placement.

Best regards,
Jeremy Weiner

Attachment:

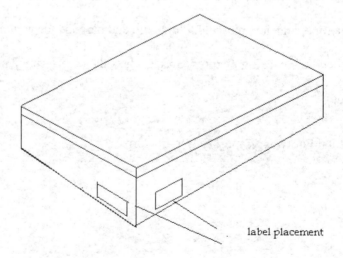

label placement

Chapter VI Order and Contracts

1. **partial** *adj.* 部分的

   partial acceptance 部分接受，partial shipment 分批装运

2. **upon receipt of:** as soon as 一……就

   Upon receipt of your instructions we will send the goods.

   一俟收到你方要求，我们将发货。

3. **entertain** *v.* 考虑（引申为接受）

   We shall be glad to entertain any constructive suggestion you make.

   我们将考虑你方所提出的具有建设性的意见。

   We are too heavily committed to be able entertain fresh orders.

   我们手头订单太多，无法接受新的订单。

4. **make up** 拼凑成，配齐，弥补

   make up an order 备齐订货

   You're requested to make up the shortage.

   请你方补齐所缺部分。

   We will do whatever we can to make up the economic losses.

   我们将尽全力弥补经济损失。

5. **shortage of** 缺乏

6. **repeated efforts** 不断的努力

7. **persuasion** *n.* 说服，劝说   persuade *v.* 说服，劝说

   In spite of my efforts at persuasion, he wouldn't agree.

   尽管我努力劝说，他还是不同意。

8. **stock** *n.* 存货（后接介词 in/of，再接商品）

   At present, we have only a limited stock in (of) linen goods.

   目前我们的亚麻货物库存有限。

   There are no stocks available at present.

   目前无货可供。

   We have run out of stock.

   我们的存货已售完。

   We can supply this quantity from stock (ex stock).

   这个数量我们可供现货。

If you have Fountain Pens in stock, please send us some samples.

如果你方有水笔现货，请给我们寄些样品。

9. **for your perusal** 供某人详阅

Regarding the details of specifications, we are faxing a copy of our illustrated catalogue for your perusal.

关于详细规格，我们传真一份带插图的目录供你方参阅。

10. **barcode** 条形码 (barcode) 是将宽度不等的多个黑条和空白，按照一定的编码规则排列，用以表达一组信息的图形标识符。条形码可以标出物品的生产国、制造厂家、商品名称、生产日期、图书分类号、邮件起止地点、类别、日期等许多信息，因而在商品流通、图书管理、邮政管理、银行系统等许多领域都得到了广泛的应用。

11. **Serial Number** S/N 是简称，就是序列号；P/N: part number

12. **label placement** 贴法；label stick 标贴

I. Translate the following expressions.

A. From English into Chinese.

1. barcode
2. label placement
3. entertain an order
4. partial acceptance
5. out of stock
6. on the basis of

B. From Chinese into English.

1. 供某人详阅
2. 急需
3. 由"胜利"轮卸下
4. 可供现货

II. Choose the best answer.

1. Our goods are _____ great demand at the moment.
   A. at   B. in   C. for   D. upon

2. Please quote us your lowest price _____ CIF London basis.
   A. in   B. for   C. of   D. on

3. Our latest design has won worldwide _____.
   A. popular   B. popularity C. popularly D. popularize

4. We have pleasure in enclosing a copy of our latest catalogue _____ for in your letter.

   A. ask   B. asks   C. asked   D. asking

5. We can supply a variety of jeans _____ very favorable terms.

   A. for   B. to   C. against   D. on

6. We have confidence _____ the quality of Chinese textiles.

   A. at   B. in   C. for   D. with

7. We thank you _____ advance for your attention.

   A. at   B. in   C. for   D. with

8. We would _____ very much if you would pass the letter on to the person responsible for the matter.

   A. appreciate   B. appreciate it   C. thank   D. thank you

9. We are glad to say that we can supply any quantity of anoraks _____ stock.

   A. for   B. from   C. of   D. on

10. We were satisfied with the products _____ S/S Wanjie when your shipment reached us.

    A. per   B. onto   C. ex   D. nearby

III. Translate the following sentences into English.

1. 随函附上标贴供参考。
2. 现在我们的库存量急剧减少，我们能供应的最大量是 200 吨。
3. 我们没有现货，请告知其他牌子可供现货的规格。
4. 订货太多，到年底交货的产品都已售完。
5. 我们很高兴确认从你处购进 1000 箱番茄酱（Tomato Paste），船期是 10 月。

Lesson 15

(A) Sending a Sales Confirmation

From: alicia0618@tchina.com
To: Jeremy Weiner@hotmail.com
Sent: Nov. 25, 2018
Subject: Sales Confirmation
Attachment: Sales Contract

Dear Jeremy Weiner,

After our recent exchange of emails, we are pleased to book your Order PO No. 03.05.GB24. for Flip Flop.

Attached is our Sales Confirmation FP992041W-1 in duplicate made out against your mentioned above. Please countersign it and return one copy for our files, and establish the covering L/C in December, 2018.

We wish to point out that the stipulations in the relevant credit should strictly conform to the terms stated in our sales confirmation thus avoiding subsequent amendments.

You may rest assured that we shall make up your order upon receipt of the credit and effect the shipment within the time you requested.

We appreciate your co-operation and anticipate your further orders.

Best regards,
Alicia
China Oriental Footwear Import & Export Corp.

Chapter VI Order and Contracts

(B) Counter-Signature Letter

From: Jeremy Weiner @hotmail.com
To: alicia0618@tchina.com
Sent: Nov. 27, 2018
Subject: Sales Confirmation
Attachment: Sales Contract

Dear Alicia,

We have duly received your Sales Confirmation FP992041W-1. Enclosed please find the duplicate with our counter-signature. Thanks to our mutual efforts, we were able to bridge the price gap and put the deal through.

The relative L/C will be established with the Banca Monte Dei Paschi Di Siena S.P.A., London, in your favor. It will reach you in due course.

Regarding further quantities required, we hope you will see your way clear to make us an offer.

Best regards,
Jeremy

Attachment:

福 建 东 方 鞋 业 进 出 口 公 司
FUJIAN ORIENTAL FOOTWEAR IMP. & EXP. CO., LTD.
售 货 合 同
SALES CONTRACT

正 本　　　　　　　　　　　合同号码：FP992041W-1
（ORIGNAL）　　　　　　　CONTRACT No. FP992041W-1

　　　　　　　　　　　　　签订日期：2018 年 11 月 25 日
　　　　　　　　　　　　　Date: Nov. 25, 2018

　　　　　　　　　　　　　签订地点：福州
　　　　　　　　　　　　　Signed at: Fuzhou

卖　方：福建东方鞋业进出口公司
The Sellers: FUJIAN ORIENTAL FOOTWEAR IMP. & EXP. CO., LTD.

地　址：
Address: 9/F MINFA BUILDING NO. 88, DONGSHUI ROAD FUZHOU FUJIAN

买　方：
The Buyer: AL ABRA SUB TRADING EST.

地　址：
Address: AL ABRA SUB TRADING EST. 94017 REGALBUTO CATANIA, ITALY

兹经买卖双方同意由卖方出售买方购进之下列货物,并按下列条款签订本合同：

This Sales Contract is made out as per the following terms and conditions confirmed by both parties:

商品名称与规格 Commodity & Specifications	数量 Quantity	单价 Unit Price	金额 Amount
'FAIL FASCIA' BRAND EVA SLIPPER ART. NO. HC13097: 928CTNS ART. NO. HC808B301: 300CTNS Assortment: SIZE:　　35 36 37 38 39 40 41 navy blue　1 2 3 3 2 1 0 black　　　0 1 2 3 3 2 1	22,272PRS 7,200PRS	FOB C2 FUZHOU USD0.71/PR USD0.81/PR	USD15,813.12 USD5,832.00
TOTAL:	29,472 PRS	--------------	**USD21,645.12**

（允许卖方在装货时溢装或短装　　％价按照本合同所列的单价计算）
The Sellers are allowed to load 　　％ more or less, the price shall be calculated according to the price)

Total Value: USD21,645.12(SAY USD TWENTY ONE THOUSAND SIX HUNDRED AND FORTY-FIVE CENTS TWELVE)

1. **Time of shipment:** JANUARY, 2019

   Transhipment: ALLOWED

   Partial shipments: ALLOWED

2. **Shipping mark:** A.B.S.T nbr—ord number—art number port of destination: CATANIA

3. **Port of loading:** FUZHOU MAIN PORT, CHINA

4. **Port of destination:** CATANIA PORT, ITALY

5. **Packing:** EACH PAIR IN POLYBAG, TIED TOGETHER IN NYLON THREAD, WITH HOOK

6. **Payment:** BY IRREVOCABLE L/C AT SIGHT

7. **Insurance:** TO BE EFFECTED BY THE BUYER

8. **Force Majeure:** The Seller shall not be held liable for failure or delay in delivery of the entire lot or a portion of the Commodity under this contract in consequence of any force majeure incidents.

9. **Arbitration:** Any or all disputes arising from or in connection with the performance of the Contract shall be settled through negotiation by both parties, failing which they shall be submitted for arbitration. The arbitration shall take place in China and shall be conducted by the CIETAC in accordance with the rules of procedures of the said commission. The arbitration award shall be final and binding upon both Buyers and Sellers. Unless otherwise awarded by the said arbitration commission, the arbitration fees shall be borne by the losing party.

10. **Other conditions**:

    验收要求：1. 抽样：按 GB2828 正常二次抽样方案和一般检查水平 II

    2. 品质：表面各配件装配牢固；（AQL=6.5）外观整洁：标志、文字、符号清晰；（AQL=6.5）平均瞬时日差：-~+s/d:(AQL=2.5)

    Buyers (Signature)　　　　　　　Sellers (Signature)

    Jeremy Weiner　　　　　　　　*Alicia Wu*

1. **Sales Contract 销售合同**

   在国际贸易中，交易的一方明示接受另一方的交易条件，交易即达成，然后签订具有合同性质的文件。由卖方按照双方认可的条款订制的合同称之为销售合同或销售确认书（Sales Confirmation）。相关词组还有：

draft/draw the contract 起草合同

make out the contract 缮制合同

sign the contract 签订合同

execute /honor/perform the contract 履行合同

break/breach the contract 违反合同

2. **book one's order** 接受某人的订货，买进或卖出

比较一下：

We are glad that we have booked your order for 150 bicycles.

我们很高兴售予你方150辆自行车。

We are glad that we have booked with you 150 bicycles.

我们很高兴向你方购买150辆自行车。

3. **in duplicate** 一式两份

in triplicate 一式三份，in quadruplicate 一式四份

一式四份及其以上也常说：in four copies, in five copies… 或 in four fold, in five fold…

4. **countersign** *vt.* 副署，会签

We attach hereto our Purchase Contract No. 356 with our signature. Please check and countersign it.

现附上我们已签署的356号购货合同，请审核并会签。

countersignature *n.* 副署，会签

We enclose our S/C No. ID-472 in duplicate for your countersignature.

现附上我方ID-472号售货合同一式两份，请会签。

5. **for one's file** 供某人存档（also: for one's records）

The copy of the invoice is sent to you for your file.

现将发票副本寄给你方，供你方存档。

6. **stipulation** *n.* 规定，条款（适合于合同、规定、信用证等）

The stipulations in the relative credit should strictly conform to the terms stated in our S/C.

信用证条款必须严格与合同条款一致。

The transaction is concluded on the stipulation that L/C (should) be opened 30 days before the commencement of shipment.

这笔交易必须包括一项条款，即信用证必须在装运开始前开立。

stipulate *v.* 规定

作不及物动词时与 for 连用；以 payment, shipment, quality 等名词或 that 引导的从句作宾语时，则不用 for，另外 that 从句用虚拟语气。

We note that your order stipulates direct shipment.

我们知道你方规定直达轮装运。

The contract stipulates that the goods (should) be shipped entire.

合同规定货物全部装运。

7. **conform** *v.* 使一致，符合

作及物动词时，宾语后接介词 to。

It is necessary to conform the specifications to the requirements.

规格与所需求的货一致是非常必要的。

The quality must conform to (with) the sample.

质量必须与样品一致。

conformity *n.* 符合，一致

主要用于 in conformity with 和 in conformity to 两个词组，二者均作"和……相一致；依照"解，前者较后者普遍。

This is not in conformity with our arrangement.

这与我们的安排不一致。

In conformity with (to) our desire to promote business, we have accepted your offer of 50 tons wool.

为了符合促进业务的愿望，我们已接受你方五十吨羊毛的报盘。

8. **subsequent** *adj.* 以后的

This applies to all subsequent transactions.

这个适合以后的交易。

subsequent to 在……之后

The date of this order is subsequent to your Order No. 68.

这笔订单的日期是你方第 68 号订单之后的。

9. **assure** *vt.* 使确信；保证

We wish to assure you of the punctual shipment of your order.

我们向你们保证准时付运订单。

We assure you that we shall revert to your enquiry as soon as fresh supplies come in.

我们向你们保证一旦有新货源我们就重提此事。

Please be assured of our readiness to cooperate with you.

你们尽可放心，我们随时愿意与你们合作。

You may rest assured that as soon as we are able to accept new orders, we shall give priority to yours.

你们尽可放心，我们一旦能接受订单，会优先考虑你们。

10. **duly /in due course** (in good time, at proper time, in due time) 适当地； 及时地

We are glad to inform you that we have duly received your feasibility report.

我们很高兴告知你们，我们已及时收到你们的可行性报告。

All your instructions have been duly acted upon.

你方要求已及时照办。

11. **bridge the gap** 弥合差距

   类似的有：close the gap / bridge over the gap

   We have done our best to bridge the gap.

   我们已尽力弥合差距。

   The price is too wide to bridge.

   价格差距太大难以弥合。

12. **put through** 做成（工作等）

   If you renew your offer for a further 3 days, we believe we can put the business through.

   如果你方再延续报盘三天，我们相信我们可以达成交易。

13. **in sb.'s favor / in favor of** 以……为受益人，以……为抬头

   We have already applied to Bank of China, Fuzhou for the establishment of an L/C in your favor.

   我方已向中国银行福州分行申请开立以你方为受益人的信用证。

14. **see one's way clear** 设法

I. Translate the following expressions.

   A. From English into Chinese.

   1. sales confirmation 2. in triplicate
   3. put through 4. GP
   5. in good condition 6. effect shipment

   B. From Chinese into English.

   1. 弥合差距 2. 会签
   3. 设法 4. 订货追踪

II. Fill in the blanks with suitable prepositions.
1. As Christmas is coming, we are _____ urgent need _____ candles.
2. Enclosed please find the duplicate _____ our counter-signature.
3. We appreciate your effort _____ pushing the sale of our products these years.
4. The L/C established _____ our favor does not conform _____ the terms stated in our S/C.
5. We hope to book _____ you a repeat order _____ the following lines _____ USD230 per set CIF London.
6. Please arrange production _____ strict conformity _____ our duplicate samples.
7. The L/C, we believe, will reach you _____ due course.
8. We have pleasure _____ sending you sales confirmation No.786 _____ duplicate _____ 3,000 metric tons _____ soybean, one copy _____ which please sign and return to us _____ our file.

III. Translate the following into English.
1. 经过最近我们双方的传真往来，我们很高兴与你方达成10吨干红辣椒（dry red chilli）的交易。
2. 如果你们认为没问题，我们希望你们签回销售合同的副本一份备查。
3. 请放心，该货的装运不会再有迟延。
4. 我们已于15日通过东京的中国银行给你方开出1758号信用证。
5. 关于下季度我们需要的数量，希望你公司能设法报盘。

Skill Training

Exercise I. Fill in the contract form with the information given below.

近日，上海太平洋贸易有限公司（SHANGHAI PACIFIC TRADING CO., LTD.）一外销员在参加2010年中国轻工业产品博览会时与南非THE SPLENIA INTERNATIONAL CO. 一采购员结识。

双方互相交换名片：

SHANGHAI PACIFIC TRADING CO., LTD.
上海太平洋贸易有限公司

刘 世 元

108 LAOSHAN ROAD, SHANGHAI, CHINA
TEL: 021-64675348   FAX: 021-64675346

THE SPLENIA INTERNATIONAL CO.

JAMAS SMITH

101 LONG STREET, CAPETOWN, SOUTH AFRICA
TEL: 732-6574211   FAX: 732-6574213

外方对中方的以下商品很感兴趣：

商品	FOREVER 牌相框（FRAME）		
货号	数量(件)	包装方式	CIFC3单价
ART. NO. ONE001	1200	6件/纸箱	8.90
ART. NO. ONE002	800	8件/纸箱	12.80

经过双方磋商，达成协议如下：
装运：2010年8月中旬之前装运至开普敦，允许分批装运和转运
付款：即期信用证，2010年6月底前开到
保险：加成10%投保协会货物A险及协会货物战争险

请根据以上信息缮制一份出口合同，号码为PAC20001，日期为2010年6月18日。
要求合同条款规范、完整、准确。

Chapter VI Order and Contracts

SALES CONFIRMATION

S/C No.: _____

Date: _____

The Seller: Shanghai Pacific Trading Co., Ltd. The Buyer:
Address: 108 Laoshan Road   Address:
         Shanghai, China
         Tel: 021-64675348 Fax:021-64675346

Item No.	Commodity & Specifications	Unit	Quantity	Unit Price (US$)	Amount (US$)
1	Art. No. ONE001				
2	Art. No. ONE002				
TOTAL CONTRACT VALUE:					

PACKING:

TIME OF
SHIPMENT:

TERMS OF
PAYMENT:

INSURANCE:

REMARKS:

Confirmed by:
　　　　　　THE SELLER　　　　　　　　　　　　THE BUYER

　　　　Shanghai Pacific Trading Co., Ltd.

　　　　　　(signature)　　　　　　　　　　　　(signature)

Exercise II. Fill in the contract form with information gathered from the following correspondences.

Email 1

Sender: Cathy Jones <cathy@hotmail.com>

Receiver: Wang Feng<wangf@yahoo.com>

Subject: Teapots

Date: 02-05-15 15:58:00

Shandong Eastern General Trading Co., Shandong, China

Dear Mr. Wang,

How are you?

I'm glad to tell you that our customers are very satisfied with your last shipment of brown ceramic teapots delivered to us two mouths ago. They have placed a new order for your teapots as follows:

    Item # TP5203E/J2 (2-cup capacity)   480PCS, 48PCS / ctn

    Item # TP5205E/J2 (6-cup capacity)   1680PCS, 24PCS / ctn

    Item # TP5208E/J2 (10-cup capacity)   1206PCS, 18PCS / ctn

Do the prices remain the same? Could you advise your earliest date of delivery when confirming the order?

Thanks and best regards,
Unitrade Co., Ltd./Cathy Jones

Email 2

Sender: Wang Feng<wangf@yahoo.com>

Receiver: Cathy Jones <cathy@hotmail.com>

Subject: Teapots

Date: 02-05-16 09:53:00

Unitrade Co., Ltd.

Dear Miss Jones,

Thank you for your new order. I'm glad to say we can supply the teapots you require on the usual terms. Our price remain unchanged, i.e.

    Ceramic Teapots, Brown   FOB Qingdao
    Item # TP5203E/J2 (2-cup capacity) USD@6.20/dz
    Item # TP5205E/J2 (6-cup capacity) USD@10.16/dz
    Item # TP5208E/J2 (10-cup capacity) USD@22.06/dz

We can deliver them in July.

If the above is acceptable, please confirm.

Thanks for your kind cooperation!

B. Rgds,
Wangfeng
For Shandong Eastern General Trading Co., Shandong, China

Email 3

Sender: Cathy Jones <cathy@hotmail.com>
Receiver: Wang Feng<wangf@yahoo.com>
Subject: Teapots
Attachment: Purchase Order
Date: 02-05-17 14:14:00

Dear Mr. Wang,

The price are quite acceptable. Attached is our Purchase Order No. 7033.

If there is any question, please don't hesitate to ask me.

Thanks and best regards,
Unitrade Co., Ltd./Cathy Jones

Attachment:

PURCHASE ORDER NO. 7033

To: Messrs. Shandong Eastern General Trading Co.
Commodity: Brown Ceramic Teapots
Specifications, quantity and price as stated in your email of May 16.
Finish: brown color

Packing: each piece in a cardboard box marked with UCP bar code and importer's address

Loading: in a 20ft container

Shipment: from Qingdao to Toronto on or before July 30, 2002

Shipping company: Panalpina

Shipping marks:

> D.J.C.L
>
> **TORONTO, CANADA**
>
> **Item # TP5203E/J2**
>
> **Item # TP5205E/J2**
>
> **Item # TP5208E/J2**
>
> **C/NO. 1-UP**

Payment: by T/T

Inspection: before shipment

Please mention the following statement on the B/L: "We hereby certify that this shipment contains no solid-wood packing material."

Please arrange 2pcs shipment sample of each item.

Special requirements:

GSP China Form A in duplicate

Consignee and Notify Party for GSE Form A and B/L:

Don Joy Canada Limited

281 Frosherbi Drive

Warterboo, Ontario

N2V 2G4 Canada

Unitrade Co., Ltd.

Authorized Signature(s)

Email 4

Sender: Wang Feng<wangf@yahoo.com>

Receiver: Cathy Jones <cathy@hotmail.com>

Subject: Teapots

Date: 02-05-18 11:33:00

Dear Miss Jones,

Your email of May 17 and P/O No. 7033 have been received. Thanks.

Everything is fine, but after recalculation, we find the quantity you order adds up to only 20CBM, which is not enough to make an FCL TEU. In order to make full use of the shipping container and save shipping cost, would you please consider increasing the quantity as follows:

    Item # TP5203E/J2   1296PCS
    Item # TP5205E/J2   2280PCS
    Item # TP5208E/J2   1638PCS

The above quantity fills a 20-foot container.

Please check and advise us if this workable.

With best regards,
Wang Feng

Email 5

Sender: Cathy Jones <cathy@hotmail.com>
Receiver: Wang Feng<wangf@yahoo.com>
Subject: Teapots
Date: 02-05-19 09:25:00

Dear Mr. Wang,

How are you!

I've discussed with my buyers the possibility of increasing the quantity. Because they have already confirmed the order in the original quantity (as attached in my email dated May 17), they find it a little difficult to increase your proposal. But they say they will consider it if you may re-quote your best price!

Thanks and awaiting your early reply!

Unitrade Co., Ltd./Cathy Jones

Email 6

Sender: Wang Feng<wangf@yahoo.com>
Receiver: Cathy Jones <cathy@hotmail.com>
Subject: Teapots
Date: 02-05-19 16:53:00

Dear Miss Jones,

I've studied your proposal with my manager and am glad inform you that we have revised the prices as follows:

Ceramic Teapots, Brown	FOB Qingdao
Item # TP5203E/J2 (2-cup capacity)	USD@6.06/dz
Item # TP5205E/J2 (6-cup capacity)	USD@10.02/dz
Item # TP5208E/J2 (10-cup capacity)	USD@21.92/dz

Other terms remain unchanged.

Please advise whether the above is acceptable.

Awaiting your early reply!

Wang Feng
For Shandong Eastern General Trading Co.

Email 7

Sender: Cathy Jones <cathy@hotmail.com>
Receiver: Wang Feng<wangf@yahoo.com>
Subject: Teapots
Date: 02-05-20 14:29:00

Dear Mr. Wang,

Please be informed that our Canadian buyer has agreed to increase the quantity at the revised prices to fill a 20ft container, but the quantity will be as below:

Item # TP5203E/J2	1296PCS, 48PCS/ctn
Item # TP5205E/J2	2616PCS, 24PCS/ctn
Item # TP5208E/J2	1206PCS, 18PCS/ctn

We will send you a revised P/O later.

Please just proceed with the order if it suit you.

Best rgds,
Unitrade Co., Ltd./Cathy Jones

Email 8

Sender: Wang Feng<wangf@yahoo.com>
Receiver: Cathy Jones <cathy@hotmail.com>
Subject: Teapots
Date: 02-05-21 08:09:00

Dear Miss Jones,

The quantity you propose is all right.

Please send your revised Purchase Order ASAP. Meanwhile, we will also send you a sales contract.

Thank you for your kind cooperation and we hope we can receive more orders from you.

Best regards,
Wang Feng
For Shandong Eastern General Trading Co.

CONTRACT No.

Sellers:
Buyers:

This contract is made by and between the buyers and the sellers, whereby the buyers agree to buy and the sellers agree to sell the under mentioned according to the terms and conditions stipulated below.

Specifications	Quantity	Unit Price	Total Value
Total amount			

Packing:

Shipping Marks:
Insurance:
Time of Shipment:
Port of Shipment:
Port of Destination:
Terms of Payment:
Done and signed in _____ on this _____ day of _____ .

Business Link

Terms and Terminologies

Agreement on general terms and conditions on business 一般经营交易条件的协议

Agreement on loan facilities up to a given amount 商定借款协议

Agreement fixing price 固定价格协议

Agreement on import licensing procedure 进口许可证手续协议

Bilateral agreement 双边协议

Commercial agreement 商业协议

Distributorship agreement 分销协议

Barter contract 易货合同

Binding contract 有约束力合同

Blank form contract 空白合同

Cross license contract 互换许可证合同

Formal contract 正式合同

Illegal contract 非法合同

Installment contract 分期合同

Useful Sentences

1. We are pleased to place an order with you for the following items on the understanding that they can be supplied from stock at the prices quoted.
2. Thank you for your quotation of March 5 and the samples of the footwears, we are pleased to place an order with you on the terms stated in your fax.
3. We are sending you our sales contract No. 5690 in duplicate. Please countersign and return one copy for our file as soon as possible.
4. If the first order is satisfactorily executed, we shall place repeat orders with you.
5. The chief difficulty in accepting your orders now is the heavy backlog of commitments. But you may rest assured that as soon as we are able to accept new orders, we shall give priority or preference to yours.
6. Your order is booked and will be executed with great care. Please open the covering L/C, which must reach here one month before the date of shipment.

Chapter VI Order and Contracts

7. We have accepted your order No. 35 for 20,000 yards of pongee silk article No. 567. Please send us color assortment immediately and open the relevant L/C according to the terms and conditions agreed upon.
8. Please follow our shipping instructions carefully and make sure that our order is executed to the entire satisfaction of our customers with the least possible delay,
9. It is regrettable to see an order dropped owing to no agreement on price, however, we wish to recommend you another quality at a lower price for your consideration.
10. While thanking you for your order, we have to say that supplies of raw materials are becoming more and more difficult to obtain, and we have no alternative but to decline your order.
11. Thank you for your quotation of March 5 and the samples of ten footwears. We are pleased to place an order with you on the terms and conditions stated in your fax.
12. In case one party fails to carry out the contract, the other party is entitled to cancel the contract.
13. Are you worrying about the non-execution of the contract and non-payment on our part?
14. This contract will come into force as soon as it is signed by two parties.
15. We always carry out the terms of four contracts to the letter and stand by what we say.

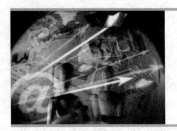

Chapter VII
Payment

> **Objectives:**
> After learning this chapter, you will
> 1. be acquainted with all types of international trade settlement;
> 2. understand the applications of different modes of payment in international trade;
> 3. master typical sentences and expressions in writing the letters on terms of payment;
> 4. learn to write reply letters concerning the above.

Introduction

Payment is an indispensable and complicated part in the course of in international trade. The final result of all business activities should be to recover the goods supplied or services rendered. Otherwise, all of them will be meaningless. Payment clause is very important in an international sales contract including such aspects as amount, time, place, currencies, modes and instruments of payment.

Remittance, collection and letter of credit (L/C) are three major modes of payment. But usually bills of exchange will be used in these modes of payment. A bill of exchange is a written order to a bank or a customer to pay someone on demand or at a fixed time in the future a certain sum of money. It is also called a draft or simply a bill.

1. Letter of Credit (L/C)

L/C is the most widely used, because it is reliable by committing the bank to honor drafts and / or documents presented by the exporter who performs in strict accordance with the L/C stipulations. It is a reliable and safe method of payment facilitating trade with unknown buyers and giving protection to both sellers and buyers. A letter of credit is a written undertaking, given at the request of the buyer, by the buyer's bank (the issuing bank) to pay a seller (the beneficiary), usually through an advising or negotiating bank in the beneficiary's country, provided the terms and conditions of the credit are complied with and documents called for by the credit are presented within the time limit specified.

The disadvantage of this method of payment is the cost, which is to be borne by the importer for opening an L/C, that is usually higher than other means of payment, and it takes a longer time.

2. Collection

Collection is a paying arrangement under which the exporter, as drawer of a bill of exchange, hands the bill of exchange to his bank, who in turn forwards it to the buyer through a collection bank in the buyer's country. There are two types of collection: clean one and documentary collection.

A collection is a "clean" one if the seller only draws a bill of exchange on the buyer without handing over any shipping documents to him; if it is one under which shipping documents accompany the bill of exchange, the collection is known as "documentary collection".

Documentary collection falls into two major categories: one is documents against payment (D/P), the other, documents against acceptance (D/A).

Documents against payment, as the term suggests, is that the collecting bank will only give the shipping documents representing the title to the goods on condition that the buyer makes payment. Under this paying arrangement, the seller may either draw a sight bill or a time (usance) bill. The former is called "D/P sight", while the later, "D/P after sight or after date".

In the case of D/P sight, the collecting bank presents a sight bill to the buyer, who must make immediate payment after presentation of the bill and gets the shipping documents in return.

If it is D/P after sight or date, the buyer must first accept the usance bill when the bank presents it to him, and will make payment when the bill falls due. At that time the buyer can obtain the relevant shipping documents.

Where the paying arrangement is D/A, the collecting bank will only give the buyer the shipping documents after buyer's acceptance of the time bill drawn on him, i.e., the buyer signs his name on the bill promising to pay the sum when it matures. In return he gets what he needs—the shipping documents. Under D/A, the seller gives up the title to the goods—shipping documents before he gets payment of the goods. Therefore, an exporter must think twice before he accepts such paying arrangement. It is very risky for him to get payment in this manner.

The major advantage of collection is the low cost, compared with an L/C. However, this is offset by the risk that the importer might for some reason or other reject the documents. Since the cargo would have already been loaded, the exporter has little recourse against the importer in cases of non-payment. Therefore the D/A or D/P arrangements involves a high level of trust between the exporter and the importer.

The fundamental difference between letter of credit and collection arrangements is that the former is bankers' credit, under which the bank is fully responsible for payment as long as the buyer has done exactly what is prescribed under the L/C; the latter is commercial credit, under which banks only act as agents to collect payment form the drawee of the bill of exchange. Banks bear no responsibility if the buyer dishonors (refuses to pay) the bill. Therefore whether the seller can get payment all depends on the creditworthiness and commercial integrity of the buyer.

3. Remittance

As the simplest method of payment in international trade, remittance means that the payer (usually the buyer) remits a certain sum of money in accordance with the parties' agreement to the payee (usually the seller) through a bank. This method of payment is often used for down payment, payment of commission and for sample, settlement of claim, or as performance bond etc. Based on the means of transferring funds, a remittance usually falls into the following three types:

a. Mail Transfer (M/T)

b. Telegraphic Transfer (T/T)

c. Demand Draft (D/D)

Mail transfer and telegraphic transfer both refer to the movement of money from one bank account to another and differ in that the former is made by airmail while the latter by cable, telex or SWIFT. Mail transfer is cheap but slow, so it is typically used for remittances of small sums or of little urgency. While telegraphic transfer is safe and fast, thus it is currently the most popular way of remitting funds.

Demand draft is a draft drawn by the importer's bank on its branch or correspondent bank in the exporter's country and is payable immediately the exporter or holder demands payment. Thus, the procedures of demand draft are quite different from M/T and T/T, and it is also called reverse remittance. Such a demand draft is a type of bills of exchange. This means that the payee can transfer the draft before it is presented to the paying bank for payment. T/T and M/T do not have the same property as D/D.

Time of payment is also an important aspect for a sales transaction. It may be earlier or later than, or the same as the time of delivery.

a. Payment in advance. After the conclusion of a sales contract, the importer pays the purchase price for the goods to the exporter before the exporter begins to make arrangement for manufacturing or delivering the goods.

b. Payment at sight. When the exporter has shipped the goods, he tenders a sight bill and the required shipping documents to the buyer or his bank, asking the latter to make payment at sight of the draft. Collections with sight draft or sight L/C arrangement are payment of such type.

c. Deferred payment. Under this arrangement, the buyer may make payment of the goods a period of time after he has taken delivery of the goods.

Writing Tips

When we negotiate the terms of payment in the letter of payment terms, we should state the payment terms clearly and accurately. Always express the accepted terms of payment explicitly and unmistakably in business correspondence in order to avoid misunderstanding and subsequent trouble.

Usually a letter focusing on negotiating payment terms by the importers often consists of the following parts:

1) Mention the Contract No., Order No. goods, etc. in the opening sentences;

2) Suggest the specific terms of payment and put forward the reason clearly;

3) In the closing part, express your hope that the method of payment will be acceptable to your business partner and expectation for cooperation and an early reply.

When the exporter received the importer's letter, the reply to such letter also often consists of the following parts:

1) State that you have received the letter in the opening sentences;

2) Mention the method of payment your company usually adopts and give the reply of accepting or declining the suggested terms of payment; Give the reasons;

3) State your good will and your wish to do business with the importer.

Lesson 16

(A) Asking for Payment by T/T

From: Jeremy Weiner @hotmail.com
To: alicia@hotmail.com
Sent: Monday, October 29, 2018 10:00 AM
Subject: Asking for Payment by T/T
Attachment: Order Sheet

Dear Alicia,

We are pleased to receive your offer for sandals and slippers, knowing that you normally required payment by confirmed and irrevocable L/C at sight. We regret to inform you that we are unable to accept your terms of payment.

As you may know, when applying for the establishment of L/C, we have to pay a deposit in the bank. Besides, the bank interest is very high at present. It has really cost us a great deal on L/C basis. So we would like to propose a different mode of payment, say, telegraphic transfer (T/T). We shall appreciate it if you will allow us to pay 30% of the total value for this order in advance by T/T and the balance against copy B/L.

We are asking for this concession so that we can give our customers a specific delivery date and also save the expenses of opening an L/C. We hope you could grant our request.

Attached herewith is our final order sheet. Kindly review and send us the final PI to proceed further. We look forward to receiving confirmation of our order and your agreement to our new proposal for payment.

Best regards,
Jeremy Weiner

Chapter VII　Payment

(B) Confirming Payment by T/T

From: alicia@hotmail.com
To: Jeremy Weiner @hotmail.com
Sent: Wednesday, October 31, 2018 9:45 AM
Subject: Confirm Payment by T/T

Dear Jeremy Weiner,

We have received your email of October 29 and thanks for your Order No.123.

With a view to encouraging our future business, we are pleased to accept your proposal for payment by T/T. We believe this modification to payment terms will be more conducive to the expansion of trade between us.

Pls kindly check the PI and your file with completed information as attached. If it is OK for you, please wire 30% deposit to us by CHINA CITIC BANK, FUZHOU BRANCH, so that we can start the production for you ASAP. The attachment explains our T/T route and account No.

Hoping to hear from you soon.

Best regards,
Alicia
Attachment: T/T route and account No.

1. **payment terms** 付款条件
   付款条件主要包括使用的货币、付款时间、地点以及支付方式等问题，与价格条件、品质条件、数量条件、包装条件以及交货条件，同为国际贸易买卖合约上应具备的主要交易条件。

2. **confirmed and irrevocable L/C** 保兑的、不可撤销的信用证
   Our payment terms are by a confirmed and irrevocable L/C payable by draft at sight.
   我们的付款条件是以保兑的、不可撤销的即期信用证支付。

3. **easier terms** 较宽松的条款

easy *adj.* (价格等)易于接受的,宽松的;(行情等)疲软的

Easy payment terms would be conducive to our business with you.

宽松的支付方式将有助于我们彼此间的业务。

4. Telegraphic Transfer (T/T) 电汇

   Mail Transfer (M/T) 信汇

   Demand Draft (D/D) 票汇

5. D/P 全称 documents against payment 付款交单

6. with a view to 为了……

It is with a view to encouraging future transactions that we grant you this price reduction.

我们给予你方降价是为了鼓励今后的交易。

7. be conducive to (常与 to 连用)有助于……的;有利于……的;助长……的

Close cooperation between us is conducive to the promotion of business.

我们之间的紧密合作有助于促进业务的发展。

8. wire *v.* 电汇

We have wired USD6,500 to you as the deposit of the goods.

我们今天已给你电汇 6500 美元作为货物的订金。

9. route *n.* (汇款)路径,由银行提供

I. Translate the following expressions.

   A. From English into Chinese.

   1. confirmed and irrevocable L/C   2. pay a deposit

   3. on L/C basis   4. be entitled to

   5. the balance   6. total value

   B. From Chinese into English.

   1. 即期信用证   2. 电汇

   3. 付款方式   4. 开立信用证

II. Decide whether the following statements are true or false. Write T for true and F for false in the brackets.

   (　　) 1. If the payment is to be made "30 days' sight", it means that the payment will have to be made 30 days after the issuing of this draft.

( ) 2. So far, documentary credits are the most ideal method of payment to provide security for both buyers and sellers. Therefore, in whatever conditions, L/C should be the first consideration in the method of payment for transactions.

( ) 3. The negotiating bank is usually referred to the issuing bank in the importing country.

( ) 4. To the seller, payment by D/P is much safer than by D/A.

( ) 5. On the basis of collection, the exporter usually demands the payment first before making shipment so as to protect his interest.

( ) 6. Whoever holds the bill of exchange, he has the right to demand the payment.

III. 1. Put the following letter into Chinese.

Dear Sirs,

    Thank you for your email of August 15.

    We are pleased that you will be able to ship our order in good time, but we are surprised to note that you still demand payment against documents. After long years of satisfactory trading we feel that we are entitled to easier terms. Most of our suppliers are drawing on us at 60 days' sight documents against acceptance, and we should be grateful if you could grant us the terms.

    We look forward to your favorable reply.

Yours faithfully,
×××

** 2. Give a reply to the above letter with the following hints.**

    1) 8 月 20 日电悉。

    2) 60 天期承兑交单不能接受。

    3) 考虑到长期友好合作关系，可同意 60 天期付款交单。

Lesson 17 Declining Payment by 60 Days' L/C

From: alicia0618@tchina.com
To: Jeremy @hotmail.com
Sent: Tuesday, Nov. 8, 2018 10:45 AM
Subject: Payment under Order No. 378

Dear Jeremy Weiner,

We confirm having received your trial Order No. 03.05.GB24. for flip flop slippers and thanks a lot for your efforts.

Regarding the coming order, although we appreciate your intention and suggestion, we regret to inform you that we are unable to entertain your request for payment by 60 days' L/C, owing to frequent fluctuation of present market. We do hope you can do more efforts and wish you can support us by L/C at sight for payment terms so as to ensure timely collection of the proceeds. We can fully understand what you mean by Messager that you have to invest much into materials purchase. So L/C at sight is much fair for both of us.

On the other hand, the offer is quite competitive. We cannot afford the US currency loss. Currently we have to stare at the exchange rate carefully. Once the offer is firm, we couldn't increase customer's price for our cost loss. If we ask for cost up suddenly when we inform you that the US exchange rate is dropping, and we will lose. That would ruin all business. We don't think you would like to see that happen.

We look forward to your confirmation of our payment by L/C at sight. Your early favorable reply will be highly appreciated.

Best regards,
Alicia Wu

Chapter VII　Payment

1. **letter of credit** 信用证

    信用证是可数的普通名词，单数为（a）letter of credit，复数为 letters of credit，但在商业书信中常作大写，单数为（an）L/C，复数为 Ls/C。即期信用证常简称"sight L/C"，远期信用证则可说 usance/time/term L/C。term L/C at 30 days after sight 见票30天议付的信用证。

    documentary L/C 跟单信用证　　　　reciprocal L/C 对开信用证
    transferable L/C 可转让信用证　　　divisible L/C 可分割信用证
    revolving L/C 循环信用证　　　　　back to back L/C 背对背信用证

2. **fluctuation** *n.* 波动

    The present price fluctuation in the world market has forced us to adjust our price accordingly.

    目前世界市场价格变化不定，迫使我们必须相应地调整价格。

3. **proceeds** *n. pl.*（常用复数）货款，收益，收入

    All the proceeds will go into our account with the Bank of China, Shanghai Branch.

    所有的货款都将进入我们在中国银行上海分行的账户。

4. **competitive** *adj.* 竞争的，有竞争力的

    To command certain share in the international market, competitive price is necessary.

    要在国际市场拥有一定的份额，商品价格必须具有竞争力。

5. **exchange rate** 汇率；兑换率

    The exchange rate changes are needed to facilitate global adjustment.

    汇率变动是促成全球调整的必要条件。

I. Translate the following expressions.

　　A. From English into Chinese.

　　1. owing to　　　　　　　2. 60 days' L/C

　　3. entertain　　　　　　　4. competitive offer

　　5. frequent fluctuation　　　6. present market

B. From Chinese into English.
1. 远期信用证   2. 汇率
3. 美国货币   4. 托收

II. Identify the one error in each of the following sentences.

1. Please see <u>to</u> it that the credit stipulations <u>are</u> <u>in</u> exact accordance <u>of</u> the terms of
    　　　A　　　　　　　　　　　　　　B　C　　　　　　　D
   contract.

2. As you have failed to open the L/C <u>in time</u>, we regret <u>being</u> unable to make
    　　　　　　　　　　　　　　　　A　　　　　　　　B
   shipment <u>within</u> the <u>stipulating</u> time limit.
    　　　　　　C　　　　　D

3. In compliance <u>with</u> your request, we exceptionally accept delivery <u>against</u> D/P
    　　　　　　　　A　　　　　　　　　　　　　　　　　　　　　　　　B
   <u>with</u> sight, but this should not be regarded <u>as</u> a precedent.
    　　C　　　　　　　　　　　　　　　　　　　D

4. We opened our confirmed and <u>irrevocable</u> letter of credit <u>in our favor</u> available by
    　　　　　　　　　　　　　　　A　　　　　　　　　　　　B
   your draft at 60 days <u>after sight</u> <u>drawn on</u> this bank.
    　　　　　　　　　　　　C　　　　　　D

5. We regret our <u>inability</u> to entertain your request that our L/C <u>establishing</u> with the
    　　　　　　　A　　　　　　　　　　　　　　　　　　　　　　B
   Bank of China <u>be confirmed</u> by X Bank <u>in</u> your city.
    　　　　　　　　　C　　　　　　　　　D

6. We shall draw <u>on</u> you by our documentary draft <u>at sight</u>, <u>in</u> collection basis, <u>without</u>
    　　　　　　　A　　　　　　　　　　　　　　　B　　　C　　　　　　　D
   L/C.

7. <u>As requested</u>, we have immediately arranged <u>for</u> our bankers to <u>extend</u> the expiry
    　　A　　　　　　　　　　　　　　　　　　B　　　　　　　　　C
   date of our L/C for 15 days <u>up to</u> May 10.
    　　　　　　　　　　　　　　　D

8. With regard of terms of payment, we regret being unable to accept documents
       A   B   C
   against payment.
       D

III. Put the following into English.

1. 为了今后的业务，我方同意不用即期信用证，而改用即期付款交单方式。
2. 我方接受保兑的、不可撤销的信用证，以即期汇票而不是以电汇形式偿付。
3. 鉴于交易总金额巨大，国际货币市场又很不稳定，所以我方无法接受除信用证外的其他支付方式。
4. 鉴于我们长期的友好贸易关系，我方破例接受见票后 60 天议付的信用证。
5. 为了节省开立信用证的大量费用，我们将在货物已备妥待运且舱位已订下时，电汇全部金额。

Lesson 18

(A) Asking for Easier Payment

From: Arne Jense @hotmail.com
To: alicia@hotmail.com
Sent: Monday, Nov. 16, 2018 10:45 AM
Subject: Asking for Easier Payment for Our Order No. 5326

Dear Alicia Wu,

As one of your regular customers, we have been dealing with you on L/C basis for many years.

On this basis, it has cost us a great deal. From the moment we open credit till the time our buyers pay us, the tie-up of our funds lasts about four months. This is currently a particularly serious problem for us in view of the difficult economic climate and the prevailing high interest rates. It'll increase the cost and leave us a much narrower profit margin.

After long years of satisfactory we feel that we are entitled to easier terms. We propose either "cash against documents on arrival of goods", or "drawing on us at D/A 60 days' sight". You may rest assured that we will pay immediately the full amount of the purchase on receipt of the shipping documents for the captioned goods.

We hope this proposal will meet with your agreement and thanks for your cooperation in advance.

Best regards,
Arne Jense

(B) Reply to the Above

From: alicia@hotmail.com
To: Arne Jense @hotmail.com
Sent: Wednesday, Nov. 18, 2018 14:45 PM
Subject: Reply to Payment under Order No. 5326

Dear Arne Jense,

Thanks for your email dated Nov. 16 concerning the matter of payment for the captioned order.

Our general practice for terms of payment is by confirmed and irrevocable L/C at sight, so we regret to inform you that we are not in a position to entertain your request for payment by 60 days' D/A.

However, in view of our long and mutually beneficial relationship, we are willing to make an exception to accept D/P at sight for this trial order. We must stress that this departure from our usual practice relates to this transaction only. We cannot regard it as setting a precedent for future transactions.

If you find our proposal acceptable, please let us know with the least possible delay and then we can expedite the transaction.

Best regards,
Alicia Wu

1. **tie-up** 占压
   tie-up of funds 占压资金
   tie-up in negotiations 谈判僵局
   tie-up of traffic 交通停顿
   The request for easier payment terms is compelled by their funds being tied up in numerous commitments.

由于资金被许多业务占用，他们迫不得已要求较宽的付款条件。

2. in view of 鉴于，考虑到

It is only in view of our longstanding business relations that we agree to accept your requirements.

只是鉴于我们之间的长期业务关系，我方才同意接受你方的要求。

3. difficult economic climate 经济不景气

4. profit margin 利润幅度；利润率

We have had many problems recently, and the recession has really cut into our profit margin.

我们最近有很多问题，尤其经济萧条更使得我们的利润下降。

5. cash against documents on arrival of goods 简称 CAD 货到后凭单付款

6. draw on sb. 表示开出汇票向某人索取某笔款项

As agreed, we are drawing on you at sight against your purchase of a sample lot.

按照商定，对你方所购样货，我们开出即期汇票向你方索款。

We regret to note that our draft drawn on you on the terms of D/P 30 days after sight was dishonored.

我们遗憾地注意到，我们开给你方的30天期的付款交单的汇票遭到了拒付。

drawings *n.* 用汇票支取的金额

drawer *n.* 出票人，发票人

drawee *n.* 受票人，（汇票）付款人

7. be in a position to 能够

be in a good position to do sth. 很有能力做某事，完全能做某事

be in a difficult position to do sth. 很难做某事

We are in a good position to meet your requirements.

我们完全可以满足你方的需求。

After repeated efforts, we regret to say that we are in a difficult position to meet your requirements.

经过再三努力，我们还是抱歉很难满足你方的需求。

8. make an exception 破例

as an exceptional case 破例地，例外地

In compliance with your request, we will accept delivery against D/P at sight as an exception.

根据你方的要求，我们将破例同意以即期付款交单的方式交货。

类似的表达还有：

make a concession 做出让步

Chapter VII   Payment

reach a compromise 妥协，折中

meet sb. half way 各让一半，折中处理

In order to close the deal, we really think we should both make some concessions.

为了做成这笔交易，我们确实认为我们双方应做出一些让步。

In view of your business amount, we would agree to meet you half way.

考虑到你们交易的金额，我们同意折中处理，各让一半。

9. **precedent** *n.* 先例

   set a precedent 开创先例

   take sth. as a precedent 将某事当作先例

   Our accommodation in this respect should not set a precedent for future transactions.

   我们在这方面的通融绝不能为今后的交易开创先例。

10. **with the least possible delay** 毫不延迟地，立即

    Please send us the goods with the least possible delay as our customers are in urgent need of them.

    因我方客户急需该货，请尽快发运。

I. Translate the following expressions.

   A. From English into Chinese.

   1. make an exception   2. easier payment terms

   3. interest rate   4. 60 days' D/A

   5. difficult economic climate   6. the shipping documents

   B. From Chinese into English.

   1. 即期付款交单   2. 占压

   3. 鉴于   4. 互利

II. Fill in the blanks in their proper forms.

Dear Sirs,

Thanks for your letter of May 16, 2010 and appreciate your intention to _____

      1. (A) promoted
      (B) promotion
      (C) promoting
      (D) promote

the sales of our electric shaver in your country.

We regret that we are unable to consider your request for payment on D/A terms. As a rule, we ask for payment by L/C.

But, _____ of our friendly relations, we will, as an _____ case,

  2. (A) in view to   3. (A) exception
     (B) in view with   (B) excepted
     (C) in view of   (C) excepting
     (D) on view of   (D) exceptional

accept payment for your trial order on D/P basis. In other words we will draw _____ you

4. (A) with
   (B) in
   (C) on
   (D) at

by documentary draft at sight, through our bank, on collection basis, without L/C.

We hope the above payment terms will be _____ to you and expect to receive your

      5. (A) accepting
       (B) acceptable
       (C) accept
       (D) acceptance

trial order in due course.

We look forward to your early reply.

Yours faithfully,
× × ×

III. Put the following into English.

  1. 应你方要求，我方破例接受即期的付款交单方式，但不能认为是惯例。

  2. 由于这次订单订货数量不大，建议其付款方式采用通过银行付款交单托收的方式，以简化手续。

Chapter VII Payment

3. 考虑到你方目前的困难，我方同意接受见票即付的付款交单方式。

4. 作为特殊照顾，我们同意你方的建议并接受即期付款交单，但这不应视为先例。

5. 考虑到我们长期的友好关系，我方这次同意你方的要求，即50%用信用证支付，其余的用即期付款交单。

Skill Training

Exercise I. Translate the following into Chinese.

Dear Alicia,

We are glad to receive your duplicate samples and feel satisfied with them.

Attached is our PO No. 123. As agreed upon, we will wire 30% of the total value to you as deposit through CHINA CITIC BANK, FUZHOU BRANCH.

BENEFICIARY'S NAME:	FUZHOU OTIENTAL FOOTWEAR TRADE CO., LTD. A/C NO. 7341 0124 8888 0009 807
BENEFICIARY'S BANKER	CHINA CITIC BANK, FUZHOU BRANCH A/C NO. 001155555 SWIFT CODE: CIBKCNBJ350
CORRESPONDENT OF BENEFICIARY'S BANKER	JPMORGAN CHASE BANK N.A., NEW YORK SWIFT CODE: CHASUS33XXX

FOR FURTHER CREDIT TO CHINA CITIC BANK, FUZHOU BRANCH MARKING THE BENEFICIARY（受益人名称）_____WITH A/C NO._____（受益人账号）

Best regards,
Jeremy Weiner

Exercise II.

场 景

你公司 SHANGHAI HUACHENG IMPORT & EXOPRT CORP. (258 YISHAN ROAD, SHANGHAI CHINA TEL: (021)646644912 E-MAIL: YYAA@H&C.COM)经过磋商，与韩国的 Myung-il Household Co. ［927-3 weolam-dong, dalseo-gu, daegu, Taegu-Kwangyeokshi, South Korea 704320 Tel: (82 53) 5823911 Fax: (82 53) 5823915］达成了一笔进口交易，主要成交条件如下：

品名：Bandi Tea Pot and Bug
货号：JY788
价格：USD 21.82 per set CFR Shanghai
数量：12000 套
包装：10 sets/ctn
装运：9月30日前等量分两批在 INCHON 装运
付款：延期付款信用证，单据到达开证行后三十天付款

昨天，双方签订了购货合同确认书 No. SN05SK，现请你据此填写一份信用证申请书。

其他资料
　　开证行：中国人民银行上海分行
　　数量证明一式三份
　　制造商签署的质量证明书一式二份
　　受益人证明的副本在装船通知发出后 48 小时发送给开证申请人

Chapter VII Payment

IRREVOCABLE DOCUMENTARY CREDIT APPLICATION

TO: **BANK OF CHINA, SHANGHAI BRANCH**

Applicant (full name and **Email Address**)	Beneficiary (full name and **Email Address**)
Advising Bank	L/C NO.
	Date and place of expiry of the credit

Partial shipments	Transhipment	Amount (both in figures and words)
[ ] allowed [ ] not allowed	[ ] allowed [ ] not allowed	

Loading on board/ dispatch/ taking in charge at / from

SHIPMENT is made not later than

for transportation to

Description of goods:

Bandi Tea Pot and Bug as per S/C NO. SN05SK

Packing:

Credit available with   ANY BANK
[ ] by sight payment   [ ] by acceptance   [ ] by negotiation
[ ] by deferred payment at   30 DAYS AFTER B/L DATE
against the documents detailed herein
[ ] and beneficiary's draft for   % of the inoice value
at
on   OPENING BANK
[ ] FOB   [ ] CFR   [ ] CIF
[ ] or other terms

Documents requied:(marked with x)
1. ( ) Signed Commercial Invoice in   copies indicating L/C No. And Contract No.
2. ( ) Full set of   clean on board ocean Bills of lading made out to   THE ORDER
        endorsed   IN BLANK   marked "freight ( ) to collect / ( )prepaid"
        and showing   FREIGHT AMOUNT   notifying   APLICANT
3. ( ) Air Waybills showing "freight[ ]to collect/[ ]prepaid[ ]indicating freight amount' and consigned to

4. ( ) Cargo Receipt issued by   consigned to

5. ( ) Insurance Policy / Certificaate in   copis, blank endorsed for   % of the invoice value showing claims payable
        at   in the currency of the drafts.
        covering
6. ( ) Packing List / Weight Memo in   copies indicating quantity / gross and net weight of each package and packing conditiions as
        called for by the L/C
7. ( ) Certificate of Quantity/Weight in   copies issued by an independent surveyor at the loading port, indicating the actual surveyed
        quantity / weight of shipped goods as well as the packing condition.
8. ( ) Certificate of Quality in   copies issed by[   ]manufacturer /[   ]public recognized surveyor / [   ]
9. ( ) Beneficiary's certified copy of cable / telex dispatched to the accountees within   hours after shipment advising [   ]name of
        vessel / [   ]flight No./ [   ] wagon No,. Date, quantity, weight and value of shipment
10. ( ) Beneficiary's Certificate certifying that extra copies of the documents have been dispatched according to the contract terms.
11. ( ) Shipping Co's Certificate atesting that the carrying vessel is chartered or booked by accountee or their shipping agents:

12. ( ) Other documents, if any:

Additional instuctions:
1. ( ) All banking charges outside the opening bank are for beneficiary's account.
2. ( ) Documents must be presented within   21   days after the date of issuance of the transport documents but within the valicity of
       this credit.
3. ( ) Third party as shipper is not acceptable. Short Form / Blank Back B/L is not acceptable.
4. ( ) Both quantity and amount   % more or less are allowed
5. ( ) Prepaid freight drawn in excess of L/C amount is acceptable against presentation of original charges voucher issued by shipping Co.
6. ( ) All documents to be forwarded in one cover, unless otherwise stated above.
7. ( ) Other terms, if any:

Account No.:   with   BANK OF CHINA, SHANGHAI BRANCH   (name of bank)

Transacted by: (Applicant: name, signature of authorized person)

Email: YYAA@H&C.COM

Business Link

I. Major Banks in China

中国银联：China UnionPay

中国银行：BOC（Bank of China）

中国工商银行：ICBC（Industrial & Commercial Bank of China）

中国农业银行：ABC（Agricultural Bank of China）

中国建设银行；CCB（China Construction Bank）

中国招商银行：CMB（China Merchants Bank）

中国光大银行：CEB（China Everbright Bank）

中国民生银行：CMBC（China Minsheng Bank）

中国进出口银行：The Export-Import Bank of China

中信银行：China CITIC Bank

兴业银行：CIB（Industrial Bank Co., Ltd.）

交通银行：Bank of Communications

上海浦东发展银行：Shanghai Pudong Development Bank

广东发展银行：Guangdong Development Bank

国家开发银行：China Development Bank

II. World Major Banks

阿比国民银行 Abbey National 英国

米兰银行 Midland Bank 英国

劳埃德银行 Lloyds Bank PLC. 英国

国民西敏寺银行 National Westminster Bank PLC. 英国

巴西银行 Banco Do Brasil 巴西

大通曼哈顿银行 Chase Manhattan Bank 美国

第一洲际银行 First Interstate Bancorp 美国

花旗银行 Citibank 美国

芝加哥第一国民银行 First Chicago Corp. 美国

梅隆国民银行 Mellon National Corp. 美国

美洲银行 Bank America Corp.（全称"美洲银行国民信托储蓄会"："Bank of America National Trust and Savings Associations"）美国

纽约银行家信托公司 Bankers Trust New York Corp. 美国

德累斯顿银行 Dresdner Bank 德国

德意志银行 Deutsche Bank 德国
西德意志地方银行 Westdeutsche Landesbank Girozentrale 德国
多伦多自治领银行 Toronto-Dominion Bank 加拿大
加拿大帝国商业银行 Canadian Imperial Bank of Commerce 加拿大
加拿大皇家银行 Royal Bank of Canada 加拿大
国民劳动银行 Banca Nazionale del Lavoro 意大利
都灵圣保罗银行 Istituto Bancario SanPaolo Di Torino 意大利
西亚那银行 Monte Dei Paschi Di Siena 意大利
意大利商业银行 Banca Commerciale Italiana 意大利
荷兰农业合作社中央银行 Cooperatieve Centrale Raifferssen-Boerenleenbank 荷兰
荷兰通用银行 Algemene Bank Nederland 荷兰
农业信贷国民银行 Caisse Nationale Credit Agricole 法国
巴黎国民银行 Banque Nationale de Paris 法国
里昂信贷银行 Credit Lyonnais 法国
瑞士联合银行 Union Bank of Switzerland 瑞士
西太平洋银行公司 Westpac Banking Corp. 澳大利亚
住友信托银行 Sumitomo Trust & Banking 日本
第一劝业银行 Dai-Ichi Kangyo Bank 日本
三菱银行 Mitsubishi Bank 日本

Useful Sentences

1. Please remit 30% of the contract value to us before the end of October 2010 as down payment so that we can start the production for you ASAP.
2. We would suggest that for this particular order you let us have a D/D, upon receipt of which we shall ship the goods on the first available steamer.
3. We ask for a 30% down payment, the remaining balance is divided in 10 equals, payments to be made monthly.
4. D/P is applicable only if the amount involved for each transaction is less than $3000.
5. In view of the amount of this transaction being very small, we are prepared to accept payment by D/P at sight (or at 30 days' sight) for the value of the goods shipped.
6. It is necessary for us to make it clear that this concession is only for your convenience to push sales of our new products, which should in no case be taken as a precedent.

7. L/C at sight is normal for our export to your country, so we can hardly make any exception this time.
8. In the event of our acceptance of your offer, we shall issue a confirmed and irrevocable L/C in your favor.
9. As agreed, the terms of payment for the above orders are letter of credit at 60 days' sight or D/P sight draft.
10. We regret having to inform you that although it is our desire to pave the way for a smooth development of business between us, we cannot accept D/A.
11. Payment is to be made against sight draft drawn under a confirmed, irrevocable, divisible and transferable L/C without recourse for the full amount of purchase.
12. We wish to draw your attention to the fact that as a special sign of encouragement, we shall consider accepting payment by D/P during this sales-pushing stage. We trust this will greatly facilitate your efforts in sales, and we await your favorable reply.
13. The request for easier payment terms is compelled by our funds being tied up in numerous commitments.
14. In order to pave the way for your pushing the sale for our products in your market, we agree to payment for this transaction on D/P terms as a special accommodation.
15. It is expensive to open an L/C and ties up the capital of a small company like ours. So it's better for us to adopt D/P or D/A.

Chapter VIII
Establishment of and Amendment to L/C

Objectives:

After learning this chapter, you will

1. be acquainted with the characteristics of the letter of credit;
2. master how to urge the establishment of L/C and the relevant sentences and expressions;
3. understanding how to examine and amend an L/C;
4. master the writing skills of amendment to the L/C or extension of the L/C and the relevant sentences and expressions.

Introduction

When a transaction is concluded on L/C terms, the buyer is usually under the obligation to establish an L/C with his bank within the time limit stipulated in the sales contract. Especially for bulk sale or the commodities produced according to buyer's request, it is very important for the buyer to open the L/C in time; otherwise, the seller can't arrange the production and commodities.

Normally, the buyer's L/C should reach the seller 15 days (or 30 days) prior to the date of shipment so as to give the seller sufficient time to make preparations for shipment. But in practice, foreign customers may fail to establish the L/C or delay opening the L/C when the market condition changes or the shortage of fund arises. Therefore, the seller should urge the buyer to expedite the L/C at an early date.

Whatever the cause may be, it is always annoying to the seller, but no suggestion of annoyance must be allowed to appear in his letter, email or fax. It would be wrong, except in special circumstances, to start off too strongly by blaming the buyer for non-performance of contract. The first message sent should therefore be a polite note saying that the goods ordered are ready but the relevant L/C has not yet come to hand. If the first message brings no reply, a second one will be sent. This one, though still restrained, will express disappointment and surprise.

Messages urging establishment of L/C must be written with tact. Their aim is to persuade the buyer to co-operate more closely and in fact to fulfill his obligations; otherwise they will give offence to the buyer and bring about unhappy consequences.

On receiving the relevant L/C, the seller (exporter) should first of all make a thorough examination to see whether the clauses set forth in the L/C are in full conformity with the terms stated in the sales contract (confirmation). This step is essential. A minor difference between the two, if not discovered or duly amended, may cause the seller much inconvenience because the negotiating bank will refuse negotiation of the documents according to the instructions given by the opening bank. Therefore, if any discrepancies or some unforeseen special clauses to which the seller does not agree are found in the L/C, the seller should send an advice to the buyer, asking him to make may arise. In this case, an amendment to the original L/C will also be required.

Not only can the seller ask for amendment to an L/C, the buyer can likewise ask for amendment if he finds something in the L/C needs to be altered. The usual procedure is that the buyer should first obtain consent from the seller and then instruct the opening bank to amend the L/C.

Sometimes the seller may fail to get the goods ready for shipment in time or the buyer may request that the shipment be postponed for one reason or another; then the seller will have to ask for extension of the expiry date as well as the date of shipment of the L/C.

Letters concerning L/C amendment and extension should be written with courtesy because a mere amendment to or extension of L/C will need time and money, which is always an annoying thing to the buyer.

Writing Tips

When urging the buyer to establish the relative L/C, the seller should draft the letter or email skillfully by using proper language to show your determination but not to harm the relationship between two parties.

Usually a letter or email focusing on urging the buyer to establish the relative L/C by the seller often consists of the following parts:

1) Mention the Contract No., Order No. of the goods in the opening sentences;

2) State the reasons why you need to inform or urge the buyer to open the L/C;

3) Urge the buyer to open the L/C ASAP.

When asking for amendment to an L/C, it is essential to:

1) in the opening sentences thank the customer for the L/C you received and give a detailed description about it;

2) give the reasons why you have to ask for the amendment to the L/C;

3) tender apologies, should we be the responsible party. If not, omit this step;

4) express your appreciation for the amendment and state your good will to make prompt shipment.

When asking for extension of an L/C, it often consists of the following parts:

1) in the opening sentences express your thanks for the L/C you received and give a detailed description about it;

2) give the reasons why you have to ask for the extension of the L/C;

3) put forward the detailed requirements of shipment and validity extension;

4) express your appreciation for the extension and make sure you will make prompt shipment.

Lesson 19

(A) Urging Establishment of L/C

From: alicia0618@tchina.com
To: Jeremy Weiner@hotmail.com
Sent: Monday, November 15, 2018 3:45 PM
Subject: Establishment of L/C for S/C FP992041W-1

Dear Jeremy Weiner,

With reference to the slippers under our Sales Contract FP992041W-1, we wish to draw your attention to the fact that the date of delivery is approaching, but up to the present we have not received the covering L/C. Please do your utmost to expedite its establishment, so that we may execute the order within the prescribed time.

In order to avoid any further delay, please see to it that the L/C stipulations are in exact accordance with the terms of the contract.

We look forward to receiving your favorable response at an early date.

Best regards,
Alicia

Chapter VIII Establishment of and Amendment to L/C

(B) Confirming L/C Application

From: Jeremy Weiner@hotmail.com
To: alicia0618@tchina.com
Sent: Tuesday, November 16, 2018 9:45 AM
Subject: Confirmation of L/C Application

Dear Alicia,

We have received your email 15th of November, urging us to establish the covering L/C for Sales Contract FP992041W-1.

We very much regret the inconvenience you were caused by the delay in opening our L/C as we had to go through the necessary formalities to apply for the relevant import licence. Now we are pleased to inform you that we have established and attached the Irrevocable Documentary Credit Application in your favor.

In order to avoid subsequent amendments to L/C, please check and confirm the terms and conditions of the L/C application. If you find it in order, pls email us your confirmation ASAP.

Should any of the clauses be unacceptable to you, please let us know your amendments. We will open and send the L/C through our bank in a few days upon receipt of your confirmation.

Your prompt attention will be appreciated.

B. rgds/ Jeremy

1. **urge** *vt.* 催促，劝说

   Recently they have been urging us for execution of their order for 3000 gross pencils.
   最近他们一直在催促我们履行有关三千罗铅笔的订单。

   Your are urged to give an early reply to our enquiry for groundnuts.
   请早日答复我们有关花生的询盘。

2. **with / in reference to…** 关于……

   With reference to payment, we cannot do otherwise than L/C.
   关于付款方式，我方只选择信用证。

3. **draw (call, attract, invite) your attention to the fact that…** 我们要提请你方注意……

   We would like to draw your attention to the expiration of the L/C.
   我们提请你方注意信用证的到期日。

   We would like to call your attention to the fact that as the goods are very easily damaged by heat, we hope that you will keep them in a cool place.
   我们想提请贵方注意，由于货物很容易受热损坏，希望贵方将货物存放在阴凉的地方。

4. **do one's utmost** 尽某人最大的努力

   We hope that you will do your utmost to get shipment ready before the deadline stipulated in the sales contract.
   我方希望贵方尽最大努力，在销售合同规定期限内装船完毕。

5. **expedite** *v.* 加快、加速（进程等）；促进（措施等）；迅速处理（事务）

   Please try your best to expedite the establishment of the relative L/C.
   请尽力加快相关信用证的开立。

6. **prescribe** *v.* 规定

   We refer you to your L/C No. 687 which prescribes that transshipment is not allowed.
   请查阅你方第687号信用证，该信用证规定不允许转船。

7. **see (to it) that** 注意（使），务必（使）

   We hope you will see to it that everything is ready before the end of this month.
   请你们务必保证本月底前一切都已准备就绪。

   Please see to it that the goods sent are what we need.
   务请确认所发货物是我们所需要的。

Chapter VIII Establishment of and Amendment to L/C

8. **go through** 办理

   How long will it take to go through the customs formalities?

   办理通关手续需要多长时间？

9. **Irrevocable Documentary Credit Application** 不可撤销的跟单信用证申请书

10. **in order** 正确的，正常的，就绪

    All the shipping documents are in order.

    所有的装运单据都已就绪。

I. Translate the following expressions.

A. From English into Chinese.

1. import license
2. see to it that
3. go through
4. with reference to
5. terms and conditions
6. in favor of

B. From Chinese into English.

1. 催证
2. 必要手续
3. 与……严格一致
4. 信用证申请书

II. Fill in the blanks with a proper word.

1. The seller should, if necessary, require the buyer to make an amendment _____ the L/C _____ shipment.

2. _____ reference _____ 8000 pairs of Sheepskin Slippers _____ the sales confirmation No. 578, we have not received your _____ L/C _____ to date.

3. We would like to _____ your attention _____ the _____ that the shipment date is _____, we must point out that unless your L/C _____ us by the end of this month, we shall not be able to _____ shipment _____ the contracted time.

4. We apologize _____ you _____ not having established the relative L/C in time.

5. We wish to call your attention to the validity _____ the L/C, since there is no possibility _____ L/C extension.

6. We would like to make it _____ that the covering L/C should be established

_____ time, otherwise it will put us _____ great trouble.

7. _____ compliance _____ the terms _____ payments _____ in the contract, please open a confirmed and irrevocable L/C _____ our favor.

8. The expiry date of your L/C falls _____ May 15, which won't leave us enough time _____ negotiation _____ the document.

III. Translate the following letter into English in a proper format.

Reindeers Home Products Distributors Plc. Ltd.
78 George Street, Derby, Middle England, QIS MKJ, UK

先生／女士，

事由：我方第 DT-123 号售货确认书

感谢贵司向我大量订购玻璃啤酒瓶，经与多家供货商洽谈并最终确定了厂家，双方达成了均感满意的意向。随后即已将售货确认书发给贵司，我方编号 DT-123 号想已收悉，可是现在三周过去了，但至今仍未收到有关信用证，特提醒如下：

关于我方第 DT-123 号售货确认书项下 200 箱玻璃啤酒瓶，拟提请注意交货日期日益迫近，请速开立信用证，以便我方顺利执行这项订单。

为了避免随后的修改，务请注意信用证的规定事项与合同条款完全一致，盼佳音。

此致

中国天津滨海玻璃制品公司
出口部经理李青
2018 年 8 月 15 日

Chapter VIII Establishment of and Amendment to L/C

Lesson 20

(A) Amendment to L/C

From: alicia0618@tchina.com
To: Jeremy Weiner@hotmail.com
Sent: Tuesday, November 18, 2018 11:16 AM
Subject: Amendment to L/C No. ELC-TFS-981520
Attachment: Letter of Credit

Dear Jeremy Weiner,

We are pleased to have received your L/C No. ELC-TFS-981520 against S/C No. FP992041W-1. However, on examining it carefully, we regretfully find it contains quite a few discrepancies and therefore, we would appreciate it very much if you will make the following necessary amendments as early as possible so as to facilitate our shipping arrangement:

1) Amend "FOB FUZHOU" to read "FOB C2 FUZHOU".

2) The place of expiry should be "Fuzhou, China" not "Palermo, Italy".

3) The Bill of Lading should be marked "freight collect" instead of "freight prepaid".

4) Pls delete insurance clause as our price is on FOB basis.

5) "TRANSHIPMENT NOT ALLOWED" should read "TRANSHIPMENT ALLOWED".

6) "PERIOD FOR PRESENTATION" should be "WITHIN 15 DAYS" instead of "WITHIN 5 DAYS".

As the stipulated time of shipment is drawing near, please make the necessary amendments by fax at an early date so that we can effect shipment in time.

Best regards,
Alicia Wu

Attachment (合同见 Lesson 15):

LETTER OF CREDIT

---

27 SEQUENCE OF TOTAL:	1/1
40A FORM OF DC:	IRREVOCABLE
20 DC NO:	ELC-TFS-981520
31C DATE OF ISSUE:	181205
40E APPLICABLE RULES	UCP LATEST VERSION
31D EXPIRY DATE AND PLACE:	190215 Palermo, Italy
50 APPLICANT:	AL ABRA SUB TRADING EST.
	94017 REGALBUTO
	CATANIA, ITALY
59 BENEFICIARY:	FUJIAN ORIENTAL FOOTWEAR I.E. CO., LTD.
	9/F, MINFA BUILDING NO. 88 DONGSHUI ROAD
	FUZHOU, CHINA
32B DC AMT:	USD21645.12
41D AVAILABLE WITH/BY:	CITIC INDUSTRIAL BANK BEIJING BY PAYMENT
43P PARTIAL SHIPMENTS:	ALLOWED
43T TRANSSHIPMENT:	NOT ALLOWED
44A LOADING/DISPATCH AT/FM:	FUZHOU MAIN PORT, CHINA
44B PORT OF DISCHARGE:	CATANIA PORT, ITALY
44C LATEST DATE OF SHIPMENT:	190131

45A GOOODS OR SERVICES:

'FAIL FASCIA' BRAND EVA SLIPPER AS PER PROFORMA INVOICE NO. WW0803015A DATED 15 NOV., 2018.

　DELIVERY TERMS: FOB FUZHOU

　PACKING: EACH PAIR IN POLYBAG, TIED TOGETHER IN NYLON THREAD, WITH HOOK AND SHOWING.

46A/DOCUMENTS REQUIRED:

　+SIGNED COMMERICAL IN 5 COPIES, STATING L/C NO. ELC-TFS-981520 AND CONTRACT NO.

　+FULL SET OF CLEAN ON BOARD BILL OF LADING, MADE OUT TO THE

ORDER MARKED 'FREIGHT PREPAID'.
+CERTIFICATE OF ORIGIN GSP FORM. A.
+PACKING LIST IN FIVE COPIES.
+INSURANCE POLICY IN THE CURRENCY OF THE CREDIT ENDORSED IN BLANKED FOR THE FULL INVOICE VALUE PLUS 10 PCT COVERING ALL RISKS OF PICC CLAUSES.

47A ADDITIONAL CONDITINONS:
+ALL DOCUMENTS MUST BE IN ENGLISH LANGUAGE.
+ALL DOCUMENTS MUST INDICATE THIS CREDIT NUMBER.
+THE OPENING BANK IS OBLIGED TO PAYMENT ONLY AFTER GOODS ARE SHIPPED TO THE PORT OF DESTINATION.
+ FOR EACH SET OF DOCUMENTS PRESENTED WITH DISCREPANCY(IES), A DISCREPANY FEE OF USD90,00 AND THE RELATIVE TELEX /SWIFT COST WILL BE DEDUCTED FROM THE PROCEEDS NO MATTER THE BANKING CHARGES ARE FOR WHOEVER A/C.

71B DETAILS OF CHARGES: ALL FOREIGN BANK CHARGES ARE ON ACCOUNT OF BENEFICIARY.

48 PERIOD FOR PRESENTATION: DOCUMENTS MUST BE PRESENTED WITHIN 5 DAYS AFTER B/L ON BOARD DATE BUT WITHIN CREDIT VALIDITY.

78 INSTRUCTIONS TO THE PAYING/ACCEPTING/NEGOTIATING BANK:
+UPON RECEIPT OF DOCUMENTS IN COMPLIANCE WITH ALL THE TERMS AND CONDITIONS OF THE CREDIT, WE WILL PAY YOU AS PER YOUR INSTRUCTIONS.

57A ADVISE THRU: CIBKCNBJ350
                CHINA CITIC BANK (FUZHOU BRANCH), FUZHOU, CHINA

(B) Reply to the Above

From: JeremyWeiner@hotmail.com
To: alicia0618@tchina.com
Sent: Monday, November 22, 2018 10:28 AM
Subject: Amendment to L/C No. ELC-TFS-981520

Dear Alicia,

Thank you for your email dated November 18 asking us to amend the subject L/C.

In compliance with your requests in your email, we have accordingly amended it through our bank. Pls read the attachment and email us your confirmation immediately.

We will ask our bank to fax the amendments to your bank upon receipt of your confirmation.

We thank you for your kind cooperation. We look forward to your timely shipment.

B. rgds/ Jeremy

1. **amendment** *n.* 修改，修改书
   We have instructed our bank to make an amendment to the L/C No. 378 as requested.
   我方已通知银行按要求修改 378 号信用证。
   amend *v.* 修改
   Please amend your L/C to allow partial shipments and transshipment.
   请修改信用证允许分批装运和转船。

2. **discrepancy** *n.* 差异；异样；不符点
   Please amend the discrepancies in the above L/C.
   请修改上述信用证中的不符点。
   In case of any discrepancy between unit prices and amounts, unit prices shall govern.
   如果单价与总金额之间有出入，应以单价为准。

Chapter VIII Establishment of and Amendment to L/C

3. **read** *v.* 内容是，读起来

   Please amend L/C No. 368 to read: "This credit will expire on 15 May, 2020 in China."

   请将第 368 号信用证改为："该信用证将于 2020 年 5 月 15 日在中国到期。"

4. **expiry / expiration** *n.* 终止；满期，届期

   What is the expiry date on your library book?

   你从图书馆借的那本书什么时候到期？

   The President can be elected again at/on the expiration of his first four years in office.

   总统第一任四年任期届满后可竞选连任。

   expire *v.*（指某事经过一段时间）期满，到期；终止

   The trade agreement between the two countries will expire next year.

   两国的贸易协议将在明年到期。

5. **instead of** 代替，而不是

   As stipulated, payment is to be made by sight L/C instead of L/C at 30 days.

   根据合同规定，付款方式应为即期信用证，而不是 30 天期信用证。

6. **freight** *n.* 运费

   freight prepaid 运费预付

   freight paid 运费已付

   freight collect 运费到付

7. **delete** *vt.* 删除，取消

   Please delete " transshipment is not allowed" from the L/C.

   请删去信用证中"不允许转船"这一条。

8. **timely shipment** 及时装运

I. Translate the following expressions.

    A. From English into Chinese.

    1. in conformity with   2. freight prepaid

    3. more or less   4. documentary L/C

    5. timely shipment   6. beneficiary

    B. From Chinese into English.

    1. 运费到付   2. 不符点

    3. 修改信用证   4. 信用证到期日

II. Translate the following L/C stipulations into Chinese.

1. Full set of clean "on board" "Freight Prepaid" Ocean Bill lf Lading, made out to order and blank endorsed, marked: "Notify China National Foreign Trade Transportation Corporation, at the port of destination."
2. We hereby agree with the drawers, endorsers, and bona-fide holders of drafts drawn in compliance with the terms of the credit that such drafts shall be duly honored on presentation and paid at maturity.
3. A certificate from the shipping company or their agent stating that the goods are shipped on vessels: covered by the institution classification clause under 15 years of age.
4. Beneficiary's statement certifying that shipment from Qingdao to Hamburg with transshipment at Hong Kong on carrier Maersk Line.
5. Documents must be presented within 15 days after the date of issuance of the transport documents but within the validity of this credit.

III. Put the following into English.

1. 由于所订货物已备妥待运，请即开信用证，我方一收到信用证，立即装运。
2. 请从信用证中删去此条款："所有银行费用由受益人支付。"
3. 在审阅信用证条款后，我方遗憾地发现某些规定与合同条款不符。
4. 我们希望在这一方面能与贵方合作，同时等候贵方银行的信用证修改书。
5. 根据我方所收到的信用证，付款方式是见票后30天付款，但根据合同应是见票即付，因此，请按说明修改信用证。
6. 请将上述信用证做如下修改："由青岛装运"改为"由大连装运"。

Chapter VIII Establishment of and Amendment to L/C

Lesson 21

(A) Asking for Extension of L/C

From: alicia@hotmail.com
To: Arne Jense@hotmail.com
Sent: Monday, January 20, 2018 10:16 AM
Subject: Extension of L/C

Dear Jeremy Weiner,

We thank you for your irrevocable letter of credit opened through your bank for Slippers under S/C No. FP992041W-1.

As stipulated in S/C No. FP992041W-1, the goods should be shipped not later than January 31. Although we have been making great efforts to book shipping on time, much to our regret we were told by the shipping companies contacted that there would be no steamship before January 31 owing to the bad weather.

Under such circumstances, we find it impossible to deliver your order in time, and regret having to request you to extend the date of shipment and the validity of the said L/C to February 15 and March 2nd respectively.

Since this is an urgent matter, please amend the L/C by fax. Your compliance with our requests will be highly appreciated.

Best regards,
Alicia

(B) Reply to the Above

From: Jeremy Weiner@hotmail.com
To: alicia0618@tchina.com
Sent: January 27, 2018
Subject: Extension of L/C

Dear Alicia,

We have received your email dated 20 January requesting us to extend the above L/C to February 15 and March 2nd for shipment and negotiation respectively.

As requested, we have instructed our bank to extend the L/C up to the date you required, which is March 2nd. We hope it can provide you with enough time to solve the space problem of the goods.

You will receive the extension advice by this Friday. We shall be much obliged if you will make a prompt shipment of our order after receipt of the amendment, thus enabling them to catch the brisk demand at the start of the season.

Best regards,
Jeremy Weiner
Sales Manager

1. **extension of an L/C** 信用证的展期
   信用证中都规定了装运日期和到期日期，有时卖方未能及时将货物备妥待运，或买方由于某种原因要求延迟装运，这时卖方将不得不要求买方将信用证中的装运日期和到期日期分别延长，即信用证的展期或信用证的展延。

2. **extension** *n.* 延长，展期
   Extension commission will be for your account. 展延手续费将由你方负担。
   We have contacted our customer today asking for a two-week extension of the L/C covering Order No. 8982.
   我们已与客户联系，要求他们将 8982 号订单信用证的有效期延长两周。

Chapter VIII　Establishment of and Amendment to L/C

extend *vt.* 延长，使展期；扩展；给予

extend...to... 将……延长到……（日期）

The L/C expires of November 30th, and we hope you will extend the validity date to December 15th.

该信用证于11月30日期满，我们希望你将其有效期延至12月15日。

Please have your letter of credit extended to July 21.

请将你信用证展期到7月21日。

They intend to extend their business to neighboring countries.

他们打算将业务扩展到邻近国家。

3. **as stipulated** 根据规定

The machine will correspond in all respects with the quality and specifications as stipulated in the contract.

机器的各个方面将符合合同所规定的质量要求和规格。

The Seller shall ship the goods within the time as stipulated in this Contract by a direct vessel sailing from the port of loading to China port.

卖方在本合同规定的时间之内应将货物装上由装运港到中国口岸的直达船。

4. **respectively** *adj.* 分别地

You are requested to extend the shipment date and the validity of your L/C to the end of September and October 15 respectively.

要求你方将信用证的装船日期和有效期分别展延至9月底和10月15日。

5. **extension advice** 延期通知

I. Translate the following expressions.

A. From English into Chinese.

1. extension advice　　　2. validity
3. expiration　　　4. get the goods ready
5. as stipulated　　　6. make great efforts

B. From Chinese into English.

1. 展证　　　2. 清洁提单
3. 装运期　　　4. 订舱

II. Choose the best answer to complete each of the following sentences.

1. The term CIF should be followed by _____.
   A. port of origin   B. port of shipment
   C. port of destination   D. port of loading

2. The bank who opens the L/C required by the buyer is called _____.
   A. paying bank   B. issuing bank
   C. negotiating bank   D. notifying bank

3. _____ the goods have been ready for shipment for some time, please establish the relative L/C _____ our favor as soon as possible.
   A. Because, on   B. Because, in
   C. As, in   D. As, on

4. We could manage to arrange the shipment in July, subject to your L/C _____ us not later than June 15.
   A. reach   B. reaches
   C. reaching   D. being reached

5. Failure to establish the L/C _____ will _____ the fulfillment of this order.
   A. on time, effect   B. on time, affect on
   C. in time, affect   D. in time, effect on

6. As the shipment date _____, we must point out that unless your L/C reaches us by the end of this month, we shall not be able to effect shipment within the _____ time.
   A. is approaching…contracting   B. is approaching…contracted
   C. approached…contracting   D. approached…contracted

7. Your L/C calls for an insurance amount for 120% of the invoice value. _____ we would request you to amend the insurance clause.
   A. The case is like this.   B. The case being it.
   C. Such being the case.   D. Such is the case.

8. Due to unforeseen difficulties, we find it impossible to make shipment in July, and would appreciate _____ the shipment date and validity of your L/C to May 31 and June 15 _____.
   A. you to extend…respectively   B. you to extend…respective
   C. your extending…respectively   D. your extending…respective

Chapter VIII Establishment of and Amendment to L/C

9. As arranged, we would ask you to open an confirmed and irrevocable letter of credit in _____ favor and shall hand over shipping documents _____ acceptance of our draft.

   A. our…against
   B. our…for
   C. your…against
   D. your…for

10. You must be aware that the terms and conditions of a contract once _____ should be strictly _____, failure to abide by them will mean violation of contract.

    A. signed…observed
    B. signed…observing
    C. signing…observed
    D. signing…observing

III. Put the following into English.

1. 如能速开信用证，我们将不胜感激。
2. 经核对信用证条款，我方遗憾地发现你方信用证要求 10 月份装运，但我方合约规定 11 月份装运，因此，务请把装运期和议付期分别展至 11 月 30 日和 12 月 15 日。
3. 我们强调货物必须在限期内装船，展期要求将不予考虑。
4. 我方已根据贵方第 308 号信用证条款，将全套清洁已装船提单连同其他单据提交中国银行福州分行。
5. 由于你方信用证装运期与有效期相同，请按惯例将信用证有效期延展十五天。
6. 由于本月没有直达轮，我方要求延长信用证有效期至 5 月 31 日。

Skill Training

Exercise I. Write a letter in English asking for amendments to the following letter of credit by checking it against the terms of the given contract.

售货合同

SALES CONTRACT

合同号码：LT07060

卖方：AAA IMPORT AND EXPORT CO.
222 JIANGUO ROAD
DALIAN, CHINA

买方：BBB TRADING CO.
P.O. BOX 203
GDANSK, POLAND

兹经买卖双方同意由卖方出售买方购进之下列货物，并按下列条款签订本合同：
This Sales Contract is made out as per the following terms and conditions confirmed by both parties:

商品名称与规格 Commodity & Specifications	数量 Quantity	单价 Unit Price	金额 Amount
65% POLYEXSTER 35% COTTON LADIES SKIRTS STYLE NO. A 101 STYLE NO. A 102 ORDER NO. HMW0501	200DOZ 400DOZ	CIF GDANSK USD60/DOZ USD84/DOZ	USD12,000.00 USD33,600.00
Total Value: USD FORTY FIVE THOUSAND AND SIX HUNDRED ONLY			

Time of shipment: DECEMBER, 2005

Transshipment: ALLOWED

Partial shipments: ALLOWED

Port of loading: DALIAN

Port of destination: GDANSK

Payment: BY TRANSFERABLE L/C PAYABLE 60 DAYS AFTER B/L DATE, REACHING THE SELLERS 45 DAYS BEFORE THE SHIPMENT.

Insurance: TO BE EFFECTED BY THE BUYER FOR 110% INVOICE VALUE COVERING F.P.A. RISKS OF PICC CLAUSE

> **Force Majeure:** The Seller shall not be held liable for failure or delay in delivery of the entire lot or a portion of the Commodity under this contract in consequence of any force majeure incidents.
>
> **Other conditions:** 略
>
> *David King*   苏进
> Buyers (Signature)   Sellers (Signature)

LETTER OF CREDIT

40A FORM OF DC:	IRREVOCABLE
20 DC NO:	70/1/5822
31C DATE OF ISSUE:	051007
40E APPLICABLE RULES	UCP LATEST VERSION
31D EXPIRY DATE AND PLACE:	060115, POLAND
50 APPLICANT:	BBB TRADING CO.
	P.O. BOX 203
	GDANSK, POLAND
59 BENEFICIARY:	AAA IMPORT AND EXPORT CO.
	222 JIANGUO ROAD,
	DALIAN, CHINA
32B DC AMT:	CURRENCY USD AMOUNT
	45,600.00
41D AVAILABLE WITH/BY:	BANK OF CHINA DALIAN BRANCH BY DEF PAYMENT
42P DEFERRED PAYM. DET.	60 DAYS AFTER B/L DATE
43P PARTIAL SHIPMENTS:	NOT ALLOWED
43T TRANSSHIPMENT:	ALLOWED
44A LOADING IN CHARGE:	SHANGHAI
44B FOR TRANSPORT TO:	GDANSK
44C LATEST DATE OF SHIPMENT:	051231
45A DESCRIPT. OF GOODS:	

    65% POLYESTER 35% COTTON LADIES SHIRTS
    STYLE NO. A 101 200DOZ@USD60/PCE
    STYLE NO. A 101 400DOZ@USD84/PCE

ALL OTHER DETAILS OF GOODS ARE AS PER CONTRACT NO. LT07060 DATED AUG. 10, 2005.

DELIVERY TERMS: CIF GDANSK (INCOTERMS 2000)

46A/DOCUMENTS REQUIRED:

1. COMMERICAL INVOICE MANUALLY SIGNED IN 2 ORIGINALS PLUS 1 COPY, INDICATING S/C NO. LT07060.
2. FULL SET(3/3) OF ORIGINAL CLEAN ON BOARD BILL OF LADING PLUS 3/3 NONNEGOTIABLE COPIES, MADE OUT TO THE ORDER OF ISSUING BANK AND BLANK ENDORSED, NOTIFY THE APPLICANT, MARKED FREIGHT PREPAID MENTIONING GROSS WEIGHT AND NET WEIGHT.
3. ASSORTMENT LIST IN 2 ORIGINALS PLUS 1 COPY.
4. CERTIFICATE OF ORIGIN IN 1 ORIGINAL PLUS 2 COPIES SIGNED BY CCPIT.
5. MARINE INSURANCE POLICY IN THE CURRENCY OF THE CREDIT ENDORSED IN BLANK FOR CIF VALUE PLUS 30 PCT MARGIN COVERING ALL RISKS OF PICC CLAUSES INDICATING CLAIMS PAYABLE IN POLAND.

47A ADDITIONAL CONDITINONS:

+ALL DOCUMENTS MUST BE ISSUED IN ENGLISH.

+SHIPMENTS MUST BE EFFECTED BY FCL.

+B/L MUST SHOWING SHIPPING MARKS: BBB,S/C LT07060，GDAND, C/NO.

+ ALL DOCS MUST NOT SHOW THIS L/C NO. 70/1/5822.

+FOR DOCS WHICH DO NOT COMPLY WITH L/C TERMS AND CONDITIONS, WE SHALL DEDUCT FROM THE PROCEEDS A CHARGE OF EUR50.00 PAYABLE IN USD EQUIVALENT PLUS ANY INCCURED SWIFT CHARGES IN CONNECTIO WITH.

71B DETAILS OF CHARGES: ALL BANKING COMM/CHARGES OUTSIDE POLAND ARE ON BENEFICIARY ACCOUNT.

48 PERIOD FOR PRESENTATION: 15 DAYS AFTER B/L DATE,BUT WITHIN L/C VALIDITY.

49 CONFIRMATION: WITHOUT

78 INSTRUCTIONS: WE SHALL REIMBURSE AS PER YOUR INSTRUCTIONS.

72 SEND TO REC. INFO: CREDIT SUBJECT TO ICC PUBL. 600

Chapter VIII　Establishment of and Amendment to L/C

Exercise II. Write a letter in English asking for amendments to the following letter of credit by checking it against the terms of the given contract.

HONGKONG & SHANGHAI BANKING CORPORATION
QUEENS ROAD CENTREAL, P.O. BOX 64, HK
TEL: 822-1111　FAX: 810-1112

Advised through: Bank of China Shanghai Branch

To: SHANGHAI TEXTILES IMP. & EXP. CORPORATION
　　27 ZHONGSHAN ROAD, SHANGHAI, CHINA

Applicant: SUPERB AIM (HONG KONG) LTD.
　　　　　RM.450 FUNGLEE COMMBLDG. KOWLOON, HONG KONG

Dear Sirs,

　　We hereby open our irrevocable L/C No. CN3099/714 in your favor for a sum not exceeding about HKD540,000.00(SAY HK DOLLARS FIVE HUNDRED AND FORTY THOUSAND ONLY) available by your draft drawn on HSBC at 30 days after sight accompanied by the following documents:

　　1. Signed Commercial Invoice in triplicate.

　　2. Packing list in quadruplicate.

　　3. 2/3 clean on board B/L made out to order notify the above mentioned applicant and marked "Freight Collect" dated not later than October 31, 2006. From Shanghai to Hong Kong, partial shipment are not permitted.

　　4. Insurance policy in 2 copies covering All Risks and War Risks for 150% invoice value as per the relevant ocean marine cargo clauses of the PICC dated 1981/01/01.

　　5. Certificate of Origin issued by China Council for the Promotion of International Trade.

　　6. A certificate issued by the beneficiary and countersigned by buyer's representative Mr. Jeremiah, his signature must be verified by opening bank, certifying the quality to conform to sample submitted on 7th June, 2006.

　　DESCRIPTION OF GOODS:

　　Textile, twill 2/1 108×54/20×20 59", Total 10,000 meters. Packed in cartons of ten meters, USD54.00 per meter CIFC2HK

　　SPECIAL INSTRUCTIONS:

　　1. Shipping advice to be sent by fax to the applicant immediately after the shipment stating our L/C No., shipping marks, name of vessel, goods description and amount as well as the bill of lading No. and date. A copy of such advice must accompany the original documents presented for negotiation.

2. 1/3 clean on board B/L sent to applicant by DHL within 24 hours after shipment.

3. We undertake to honour all the drafts drawn in compliance with the terms of this credit if such drafts to be presented at our counter on or before Oct. 31st, 2006.

4. The negotiating bank is kindly requested to forward all documents to us (HONGKONG & SHANGHAI BANKING CORPORATION QUEEN'S ROAD CENTERAL, P.O. BOX 64, HK) in one lot by airmail.

It is subject to the Uniform Customs and Practice for Documentary Credit (1993) Revision, International Chamber of Commerce Publication No. 600.

Yours faithfully,
For **HONGKONG & SHANGHAI BANKING CORPORATION**

SHANGHAI TEXTILES IMP. & EXP. CORP.
27 ZHONGSHAN ROAD, SHANGHAI, CHINA
TEL: 86-21-63218467   FAX: 86-21-63291267

SALES CONFIRMATION

No.: ST 060311
Date: Aug.15, 2006

TO: SUPERBAIM (HONG KONG) LTD.
RM. 504 FUNGLEE COMM BLDG KOWLOON, HONG KONG

We hereby confirm having sold to you the following goods on terms and conditions as stated below.

NAME OF COMMODITY: textile
SPECIFICATION: Twill 2/1 108×54/20×20 59"
PACKING: Packed in cartons of ten meters
QUANTITY: Total 10,000 meters
UNIT PRICE: USD54.00 per meter CIFC2 HK
TOTAL AMOUNT: USD540,000.00
                         (SAY US DOLLOARS FIVE HUNDRED AND
                         FORTY THOUSAND ONLY)

SHIPMENT: During Oct./Nov. 2006 from Shanghai to HK with partial shipments permitted.

INSURANCE: To be covered by the seller for 110% of total value against all risks

Chapter VIII Establishment of and Amendment to L/C

and war risk as per the relevant ocean marine cargo clauses of the PICC dated 1981/01/01.

PAYMENT: The buyer should open through a bank acceptable to the seller an irrevocable L/C payable at 30 days after B/L date to reach the seller 30days before the month of shipment valid for negotiation in China until the15th day after the date of shipment.

REMARKS: Please sign and return one copy for our file.

The Buyer: The Seller:
Alice   SHANGHAI TEXTILES IMP. & EXP. CORP.

Business Link

I. Basic Rules for Checking the L/C
信用证的审核技巧
（一）操作口诀：合约依据、谨慎审证、通领全局、一次改证
（二）审核信用证的基本要点如下：
1. 信用证本身的审核
（1）信用证的性质：是否为不可撤销。
（2）适用惯例：是否申明所适用的国际惯例规则。
（3）信用证的有效性：检查是否存在限制生效及其他保留条款，注意电开信用证是否为简电信用证。
（4）信用证当事人：对开证申请人和受益人的名称和地址要仔细加以核对。
（5）信用证到期日和到期地点：到期日应符合买卖合同的规定，一般为装运后15天或20天，到期地点一定要规定在出口商所在地，以便做到及时交单。
2. 专项审核
（1）信用证金额、币种、付款期限是否与合同一致。
（2）商品品名、货号、规格、数量规定是否与合同一致。
（3）信用证中的装运条款包括装运期限、装运港、卸货港、分批装运之规定是否与合同一致。
（4）对信用证项下要求受益人提交议付的单据通常包括：商业发票、保险单、海运提单、装箱单、原产地证明、检验证书以及其他证明文件，要注意单价由谁出具、能否出具，信用证对单据是否有特殊要求，单据的规定是否与合同条款一致，前后是否有矛盾之处。

II. Types of L/C

sight L/C	即期信用证
time / usance / term L/C	远期信用证
documentary L/C	跟单信用证
clean L/C	光票信用证
revolving L/C	循环信用证
back to back L/C	背对背信用证
reciprocal L/C	对开信用证
stand-by L/C	备用信用证或反担保信用证
confirmed L/C / unconfirmed L/C	保兑信用证 / 不保兑信用证
revocable L/C / irrevocable L/C	可撤销信用证 / 不可撤销信用证
transferable L/C / Non-transferable L/C	可转让信用证 / 不可转让信用证
divisible L/C / indivisible L/C	可分割信用证 / 不可分割信用证
without recourse L/C / with recourse L/C	无追索权信用证 / 有追索权信用证
L/C with T/T reimbursement clause	带电汇条款信用证
deferred payment L/C / anticipatory L/C	延期付款信用证 / 预支信用证

Useful Sentences

1. Payment will be made by irrevocable Letter of Credit against presentation of documents to the issuing bank.
2. We only accept payment by confirmed, irrevocable letter of credit available against presentation of shipping documents.
3. We have instructed our Bank to open in your favor a confirmed, irrevocable L/C with partial shipment and transshipment allowed clause, available by draft at sight, against surrendering the full set of shipping documents to the negotiating bank.
4. We ask for payment by confirmed, irrevocable L/C in our favour, available by draft at sight, reaching us one month ahead of the stipulated time of shipment, remaining valid for negotiation in China until the 15th day after the time of shipment, and allowing transshipment and partial shipments.
5. As clearly stipulated in the Sales Contract No. GB245, the commission for this transaction is 2%, but we find your L/C No.245 demands a commission of 5% which is obviously not in line with the contract stipulations. Therefore, please amend the

Chapter VIII　Establishment of and Amendment to L/C

L/C to read "commission 2%".

6. As stipulated in our Sales Confirmation No. 695, the covering L/C should reach us not later than the end of this month and we hope you will open it in time, so as to ensure early shipment.

7. If you do not establish the L/C in time, you will be responsible for any loss resulting from the delay.

8. Since there is no direct steamer sailing for your port, we would request you to amend your L/C to allow transshipment.

9. Owing to your failure to open the L/C in time, we regret that we are not able to ship the goods within the stipulated time.

10. The goods are ready for dispatch. Please do your utmost to expedite the L/C, or we can but rescind the contract and ask you to refund to us the storage charges we have paid on your behalf.

11. On receiving your letter, we have contacted our bank and urged them to open the relevant letter of credit.

12. When you find anything to the contrary in the L/C, please let us know so that we can make amendment accordingly.

13. We thank you for your L/C No. 586, but on checking its clauses we find with regret that your L/C calls for shipment in March, whereas our contract stipulates for April shipment.

14. We are sorry that owing to our negligence, we made some mistakes in the establishment of the L/C.

15. Under the circumstances, we find it necessary to request you to amend your L/C as allowing transshipment, failing which the delivery of this order will by force be delayed beyond the contractual date.

Chapter IX
Packing & Marking

> **Objectives:**
> After learning this chapter, you will
> 1. know the importance of proper packing and terms of packing in foreign sales contract;
> 2. grasp the essential components of a letter about packing;
> 3. master typical sentences and expressions in writing the letters on packing.

Introduction

Packing is of particular importance in international trade. It is one of the essential components of commodity production or the continuation of production. The ultimate purpose of packing is to keep the transported goods in perfect condition and prevent loss and leakage during transportation, and even raise their marketing value.

Packing can be divided into two types: outer packing and inner packing. Outer packing, also known as transport packing, is done mainly to keep the goods safe and sound during transportation. The outer packing should be suited for long distance transportation and easy to load and unload. Inner packing, also known as small packing or sales packing, is done mainly to push sales. It can be realized in various forms and with different materials as long as it is nice to look at, easy to handle and helpful to the sales. The inner packing should be attractive, modern, easy to publicize and raise the marketing value.

Packing Containers

Bag: May be made of strong paper, linen, canvas, rubber, etc. It is light and cheap and commonly used for powder and granular materials.

Bale: A package of soft goods (e.g. cotton, wool, sheepskin) tightly pressed together and wrapped in a protective material. Usual size 30×15×15 in. To avoid the damage, bales can be wrapped in waterproof covering and strengthened by metal bands.

Carton: Made of light but strong cardboard, or fiberboard with double lids and bottoms, fixed by glue, adhesive tapes, metal bands or wire staples. Sometimes a bundle of several cartons is made up into one package, held by metal bands. It is lighter and cheaper than the wooden case or the drum. But the disadvantage is that it can be easily opened and its contents pilfered. It is most suitable when carried within a metal container.

Case: A strong container made of wood. For extra strength it may have "battens". Sometimes thinner wood may be used with metal bands or wires passed around the case. The inside of the case may be "lined" with various materials, e.g. damp resisting paper, tin foil, etc., to prevent damage by water, air or insects.

Box: A small case, which may be of wood, cardboard or metal, and may have a folding (hinged) lid.

Crate: This is a case, but one not fully enclosed. It has a bottom and a frame, sometimes open at the top. Crates are often built for the particular thing they have to carry. Machinery packed in crates needs a special bottom (a skid) to facilitate handling.

Drum: A cylinder-shaped container for carrying liquids, chemicals, paint, etc. It is usually made of metal. Certain dry chemicals (non-inflammable) or powders are sometimes packed in wood or cardboard drums.

Can (or Tin): A small metal container in which small quantities of paint, oil or certain foodstuffs are packed.

Carboy: A large glass container protected in a metal or wicker cage with soft packing between glass and cage. It is used for chemicals.

Container: A very large metal box for transport of goods by road, rail, sea or air. Packing goods in a large container facilitates loading and unloading by mechanical handling; thus time is saved.

Pallet: A large tray or platform for moving loads (by means of slings, etc.), e.g. from a lorry into a train or onto a ship, and so save time for handling of separate items. Usually the pallet is constructed so that it has space under it to permit lifting by mechanical equipment.

Shipping Marks

Packing must be strictly marked. Generally speaking, outer packing marks mainly include transport marks, directive marks and warning marks, all of which can greatly facilitate identification and transportation. The transport marks consist of the following parts: consignor's or consignee's code name; number of the contract or the L/C; the port of destination; numbers of the packed goods; weight and dimension.

Directive marks are eye-catching figure and concise instructions concerning manner of proper handling, storing, loading and unloading of the packed goods, such as

THIS SIDE UP
USE NO HOOKS
OPEN THIS END
LIFT HERE

Warning marks are obvious symbols or words to warn people against the hidden danger of inflammable, explosives and poisonous products. Such as

DANDEROUS GOODS
ACID—WITH CARE
INFLAMMABLE
GLASSWARES—WITH CARE
PERISHABLE GOODS

Writing Tips

Letters about packing issues should be concise and clear. In such letters, the buyer can inform the seller of any formerly unexpected requirements about packing. The seller can describe in detail to the buyer his customary packing of the goods concerned and also indicate clearly that he may accept and required packing at the expense of the buyer. Any changes regarding packing stipulated in the contract should be mutually discussed before shipment.

Usually a letter regarding the packing often consists of the following parts:

1) Sometimes, mention the Contract No. or Order No. to make sure the reader knows what the letter is about in the subject line, if any;

2) State clearly the letter you are replying to by specifying the exact date and sometimes the order number at the very beginning of the letter;

3) State clearly the purpose of your letter;

4) Present your packing requirements specifically and clearly, and sometimes explain why you have these requirements;

5) Express your expectations and thanks for your partner's cooperation.

Lesson 22 Inner Packing & Labeling

From: Jeremy Weiner@hotmail.com
To: alicia0618@tchina.com
Sent: November 21, 2018
Subject: Inner Packing Requirements

Dear Alicia,

Thanks for your email. In order to avoid possible future trouble, we would like to make clear beforehand our packing requirements, especially inner packing as follows:

For ART. NO. HC13097, each pair must be on a strong good quality hanger and packed in a polybag then 24 pairs to a carton. The polybag can be self sourced and should be self sealing with a gummed strip. No health warning is required on this bag. Each foot must contain a woven insole label and a price label. Exact color instructions can be found in the instruction manual sent by separate mail. Attached with a Nylon string to each pair must be a hangtag with PRICE on the front and the bar code on the back. The BLACK hanger must have a multi- coloured size sticker attached on the oval shape. Photos as below:

For ART. NO. HC808B301, each pair still need to be wrapped with tissue paper and packed in **PLAIN WHITE SHOE BOX** with finger hole. The shoes/tissue paper/ shoe box should be with **no reference of xxxxx**. After assessing this style, we have decided that the shoes are not required to be lined with cardboard skillets or tissue paper. This shoe should hold its own shape during transit without any additional packaging. Be sure to put the following wording on the shoe box bottom both in English and Italian.

Looking forward to your early reply.

Best regards,
Jeremy Weiner

1. **packing requirements** 包装要求

   业务中产品包装需严格按照购货合同规定，出口商品的包装要求各不相同，供货方应征得购货方同意的包装方式，或根据购货方的具体要求进行包装。

2. **packing** *n.* 包装

   Your price is to include packing in crate, and delivery to our warehouse.

   贵方报价应包括板条箱包装费以及到我方仓库的运费。

   pack *v.* 包装，把……装箱

   The pens are packed in boxes of one dozen each, 200 boxes to a wooden case.

   钢笔应装在盒子里，每盒装一打，每 200 盒装一木箱。

   关于包装方式的几种表达法：

   (1) in... 用某种容器包装

   The goods must be packed in 5-ply strong paper bags as contracted.

   货物应按合同规定用五层坚固纸袋包装。

   (2) in... of...each... 用某种容器包装，每件若干重量

   Men's Shirts are packed in wooden cases of 10 dozen each.

   男式衬衫用木箱装，每箱十打。

   (3) in... each containing... 用某种容器包装，每件内装若干

   Nylon Socks are packed in wooden cases, each containing 50 dozen.

   尼龙袜用木箱包装，每箱装五十打。

   (4) ...to... 某种商品装于某一容器中

   Folding Chairs are packed 2 pieces to a carton.

   折叠椅两把装一个纸板箱。

   (5) each... in...and...to... 每单位装某种容器，若干单位装另一种较大的容器

   Each pair of Nylon Socks is packed in a polybag and 12 pairs to a box.

   每双尼龙袜装一个塑料袋，十二双装一盒。

   (6) ...to...and...to... 若干单位装某种较小容器，若干单位再装入另一种较大的容器

   Pens are packed 12 pieces to a box and 200 boxes to a wooden case.

   钢笔十二支装一盒，二百盒装一木箱。

3. **polybag** *n.* 塑料袋

   Each pair of nylon socks is packed in a polybag and 12 pairs to a box.

Chapter IX　Packing & Marking

尼龙袜子每双包装用聚乙烯袋包装，每 12 双装一个盒。

4. **woven insole label** 布标

5. **price label** 定价标签

6. **instruction manual** 使用手册，说明书

   Refer to the instruction manual before installation and operation.

   请在安装和操作前阅读说明书。

7. **hangtag** *n.* 挂牌，吊牌

   指挂在产品上用以说明所用材料、规格、产品的牌子或公司联系方式等信息的纸质或 PVC 的标牌。

纸质挂牌

PVC 挂牌

8. **the BLACK hanger** 黑色挂钩

   一些鞋子需要用挂钩托住以保持形状。

9. **wrapped with/in** 包在

   For the above order, the goods should be packed in tin-lined water-proof woolen bale, each bale wrapped in oilcloth, and 10 bales packed in one case.

   这批货物必须装在内衬锡纸的防水毛纺布里，外用油毡布包，每十包装一箱。

10. **finger hole/grip hole** 指孔

11. **be lined with** 内衬

    Each carton is lined with a polythene sheet and secured by overall strapping.

    纸板箱均内衬一层聚乙烯塑料布，并用带子全面捆扎加固。

    lining *n.* 衬里，衬套，内层

    The wool sweaters must be packed each in a poly bag with an inner lining of stout waterproof material and then in cardboard box, 10 dozen to a carton.

    羊毛衫必须一件装一个聚乙烯塑料袋，内衬坚固防水材料，然后装入硬纸盒，10 打装一纸箱。

12. **hold shape** 保持形状

13. **additional packaging** 额外的包装费用

I. Translate the following expressions.

A. From English into Chinese.

1. hangtag
2. bar code
3. European size
4. price label
5. inner packing
6. packing clause

B. From Chinese into English.

1. 使用手册
2. 内衬……
3. 另邮
4. 包装要求

II. Choose the best answer to complete each of the following sentences.

1. We would suggest that you _____ the carton with double straps.
   A. securing   B. will secure   C. secure   D. are secured

2. The exporting sewing machines _____ in stout waterproof material, and _____ in pairs in lightweight crates.
   A. are wrapping; packing   B. are wrapped; being packed
   C. being wrapped; are packed   D. are wrapped; packed

3. We have made it clear that the packing must be _____ to withstand rough handling.
   A. strong enough   B. enough strongly
   C. enough strong   D. strongly enough

4. The shirts should be packed _____ plastic bags, six dozen _____ one carton, 12 carton _____ a pallet, 10 pallets _____ an FCL container.
   A. in; in; in; in   B. in; in; on; in
   C. in; on; in; in   D. in; in; in; on

5. Packing charges _____ in the price, and we can make delivery whenever you wish.
   A. include   B. included   C. are included   D. in included

6. Requirements for inner packing are _____ high, _____ beautiful color, creative design and convenient handling _____ its chief concern.
   A. increasing; with; as   B. increasingly; with; as
   C. increasing; in; of   D. increasingly; in; of

7. Pls pack the goods _____ small barrels, which must be lined _____ polythene.
   A. by…in   B. in…by   C. in…with   D. on…in
8. Your comments on packing will _____ on to our manufacturers for their reference.
   A. be passed   B. passed   C. be passing   D. passing

III. Put the following into English.

1. 条形码贴于挂卡上以及贴于胶袋右上角。
2. 我们要求将每件女式衬衫装一个塑料袋，每12打装入一个有防水衬里的纸箱。
3. 我们必须说明的是，采用不同的包装材料，包装费用会不一样。
4. 根据你方的建议，我们已改进了内包装，以满足你方市场消费者的需要。
5. 木箱上不需要印刷警告语。

Lesson 23　Outer Packing

From: Jeremy Weiner@hotmail.com
To: alicia0618@tchina.com
Sent: November 23, 2018
Subject: Outer Carton Information

Dear Alicia,

Thank you for your email of November 12 inquiring for outer packing.

As regards outer carton, egg-crating within a carton is no longer permitted because we'll select goods through the punch panel on the side mark. This is to be replaced with "S" crating. Please use a piece of 5-ply corrugated cardboard and curve the cardboard around the bulk goods to protect goods and strengthen the carton. Please see example below.

Our customers accept only 2 sizes of outer carton. GCOS1 is most commonly used and measured 600 × 300 × 400mm (LWH). The only other carton acceptable is the smaller GCOS2 measuring 400 × 300 × 400mm (LWH). Carton size is critical & cannot be amended.

Cartons should NOT be made from recyclable cardboard as such kinds of recycled materials are not strong enough to protect the goods from suffering the damp or damage during container transit / sea freight. We have already confirmed that the number of pairs per carton is 24—this cannot be changed.

Cartons must be sealed with tape. Under no circumstances should staples be tied, stapled, glued or shrink wrapped. It does not need to be secured outside with plastic straps. All cartons must be perforated with a "punch panel" for ease of warehouse picking with a thumb tab for ease of opening. You will find the other detailed requirements for the carton in our attachment.

Please see separate instructions for shipping mark (main mark) and side marks in the attachment. We trust that you can meet the above requirements and thank you in advance for your cooperation.

Best regards,
Jeremy Weiner
The attachment:

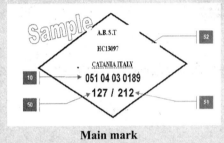
Main mark

Side mark

With reference to the main and side mark of the above order, we would like to draw your special attention to the packing instructions listed as follows:

1. The carton label must be attached to the perforated end of the carton in the upper half of the perforation. Please see example below.

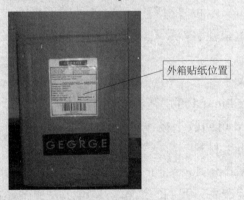

2. The carton perforations for the "punch panel" should only be 4-ply deep, leaving the 5th ply unperforated to assist with carton strength. The carton perforations should be no less than 7.5mm apart.
3. Silica gel packs—Our customers have requested that we can not use packets containing beads of silica gel as these can split open on the shop floor and can be

dangerous. They have requested us to use Microban / Microgarde instead. Please affix one sticker per carton.

4. The pre-pack part of this order will require a red NEW PRODUCT label to be attached to the outer carton.

5. Please mark our initials in a diamond, under which the port of destination and our order number should be stenciled or printed.

1. **egg crate, egg-crate packing** 蛋格包装，像蛋一样一对对插入，如下图：

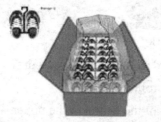

2. **punch panel** 冲孔

是指在钢板、革、布、木板等材料上打出各种图形以适应不同的需求，具体有：十字孔、菱形孔、鱼鳞孔、八字孔、六方孔、冲孔板、长孔、四方孔、圆孔、冲孔板网、三角孔等。

3. **"S" crating** S 形纸板

4. **5-ply corrugated cardboard** 五层瓦楞纸

5. **recyclable cardboard** 可回收纸板，再生纸板

   recycled materials 再生材料

   As with our other boxed products, our cardboard boxes are both recycled and recyclable.
   如同我们的其他盒装产品，我们的纸箱都是可回收和循环再造的。

6. **be sealed with** 用……密封

   The powder must be packed in plastic bags and then put into drums which are to be sealed with adhesive tape.
   所有的粉末都要用塑料袋包装，并装到罐子里，罐子要用胶袋封紧。

7. **to be secured with** 用……加固

   We do not object to packing in cartons, provided the flaps are glued down and the cartons secured with metal bands.

如果箱盖封牢，外打铁箍加固，我们不反对用纸箱包装。

8. plastic straps 塑料箍，塑料带

Please pack the Men's Shirts each inside a polythene bag, with a paper box outside, 100 boxes to a carton, bound with two plastic straps.

请用纸盒包装男式衬衫，每件装一盒，内套一个塑料袋。一百盒装一个纸箱，箱外打两道塑料带。

9. be perforated with 在……钻孔

A board perforated with regularly spaced holes into which pegs can be fitted.

这块板子上面被均匀地凿上了孔，这些孔可以插钉子。

10. carton labels 外箱贴纸

11. mark 唛头或包装标志

指在每件已包装货物上用模板印刷的标志。不同货物的标志的内容及印刷形式不尽相同，一般包括受货人的名称编码、货物抵达目的港的名称、每件的序号以及储运指示标志等。唛头又分为主唛（或正唛 main marks）和侧唛（side marks）。主唛一般是由客户提供，通常由型号、图形（字母、数字及简单的文字）或收货单位简称、目的港、件数或批号等组成。而侧唛则显示商品的尺寸、毛重、净重等资料，用于客户在目的国收货拆柜后，辨认货物。

12. perforated plate 穿孔板

原名冲孔板，就是在不同材质的板材上打孔，如不锈钢板、铝板、铁板、低碳钢板、铜板等。穿孔板在现实生活中的应用非常广泛，可作为装饰用板，美观大方。

13. to be stenciled or printed with 被印上……；刷唛

Please stencil our initials and order number on the outer packing.

请在外包装上印上我公司名称的首字母和订单号。

I. Translate the following expressions.

A. From English into Chinese.

1. plastic straps
2. 3-ply corrugated cardboard
3. be sealed with
4. perforated plate
5. egg crate
6. recycled materials

B. From Chinese into English.
1. 主唛
2. 用……加固
3. 包装须知
4. 侧唛

II. Identify the one error in each of the following sentences.
1. Pens are packed 24 pieces to a box and 200 boxes in a wooden case.
      A   B   C   D
2. Styrol boxes are used to reducing weight, and they are so easy to carry.
          A   B   C   D
3. Our cartons for canned food are not only seaworth but also strong enough to protect
         A   B   C
   the goods from possible damage.
             D
4. Since cartons are comparatively light and compact, they are more convenient to
                A   B
   handle at the course of loading and unloading.
     C   D
5. The boxes are packed in strong cardboard cartons, twelve for a carton, separated
               A   B
   from each other by paper dividers.
    C   D
6. The crates are lined with waterproof, airtight material. The lids are secured by
             A   B   C
   nailing, and the crates are strapped in metal bands.
                             D

III. Put the following into English.
1. 考虑到货物的易碎性和昂贵的包装费用，请采用耐用包装和经济包装。
2. 衬衣装在衬有塑料袋的纸箱里比装在木箱里不易受潮。
3. 12双装一个外箱，外箱贴纸应该贴在外箱正唛头的一面，供应商信息如下。
4. 请确保箱子上标有"易碎品""小心搬运"字样。
5. 经查，发现约有10袋未按合同规定以五层坚固纸袋包装，以致在运输途中造成破损。
6. 磁带应包装在塑料袋里，并用胶带封紧。

7. 在包装和装板条箱时，必须非常小心，因为在运输途中的任何损坏将给我们造成严重损失。

IV. Writing practice

　　Jeremy Weiner approached his clients and found his clients prefer cartons to wooden cases for slippers. Based on the feedback, Jeremy Weiner sent an email to Alicia to specify the outer packing. Now suppose you are Jeremy Weiner, write the email and state at least three reasons for choosing cartons for outer packing.

Lesson 24 Container Loading

From: JeremyWeiner@hotmail.com
To: alicia0618@tchina.com
Sent: November 29, 2018
Subject: Container Loading

Dear Alicia Wu,

We experienced a high number of items delivered that were damaged and covered in mould. This resulted in lost sales and high costs in cleaning the products. We would ask you to monitor the following points on container loading and confirm back to us that these procedures are in place.

1. All PO's must be loaded separately. No mixing of PO's within a container is permitted. Within each PO, goods must be sorted in size, so that in effect every order is segregated and consolidated. Each SKU must be loaded into the vehicle moving left to right, known as "snake loading".

2. If the bulk goods is not sufficient to fill the container in height and length, the goods should be "snake loaded" flat to fill up all length space, leaving spare volume at the top of the container. This helps to prevent collapsed loads whereby goods are loaded to fill height at rear of container, leaving space forward of the goods within the container.

3. Containers must NOT be overloaded as this risk damaging the cartons within.

4. Care should be taken to ensure bulk stock stay dry in packing and loading areas within the factory. Damp cartons can lead to mould found upon arrival.

5. All carton labels MUST be forward facing. If carton labels are mixed with some facing inwards, the bulks will be rejected.

6. Pallet loads are not acceptable.

We thank you for your co-operation in this matter.

Best regards,
Jeremy Weiner

1. **container loading** 装柜要求

   集装箱种类有：杂货集装箱（Dry Container）、冷藏集装箱（Refrigerated Container）、散货集装箱（Solid Bulk Container）、开顶集装箱（Open Top Container）、框架集装箱（Flat Rack Container）、灌装集装箱（Tank Container）。

2. **load** *v.* 装货，装载 *n.* （一船）货物，装载量

   The steamer is loading for London.
   该轮正在装货运往伦敦。
   The goods ordered have been forwarded to you in three ship loads.
   所订货物分三次运往你方。
   loading *n.* 装货
   loading and unloading 装卸
   loading charges 装货费
   port of loading 装货港

3. **segregate** *v.* 分离

   segregate full and empty cylinders 隔开满瓶和空瓶

4. **snake loading:** loading products into a container in the sequence with which the goods will be unloaded and stored in at destination 蛇形装柜，集装箱的一种装箱方法，就是"S"形装箱。先从集装箱最里面装，例如：第一排1—10箱，第二排就是11—20，第三排21—30……箱号顺序保持连贯。主要是按照客人的意图，分色或分PO号或分码段，把纸箱连续逐段，有如长蛇似的装入集装箱。客人收到货柜后，也会按照相反的次序卸下纸箱，不会发生混乱。

5. **lead to** 导致

6. **"snake loaded" flat** 平铺装柜

7. **mould** 发霉

8. **forward facing** 朝柜门装柜

9. **pallet** 货盘

   拼装货物多装托盘便于搬运。托盘根据材料不同可分为木制托盘、塑料托盘、纸质托盘等。在目前的国际贸易中，木制托盘使用较少，因为大多数国家要求对进口的木质材料熏蒸。
   We have packed 168 boxes in 7 pallets of 24 boxes each.
   我们已将168盒货物装于7个货盘，每个货盘装24盒。

I. Translate the following expressions.

A. From English into Chinese.

1. carton labels
2. polybag
3. in good order
4. container
5. PO
6. snake loading

B. From Chinese into English.

1. 整箱
2. 拼箱
3. 货盘
4. 包装要求

II. Fill in the blanks in the following letter with the proper words given below.

| packed   warning   requirements   stand   secured   suitable   hangtags |

Dear Sirs,

As to our PO No. CE578 for 5,000 cartons of wool sweaters to be shipped to us during May, we would like to make clear our packing _____ as follows:

The packing should be novel, _____ for supermarket sales and each one should have _____, bar codes. One dozen should be _____ to a box with a cardboard tray inside, 20 boxes to a carton. The cartons should be strong enough to _____ the dropping test without breakage and _____ outside with plastic straps. On the left side of the carton there should be a _____ mark: "Do not use a hook."

We will email you the pictures of the bar codes and hang tags for each item next time. We trust that you can meet the above requirements and thank you in advance for your cooperation.

We look forward to your early reply.

Yours faithfully,

×××

Chapter IX Packing & Marking

III. Put the following into Chinese.

Containerization has gained popularity from the 1960s onwards, mainly on the deep-sea trade routes and between the industrial countries of North America, Western Europe, Australia and Japan. Smaller types of container ships have also been developed for shorter distance trade in and around Western Europe, the Mediterranean and Australia.

Inside a container the goods are almost completely protected from corrosion or pilferage. The possibility of rough handling is reduced and so a lighter packing can be used. Perhaps the same packing used for domestic shipments. This can save the exporter a good deal of money and means that he can quote a lower price to his customer.

Skill Training

Exercise I. Write out the following packing containers.

_____

_____

_____

_____

_____

_____

Exercise II. Design main mark and side mark based on the information below.

Net Weight	11.5 KGS/CTN
Gross Weight	13 KGS/CTN
Gift Box Dimensions	19CM × 14CM × 23.5CM
Outer Carton Dimensions	59.5CM × 30CM × 48.5CM
Quantity per Carton	12 PCS /CTN

Packing	• For each goods with a poly bag and gift box (inner box), 12PCS/ctn.
	• Recycle marks must be printed on each polybag, gift box and outer carton.
	• Export carton must be strong.
	• Shipping marks.
	    Export carton's main mark on 2 long sides, including JACKEL, port of destination, P.O. No., model No., quantity per carton and carton No.
	    Export carton's side mark on 2 short sides, including G.W., carton dimensions and origin of goods.

1) Design main mark and side mark.
2) Fill in the letter.

Dear Sirs,

                P.O. No. _____

    In reply to your letter of the 31st August inquiring about the packing of our _____, we wish to state as below:

    Our export _____ are packed in boxes of _____ each, _____ boxes to a carton. The dimensions are _____ cm high, 30cm wide and _____ cm long with a volume of about 0.026 cubic meter. The gross weight is _____ kg while the net weight is _____ kg. As to the shipping marks outside the carton, in addition to the gross, net weights and tare, the wording "_____" is also stenciled on each polybag, gift box and outer packing. Port of destination is _____. Should you have any special preference in this respect, please let us know and we will meet you to the best of our ability.

    We thank you in advance for your early reply.

                                              Yours faithfully,
                                                    × × ×

Chapter IX Packing & Marking

Exercise III. Fill in the blanks according to the picture.

装柜顺序：

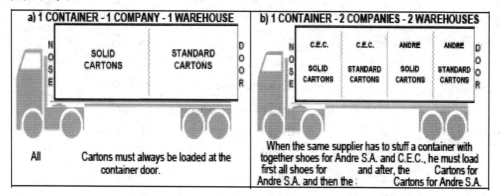

1) All _____ cartons must always be loaded at the container door.

2) When the same supplier has to stuff a container for both Andre S.A. and C.E.C., he must load first all shoes for _____ and after, the _____ cartons for Andre S.A. And then the _____ Cartons for Andre S.A.

Business Link

I. Some Phrases Concerning Packing

packing mark	包装标志	packing design	包装设计
packing cost	包装成本	packing industry	包装业
packing test	包装试验	bulk packing	散装
vacuum packing	真空包装	sealed packing	密封包装
durable packing	耐用包装	economical packing	经济包装
packing free	免费包装	packing included	含包装费
neutral packing	中性包装	packing instructions	包装指示
packing list	包装单	packing method	包装方法
packing material	包装材料	unitary packing	个别包装
inner packing	内包装	outer packing	外包装
export packing	出口包装	seaworthy packing	适于海运的包装
packing clause	包装条款	delicate packing	精致的包装

II. Terms Related to Packing Container

bag	袋，包	sack / gunny bag	麻袋
poly bag	塑料袋	bale	包，布包
bundle	捆	box	盒，箱
carton	纸板箱	case	箱
wooden case	木箱	plywood case	三合板箱
crate	板条箱	cardboard cartons	纸板箱
iron case	铁箱	fiber board case	纤维板箱
cask	木桶	barrel	桶
drum	铁皮圆桶	keg	小圆桶
tin/can	听，罐	bomb/cylinder	钢桶
polythene bag	聚乙烯袋	plastic bag	塑料袋
canvas bag	帆布袋	paper bag	纸袋

III. Some Expressions Concerning Shipping Marks

diamond	菱形	triangle	三角形
rectangle	长方形	square	正方形
heart	心形	circle	圆形
cross	十字形	star	星形
down triangle	倒三角形	oval	椭圆形
hexagon	正六角形	three diamond	三菱形

IV. Special Directions or Warnings

此端向上（THIS SIDE UP）

顶端 (TOP)

易碎物品 (FRAGILE)

保持干燥 (KEEP DRY)

避免日光直射（KEEP OUT OF THE DIRECT SUN）

危险品 (DANGEROUS GOODS)

禁止潮湿（GUARD AGAINST DAMP）

酸——小心 (ACID—WITH CARE)

请勿用钩 (USE NO HOOKS)

请勿平放（NOT TO BE LAID FLAT）

切勿下扔（DO NOT DROP）

切勿受热，隔离热气（KEEP AWAY FROM HEAT）

Chapter IX Packing & Marking

此端开启 (OPEN THIS END)
低温存放，保持冷藏 (KEEP COOL)
禁放甲板上 (DO NOT STOW ON DECK)
小心搬运 (HANDLE WITH CARE)
易燃物品 (INFLAMMABLE)
玻璃器皿——当心 (GLASSWARES—WITH CARE)
在此起吊 (LIFT HERE)
易腐物品 (PERISHABLE GOODS)

Useful Sentences

1. The goods should be packed in a manner that ensures safe and sound arrival of goods at the destination and facilitates handling during transshipment.
2. Each carton is lined with a polythene sheet and secured by overall strapping, thus preventing the contents from dampness and possible damage through rough handling.
3. Please pack the socks each pair in a polybag, 12 dozen to a cardboard box, and 25 boxes to a carton.
4. Our packing is not only seaworthy but also strong enough to protect the goods from possible damage.
5. Our cotton prints are packed in cases lined with draft paper and waterproof paper, each consisting of 30 pieces in one design with 5 colorways equally assorted.
6. Our cartons for canned food are not only seaworthy but also strong enough to protect the goods from possible damage.
7. Please take necessary precautions that the packing can protect the goods from dampness or rain, since these goods are liable to be spoiled by damp or water in transit.
8. Pls note that glass wares are fragile goods, so they need special packing precautions against jolting in transit.
9. 30 packets × 600 grams per wooden case or carton, each packet lined with white pater and outside wrapped up in cellophane paper, 2% more or less in weight for each case allowed.
10. In fact, this packing is both shockproof and waterproof. Nevertheless we have still marked the cartons with warnings like "THIS SIDE UP", "HANDLE WITH CARE", "FRAGILE" and "USE NO HOOKS".

11. In order to avoid the fungus problem for any of our merchandise, please pay special attention and make sure that all the merchandise are totally dried before packing.
12. The goods have been packed and marked exactly as directed so that they may be shipped by the first ship available towards the end of this month.
13. We trust that you will give special care to the packing in order to avoid damage in transit.
14. Please let us have your shipping advice by fax immediately stating the name of vessel so that we may effect insurance at this end.
15. Shipment is to be made during May to July in three equal lots.
16. The cigars are packed 5 pieces to a small packet, 20 packets to a carton, 144 cartons to a cardboard container.
17. The green beans can be supplied in bulk or in gunny bags.
18. Fibreboard boxes are used to reduce freight. These boxes are not returnable.
19. Overall measurements of each case must not exceed $4'\times 2'\times 2'$.
20. Please use normal export containers unless you receive special instructions from our agents.
21. Please see that the cases are marked "Fragile" or "Handle With Care".
22. Cases must have an inner lining of stout, damp-resisting paper.

Chapter X
Shipment

Objectives:

After learning this chapter, you will

1. be familiar with some trade terms and terminologies on shipping;
2. be familiar with the procedure of arranging the shipment;
3. be able to write letters on shipment.

Introduction

The effectuation of shipment signifies the seller's fulfillment of the obligation to make delivery of the goods. There are many modes of transportation in international trade, such as seaway, airway, road and railway transportation. The most commonly used mode of transportation is seaway because of its low freight cost. Basically there are two types of ocean freight according to the assorted shipping vessels used—tramp and liner. A tramp is a freight-carrying vessel which has no regular route or schedule of sailings. It is first in one trade and then in another, always seeking those ports where there is a demand at the moment for shipping space. A liner is a vessel with regular sailings and arrivals on a stated schedule between specified ports.

Shipment covers rather a wide range of work, such as booking shipping space, chartering ships, making customs declaration, etc. The complex process shall usually be handled by a professional shipping and forwarding agent.

Before Shipment, the buyers generally send their shipping requirements to the seller by Shipping Instructions. After the goods are loaded on board the ship, the sellers usually send a notice to the buyers immediately, advising them of the details of the shipment, by a Shipping Advice. For FOB and CFR transactions, the buyer will have to effect insurance on the shipment upon receipt of shipping advice from the seller.

Letters regarding shipment are usually written for the following purposes: to urge an early shipment; to amend shipping terms; to give shipping advice; to dispatch shipping documents and so on.

Writing Tips

Letters on shipment or delivery should be clear and concise so as to avoid confusion.

A letter of Shipping Advice/Instruction usually includes the following contents:

1) identify reference;

2) confirm shipping details, such as name of commodity, number of packages, total value, etc;

3) confirm shipping documents draft;

4) forwarder information if the transaction is concluded on FOB basis;

5) other requirements concerning packing and shipping.

Letters on urging shipment or allowing partial shipment/transshipment usually cover the following points:

1) identify reference;

2) reasons for urging shipment or allowing partial shipment/transshipment;

3) your expectations.

Chapter X Shipment

Lesson 25

(A) Shipping Instructions

From: Jeremy Weiner@hotmail.com
To: alicia0618@tchina.com
Date: 25 Oct., 2018 11:49
Subject: Forwarder Information

Dear Alicia,

Thank you very much for your information covering the readiness of our goods under Order No. 123 and Order No. 03.05GB24. Please contact our forwarder—NYK for shipment. NYK only handles CY (or FCL) in Xiamen port. LCL shipment (less container line) should be shipped to Hong Kong (YanTian or ShenZhen port).

Contact person: Wen Shuen - Guangdong, China
Phone: 86-75757575757 (Mr. Wang or Mrs. Wang)
Fax: 86-75758663176
Email: wenshuen@ms37.hinet.net

Please make the order stated with the correct FOB point, depending on whether it's LCL or FCL cargo.

Booking must be done 14 days prior to shipping to ensure the shipping space. Late booking will result in $350.00 charge back. Please surrender the original BL to shipping agent to make telex release to allow us to make clearance of the goods right away as the storage fee is $300 per day.

For full container shipments loaded by the factory, A.B.S has requested that before container leaves the factory, photos or video clip MUST be taken to show full quantity of the merchandise which has been packed and sealed into the container properly.

Please also note that factory must take pictures once seal lock bar is installed and maintain records. The photos need to include both seal lock numbers and container numbers clear to read. A compliance charge of $150.00 US Dollars will be charged to those who don't document seal procedures.

Thank you in advance for your cooperation.

Best regards,
Jeremy Weiner

(B) Reply to the Above

From: alicia0618@tchina.com
To: Jeremy Weiner@hotmail.com
Sent: 27 Oct. 2018, 10:07 AM
Subject: Forwarder Information

Dear Jeremy Weiner,

Thanks for your kind information about forwarder. I have contacted her accordingly.

As contracted in PO. NO.123, we will receive the balance first, and then release cargo by telex. We are waiting for your bank receipt. Here is revised PI and other shipping DOCs for your confirmation, including CI, CO, PL and BL. Please advise back soon.

Thank you for your attention.

Best regards,
Alicia

1. **Shipping Instructions** 装运指示，装运须知
   装运前买方将装运要求以书面形式通知卖方洽办，说明装船方式、包装规定和唛头等，称为"装运须知"。在FOB条件下也叫装运通知。
   Shipping Advice 装船通知
   装船通知也叫装运通知，主要指的是出口商在货物装船后发给进口方的包括货物详细装运情况的通知，其目的在于让进口商做好筹措资金、付款和接货的准备。

2. **forwarder** n. 货运代理, 指在流通领域专门为货物运输需求和运力供给者提供各种运输服务业务的总称。它们面向全社会服务，是货主和运力供给者之间的桥梁和纽带。

3. **CY**（Container Yard）集装箱（货柜）堆场，实际操作上，CY一般代表整箱装运，而CFS（Container Freight Station）代表拼箱装运。

   FCL整箱（Full Container Load）是指货主自行将货物装满整箱以后，以箱为单位托运的集装箱。

   LCL拼箱（Less Than Container Load）是指承运人（或代理人）接受货主托运的数量不足整箱的小票货运后，根据货物种类性质和目的地进行分类整理。把去同一目的地的货物，集中到一定数量拼装入箱。由于一个箱内有不同货主的货物拼装在一起，所以叫拼箱。

4. **book shipping space** 订舱位

   shipping space broker 舱位经纪人

   congestion of shipping space 舱位拥挤

   subject to shipping space available 以有舱位为准

5. **prior to** 在……之前

   Please open the L/C one month prior to the shipment.

   请在装运一个月前开出信用证。

   Please try your best to ship one third of the goods prior to the shipment.

   请尽量在装运前发运1/3货物。

6. **NYK (Nippon Yusen Kaisha Line Ltd.)** 日本邮船株式会社，是日本最大的从事集装箱运输服务以及其他相关运输业务和物流服务的航运公司之一，从成立至今已有一百多年的历史，其规模和业务量在世界航运企业中排名前列，是世界500强企业之一。

7. **storage fee** 仓储费

   demurrage charges（车、船）滞期费

   dead freight 空舱费

8. **seal lock number** 铅封号

货物装好之后，给集装箱锁上一个"锁"其实是铅封，每个铅封上面都有一个号码，铅封只有破坏才可以打开。集装箱装运，提单上应注明装载货物的集装箱号，通常在集装箱号之后还加注海关查验后作为封箱的铅制关封号。如是集装箱

提单，应将这些内容填入专门设置的集装箱号铅封号栏目。如是其他类型的提单，可随意填在提单空白处。

9. **telex release** 电放，指的是海上货物承运人或者其装货港代理在收到货物签发或应该签发而未签发提单时，根据托运人要求在装货港收回提单或不签发正本提单，以电传形式通知卸货港代理将货物交付给提单收货人或者是托运人指定的收货人的一种方式。

10. **bank receipt** 银行付款回执单（银行水单）。T/T 付款在一般情况下，3个工作日即可入账。在客户转账后，通常都会要求客户提供银行水单。

11. **DOCs** 即 **documents**。如果是信用证付款，信用证上会明确陈述所有关于出货的细节。如果不是信用证付款，在出货之前，必须向客户了解并核实出货的细节要求。因为这些文件关系到客户在当地是否可以出关，或者是否容易出关。出货后需要提交：packing list / commercial invoice / BL。

BL=Bill of Lading，正规写法为B/L，海运提单Marine Bill of Lading 或 Ocean Bill of Lading，或简称为提单Bill of Lading，B/L是指用以证明海上货物运输合同和货物已经由承运人接收或者装船，以及承运人保证据以交付货物的单证。相关的表达用语有：

DIRECT B/L直达提单，THROUGH B/L联运提单或称转船提单

MT B/L多式联运提单，STRAIGHT B/L记名提单

CLEAN B/L清洁提单，FOUL B/L不清洁提单，ANTI-DATED B/L倒签提单

CO=certificate of origin 货物原产地证书

CI=commercial invoice 出货之前要做的商业发票

PL=packing list 出货之前要做的装箱单

I. Translate the following expressions.

A. From English into Chinese.

1. shipping instructions
2. prior to
3. bank receipt
4. FCL
5. seal lock numbers
6. STRAIGHT B/L
7. shipping marks
8. take delivery of

B. From Chinese into English.

1. 货物备妥
2. 导致
3. 装运单据
4. 散货装运

II. Complete the following sentences in English.

1. Thank you very much for your information _____
   _____（关于483号订单项下货物备妥的消息）.

2. Please _____ (联系我们的货代——"马士基航运有限公司"安排装运).

3. _____（订舱）must be done _____
   _____(装运期前14天进行以确保舱位).

4. Photos must be taken to show enough _____ (全部商品数量) which _____ (被包装并封入集装箱) properly.

5. We have pleasure in informing you that we have completed the shipment _____
   _____（根据第KH40483NR的规定）.

III. Translate the following sentences into English.

1. 第2048号订单的货物70%在11月装运，其余在12月装运。
2. 10,000吨大豆因舱位不够，无法全部在10月份装运，请修改信用证，允许分批装运。
3. 由于你方要求提前装运，额外的运费由买方承担。
4. 我国传统的春节即将临近，订舱会比较困难，请尽早发送装运指示，以便尽早订舱。
5. 我们即将执行装运，货代跟上批货为同一家，但希望你们可以找一家报价更低的船公司。

Lesson 26

(A) Requesting for Prompt Shipment

From: Jeremy Weiner@hotmail.com
To: alicia0618@tchina.com
Date: 12 Dec., 2018 11:49
Subject: Prompt Shipment

Hi, Alicia,

Thanks for your kind reception at your booth!

First of all, you confirmed me the L/C before I confirmed it to the bank and the time for the order is right! But up till now nothing about shipment has been received from you.

Second, I'm arranging your shipment with another supplier in the same containers. So if you are late, the other goods will also be late!

Third, I need to receive these goods ASAP since I have to arrange it for Christmas promotions and there isn't much time!

Fourth, if the supplier delays the shipment after the requested date, you will pay the 0.004% of the total amount for each delayed day to us for the damage you cause!

So, kindly proceed in time with the shipment and release the goods to NHK within this week!

Please, Alicia, this is our first business. Don't start with delay and consequently cause our customers to cancel the order!

Hope you can understand.

Rgds,
Jeremy Weiner
Corporate Development Manager

(B) Reply to the Above

From: alicia0618@tchina.com
To: Jeremy Weiner@hotmail.com
Sent: 27 Dec., 2018 10:07 AM
Subject: Prompt Shipment

Dear Jeremy Weiner,

Thank for your comments.

Yes, we confirmed the L/C to you. We hopefully could fulfill it on time. It is good for us too. But sometimes material purchase is a bit different from production arrangements. We are sorry for the inconvenience caused. We have discussed the project for a long time, and finally concluded the deal. We value the chance to cooperate with you. You already visited us in Berlin Show and Canton Fair. We hope you can feel our sincerity for cooperation and now we need some support from you for this shipment. Trust me, we want to do better for you.

We understand your efforts to approve all files for us to guarantee prompt shipment. And we understand that the goods are for Christmas sales. We also have other orders too. We don't mean to delay the shipment but to ensure good quality for you.

The production will be completed on Nov.11 and we will catch the latest vessel which is due to sail for your port on or about Nov. 13.

Looking forward to your comments soon. Thank you.

Best regards,
Alicia
China Oriental Footwear Imp. & Exp. Corp.

1. **reception** *n.* 盛情，热情款待
2. **delay** *vt.* 延缓 *vi.* 拖延，耽搁 *n.* 延迟；耽搁
   We decided to delay our production until next month.
   我们决定把生产推迟到下个月。
   I'm sorry that I've delayed so long.
   我很抱歉拖了这么久。
   The buyer advised me to arrange shipment without delay.
   买方通知我立即安排装运。
3. **consequently** *adv.* 从而，因此
4. **cause the inconvenience**: put sb. to too much trouble
5. **Berlin Show** 德国柏林展览会
6. **penalty** *vt.* 罚款
   The penalty for spitting is US$10.
   随地吐痰罚款十美元。
   The penalty for nonperformance of contract is heavy.
   不履行合同的罚款是很重的。
7. **due to** 由于，预计，应付的
   The delay in shipment is due to force majeure.
   The amount due to you is US$300.
   M/V Red Star is due to arrive here today.
   duly *adv.* 及时
   We have duly noted the contents of your email of April 5.

I. Translate the following expressions.

   A. From English into Chinese.

    1. port of loading   2. book shipping space

    3. freight collect   4. Container Freight Station

5. congestion of shipping space   6. tramp

B. From Chinese into English.

1. 滞期费   2. 多式联运提单

3. 罚金   4. 原产地证书

II. Fill in the blanks with the following words and phrases in their proper forms.

ship	forward	regard	regret

1. Please advise whether you can _____ our order from stock.
2. With _____ to your request for a refund, we have referred the matter to our main office.
3. Buying _____ or _____ buying means buying shares or currencies or commodities at today's price for delivery at a later date.
4. Much to our _____, no more orders can be accepted this year.
5. Please arrange _____ of the goods booked by us with the least possible delay.
6. We hope this initial _____ will prove entirely satisfactory to you.
7. The transport of the goods was done by the _____ agent.
8. We are _____ that we didn't open L/C in time.
9. All the figures are _____ as estimates only and not in the least binding on us.
10. We have faxed you this morning in _____ to this matter.

III. Complete the sentences.

1. Please advise us whether you can _____ (用下个月第一艘可订舱位的船只装运货物).
2. _____ (由于货物要在香港转船), we shall require through B/L.
3. According to the stipulations in the foregoing sales confirmation, _____ _____ (货物应在三四月间装运).
4. Sometimes the buyer may request _____ (延迟装运).
5. You may make all the necessary preparations to _____ (提货) when they duly _____ (到达你方港口).

Lesson 27 Requesting for Partial Shipment and Transshipment

From: bolsen@paemaesales.com
To: jdeal@paemaesales.com
Date: 5 August, 2018 11:49
Subject: Transshipment Allowed or Not

Dear Tony,

We are in receipt of your email of yesterday requesting us to ship all the 4×40' HQ of Baby Joggers against Order No. 4930 in one lot in December. Unfortunately we are unable to comply with your wishes, due to the preparation of raw materials and our tough producing schedule.

As contracted, the delivery time of this order is up to January 31, 2021. If you desire earlier delivery, we can only make a partial shipment of 2×40' HQ in December and the remaining in January, 2019. This would speed matters up if we could ship immediately the goods we have in stock instead of waiting for the whole shipment to be completed.

At present, we are advised by the forwarder that because direct vessels, either liner or tramp, sailing for Liverpool, are infrequent, and the shipping space has been fully booked up to the end of March. In the circumstances, we have to ship via Hong Kong more often than not. As a result, transshipment may be necessary. If you allow transshipment, we would do our best to make further contacts with the forwarder. In this case, you must bear the additional charges.

Please take the above into consideration and let us know your decision as early as possible.

Best regards,
Julie

Chapter X Shipment

Notes

1. **transshipment** *n.* 转运

   Transshipment will be made at Hong Kong.

   这次运输将在香港转船。

   transship *v.* 转运

   The goods should be transshipped at Kaohsiung.

   货物将在高雄转船。

2. **partial shipments** 分批装运，指一个合同项下的货物分若干批或若干期装运。

3. **comply with** 依照，符合

   Visitors to the factory must comply with the rules.

   来工厂的访客必须遵守规章。

   to comply with one's request / demand / wishes 满足某人的要求/愿望

4. **liner service** 班轮运输

   tramp 不定期航线运输

5. **sail for** 船舶驶往某目的港

   The carrying vessel will sail for your port in early March.

   承运船只将在3月初驶往你方港口。

   sailing *n.*（轮船的）航班 *v.* 驾驶；起航

   sailing port 启航港

   sailing schedule 船期表

   As there is no direct sailing to your port, we regret being unable to ship the goods in April.

   由于没有直达你方港口的船舶，我们很遗憾无法在4月发货。

6. **bear** *v.* 负担，承担

   Owing to your negligence, you have to bear the responsibility.

   由于你方疏忽，你们不得不承担责任。

   The extra expenses are to be borne by you.

   额外的费用由你方承担。

I. Translate the following expressions.

　　A. From English into Chinese.

　　1. in one lot　　　　　　　2. tough producing schedule

　　3. expedite the production　　4. through B/L

　　5. shipper　　　　　　　　6. telex release

　　B. From Chinese into English.

　　1. 充足的库存　　　　　　2. 同时通知我们

　　3. 两批等量货　　　　　　4. 班轮运输

II. Fill in the blanks with appropriate prepositions.

1. Owing _____ the delay _____ the part of our suppliers, we must ask you to postpone the shipping date _____ October 10.

2. We wish to draw your attention _____ the fact that the date _____ delivery is approaching, but up to the present moment we have not received any news _____ you.

3. Shipment is to be made in June _____ three equal lots.

4. Today we shipped the above consignment _____ board S.S. Nellore which sails _____ your port tomorrow.

5. Any delay _____ shipment would cause us much inconvenience.

III. Put the following letter into English.

> 执事先生：
> 　　我方近期内将有20箱瓷器（chinaware）从香港运往鹿特丹（Rotterdam），货箱尺码为5×4×3英尺，每箱重约250公斤。
> 　　请告知货物运价，以及航运班期、运货所需要的时间等详细情况。据悉"恒星"号轮定于8月10日启航，但我方希望有启航日期较早的货轮。
> 　　盼早复。
>
> 　　　　　　　　　　　　　　　　　　　　　　　　　　　　谨启
> 　　　　　　　　　　　　　　　　　　　　　　　　　　　　×××

Chapter X Shipment

Skill Training

Exercise I. Fill in the blanks with the hints below.

装货港：福建福州
提单号：DDC123456
集装箱铅封号：GATU12345/65432
预计到达时间：2021年1月20日
货物名称：时尚拖
总重量：3000KGS
净重：2340KGS
数量：5200双
总金额：21,645.12美元
开证行：the Banca Monte Dei Paschi Di Siena S.P.A.
唛头：A.B. S/C nbr——ord number——art number

发票号码：HJ20100098
提单号码：DDC123456
船名：VICTORY. NO. 345P
装运日期：2020年12月30日
签发日期：2021年1月2日
合同号码：BP12345
信用证号码：HS84283AF
通知日期：2020年12月30日
目的港：CATANIA PORT, ITALY

FUJIAN ORIENTAL FOOTWEAR IMP. AND EXP. CO., LTD.

Add: 9/F MINFA BUILDING NO. 88, DONGSHUI ROAD, FUZHOU, CHINA
Tel: 0086-0591-345678   Mobile: 86-12345678
Web: www.orientalfootwear.com   Email: alicia0618@tchina.com

SHIPPING ADVICE

TO:	AL ABRA SUB TRADING EST. 94017 REGALBUTO CATANIA, ITALY	ISSUE DATE:	
		S/C NO.	
		L/C NO.	
		DATE	
		NAME OF ISSUING BANK	

Dear Sir or Madam:

  We have pleasure in informing you that we have completed the shipment in accordance with the stipulations set forth in L/C No. HS84283AF. The details of shipment are stated below:

Invoice Number:	
Bill of Lading Number:	
Ocean Vessel:	
Port of Loading:	
Date of Shipment:	
Port of Destination:	
ETA	
Containers/Seals Number:	
Description of Goods:	
Shipping Marks:	
Quantity:	
Gross Weight:	
Net Weight:	
Total Value:	

  Thank you for your patronage. We look forward to the pleasure of receiving your valuable repeat orders.

Sincerely yours,

FOR AND ON BEHALF OF:
    FUJIAN ORIENTAL FOOTWEAR IMP. AND EXP. CO., LTD.
      Alicia

Exercise II. Try to make an investigation on the fluctuations of freight rates during the past two years from your local port to other main ports in the world.

Chapter X　Shipment

Business Link

I. 海运出口货物流程

1. 订舱并填写订舱单：出口商根据合同中的最迟装运时间，提前8—10个工作日向货运代理公司订舱。
2. 货运公司确认了出口商的订舱后，出口商即可获得出口运输方面最重要的信息：船公司的名称、航班号、转船时间、开船时间、预计到达目的港的天数。
3. 获得场站收据：货运公司把货物运到装运港集装箱码头堆场后方，货运公司获得场站收据，转交给出口商，以便出口商自行报检和报关。
4. 准备装船：出口货物通过报检和报关后，把有关单据交给货运公司，货运公司则将有关单据交给场站工作人员，工作人员把集装箱运到集装箱码头堆场前方，等待装船。
5. 装船并获得海运提单：场站工作人员根据集装箱的转船时间（此时间写在订舱单上）装船。装船后，货运公司从船公司获得海运提单。
6. 支付海运费：出口商支付海运费，货运公司把海运提单交给出口商。
7. 出口商即可向进口商发送装船通知。

II. 船务术语简写

1. ORC（Origin Receive Charges）本地收货费用（广东省收取）
2. THC（Terminal Handling Charges）码头操作费（香港收取）
3. BAF（Bunker Adjustment Factor）燃油附加费
4. CAF（Currency Adjustment Factor）货币贬值附加费
5. YAS（Yard Surcharges）码头附加费
6. EPS（Equipment Position Surcharges）设备位置附加费
7. DDC（Destination Delivery Charges）目的港交货费
8. PSS（Peak Season Surcharges）旺季附加费
9. PCS（Port Congestion Surcharge）港口拥挤附加费
10. DOC（Document Charges）文件费
11. O/F（Ocean Freight）海运费
12. B/L（Bill of Lading）海运提单
13. MB/L（Master Bill of Lading）船东单
14. MTD（Multimodal Transport Document）多式联运单据
15. W/T（Weight Ton）重量吨（即货物收费以重量计费）
16. M/T（Measurement Ton）尺码吨（即货物收费以尺码计费）

17. W/M（Weight or Measurement Ton）即以重量吨或者尺码吨中从高收费
18. CY（Container Yard）集装箱（货柜）堆场
19. FCL（Full Container Load）整箱货
20. LCL（Less than Container Load）拼箱货（散货）
21. CFS（Container Freight Station）集装箱货运站
22. TEU（Twenty-feet Equivalent Units）20英尺换算单位（用来计算货柜量的多少）
23. A/W（All Water）全水路（指由美国西岸中转至东岸或内陆点的货物的运输方式）
24. MLB（Mini Land Bridge）迷你大陆桥（主要指由美国西岸中转至东岸或内陆点的货物的运输方式）

III. 货运英语名词汇总

定期租船 time charter

允许装卸时间 lay days / laying days

工作日 working days

连续天数 running days / consecutive days

滞期费 demurrage

滞期日数 demurrage days

速遣费 despatch money

空舱费 dead freight

退关 short shipment / goods short shipped / goods shut out / shut-outs

赔偿保证书（信托收据）letter of indemnity / trust receipt

装运重量 shipping weight / in-take-weight

卸货重量 landing weight

压舱 ballasting

压舱货 in ballast

舱单 manifest

船舶登记证书 ship's certificate of registry

航海日记 ship's log

船员名册 muster-roll

（船员、乘客）健康证明 bill of health

Chapter X Shipment

Useful Sentences

1. Please be assured that we will effect shipment in compliance with the contracted terms.
2. However, up to now we have not received from you any information concerning this lot.
3. As the selling season is rapidly approaching, we shall appreciate it very much if you will book shipping space and arrange shipment as soon as possible, thus enable the goods to catch the brisk demand at the start of the season.
4. Enclosed please find one set of duplicate shipping documents for the goods, the original of which are being sent to you through our bankers.
5. We take pleasure in notifying you that the consignment under S/C No. 409 have been made on board S.S. Victoria which is sailing from Hong Kong to New York via Panama Canal on July 20 and is due to arrive at New York on or about Aug. 8.
6. We have to advise you that we are unable to dispatch your order in full owing to a great shortage of shipping space.
7. The goods ordered in May are ready for dispatch and as the transaction is concluded on FOB basis you are to arrange the shipment. We should be glad to have your immediate shipping instructions.
8. The ETS would be two weeks after receipt of order. However, with the port workers now on strike, we doubt if if we could make shipment in time. We assure you that we are doing everything we can to get the goods away.
9. Please advise us 30 days before the month of shipment of the contract number, name of commodity, quantity, port of loading and the time when the goods reach the port of loading.
10. Much to our regret, we cannot ship the goods within the time limit of the L/C owing to the unforeseen difficulties on the part of mill.
11. The duplicate shipping documents including bill of lading, invoice, packing list and inspection certificate were airmailed to you today.
12. In the event of force Majeure or any contingencies beyond our control, we shall not be held responsible for the late delivery or non-delivery of the goods.
13. We hope you will understand that we would not ask for earlier delivery if we did not have compelling reasons for doing so.
14. The shipment must be made within the prescribed time limit, as further extension will not be considered.
15. As our traditional Spring Festival holiday is approaching, it will be very difficult for us to book shipping space. To make it easier, we hope transshipment and partial shipments are allowed.

Chapter XI
Insurance

Objectives:
After learning this chapter, you will
1. be familiar with terms related to insurance;
2. be familiar with insurance policies;
3. be able to write letters on insurance.

Introduction

In the international trade, it is quite possible for goods to encounter various kinds of risks and losses during the long distance transportation from the seller to the buyer. So exporters or importers need to cover insurance on their goods with insurance companies against different risks.

Insurance is defined as financial protection against loss and harm. It is an arrangement by which a company gives customers financial protection against loss, damage, and delay in transit, in return for payment that is called a premium. The insurance company agrees to pay if a specified undesirable event occurs. Arrangements for insurance may be made by either the buyer or the seller, in accordance with the terms of sale.

There are many different kinds of insurance and most are rather specific and complicated. All of them have different terms of when money will be paid and different costs. The buyer and the seller must decide on which policies are most beneficial. Sometimes the buyer and the seller pay for different parts of the coverage, especially when the buyer wants extra clauses or terms that the seller does not generally pay for.

There are a great number of insurance companies in the world. Lloyd's is a famous organization incorporated in London in 1871. It is the center of marine insurance which started in a seventeenth century coffee house, through which, insurance brokers may pace their business. In China, PICC, established in 1949, is the stated-owned insurance organization which underwriters almost all kinds of insurance and has agents in almost all main ports and regions over the world. Since the establishment of the PICC, it has become the practice of Chinese foreign trade corporations to have their imports insured with the PICC. China Export & Credit Insurance Corporation (SINOSURE) is China's only policy-oriented insurance company specializing in export credit insurance. It began operations on December 18, 2001, with capital coming from the Export Credit Insurance Risk Fund as arranged by the State fiscal budget. SINOSURE has formed a nationwide service network. SINOSURE's main products include short-term export credit insurance, domestic trade credit insurance, medium- and long-term export credit insurance, investment insurance and bonds & guarantees. The role of export credit insurance in supporting China's foreign trade and economic cooperation has become more and more evident. Since founded, SINOSURE has supported exports, domestic trade, and investments with a total value of more than 290 billion U.S. dollars, with thousands of policyholders and hundreds of medium and long term projects covered.

Writing Tips

A letter on insurance from the seller often includes the following contents:

1) Giving and explaining coverage;
2) Providing terms of payment for the coverage;
3) Asking for agreement.

A letter on insurance from the buyer often covers the following points:

1) Mention the goods, contract, etc.;
2) Suggest the terms of payment and the reason;
3) Wish the reader to accept and ship the goods early.

Lesson 28 Insurance Information

From: Angela@timbag.com
To: jan@busytrade.co.nz
Date: 8 May, 2018 10:49
Subject: Information on Our Insurance Terms

Dear Jan,

In reply to your email of last Friday enquiring about the insurance on our CIF offer for QX-508 Leather Bag, we wish to give you the following information.

For transactions concluded on CIF basis, we usually effect insurance with the People's Insurance Company of China against All Risks, as per Ocean Marine Cargo Clauses of the People's Insurance Company of China, dated the 1st January, 1981. Should you require the insurance to be covered as per Institute Cargo Clauses we would be glad to comply but if there is any difference in premium between the two, it will be charged to your account.

We are also in a position to insure the shipment against any additional risks if you so desire, and the extra premium is to be borne by you. In this case, we shall send you the premium receipt issued by the relative underwriter.

Usually, the amount insured is 110% of the total invoice value. However, if a higher percentage is required, we may do accordingly but you have to bear the extra premium as well.

We hope our above information will provide you with all the information you wish to know and we are now looking forward to receiving your order.

Best regards,
Angela

Chapter XI Insurance

1. **insurance** *n.* 保险

    effect / cover / provide / take out insurance 投保

    insurance amount 保险金额

    insurance policy 保单

    insurance certificate 保险凭证

    insurance coverage 保险范围

    Insurance is to be covered by the sellers for 110% of the invoice value.

    由卖方以发票价值110%投保。

    表示投保的货物，后接on；表示保险金额，后接for；表示投保的险别，后接against；表示保险费或保险费率，后接at；表示向保险公司投保，后接with。例如：

    We have covered insurance on the 5000 sets "LENOVO" Brand computer for 110% of the invoice value against All Risks and War Risk with the People's Insurance Company of China.

    我们已将5000台"联想"牌电脑按发票金额的110%向中国人民保险公司投保一切险。

    insure *v.* 投保；承保

    We will insure the shipment with the People's Insurance Company of China.

    我们将向中国人保为这批货投保。

    What risks are to be insured against? 要投什么险？

    insurer 承保人，保险人

    the insured 投保人

2. **as per** 根据

    Please quote us as per the attached enquiry sheet. 请根据所附询价单给我们报价。

3. **the People's Insurance Company of China** 中国人民保险公司

    中国人民保险公司1981年1月1日制定的中国保险条款（China Insurance Clauses，缩写为C.I.C.或CIC），包括海洋(Ocean Marine Cargo Insurance)、陆上(Overland Transportation)、航空(Air Transportation)及邮包(Parcel Transportation)运输方式的货物运输保险条款，以及适用于以上四种运输方式货物保险的附加条款。

4. **Ocean Marine Cargo Clauses** 海洋运输货物保险条款

    海运货物保险分为基本险和附加险两类。基本险所承保的主要是自然灾害和意外事故所造成的货物损失与费用,分为平安险(Free from Particular Average,简称FPA)、水渍险(With Average或With Particular Average,简称WA或WPA)和一切险(All Risks,简称AR)三种。附加险(Extraneous Risks)是对基本险的补充和扩大,附加险只能在投保某一种基本险的基础上才可加保。附加险有一般附加险(General Additional Risk)和特殊附加险(Special Additional Risks)之分,请参见本章的"Business Link"和"Useful Sentences"部分。

基本险	平安险(FPA)	主要是自然灾害
	水渍险(WPA)	自然灾害+意外事故
	一切险(AR)	水渍险+一般附加险
附加险	一般附加险(Additional Risk)	十一种
	特殊附加险(Special Additional Risks)	八种

5. Institute Cargo Clauses 伦敦保险协会货物保险条款

该条款共包括六种险别:(1)协会货物条款(A)[简称ICC(A)];(2)协会货物条款(B)[简称ICC(B)];(3)协会货物条款(C)[简称ICC(C)];(4)协会战争险条款(货物)(IWCC);(5)协会罢工险条款(货物)(ISCC);(6)恶意损害险(Malicious Damage Clause)。恶意损害险,属于附加险别,不能单独投保。

6. account *n.* 账户;理由;描述

take account of sth. / take sth. into account 考虑,注意到

They should have taken into account the need of foreign customers.

settle your account 付账,结账

Accounts must be settled within 30 days.

on account of 因为,由于

The shipment is delayed on account of the late arrival of some raw materials.

account for 占有;解释

Oil and gas account for 60% of the country's export.

石油和天然气占到这个国家出口的60%。

How do you account for the sudden change of export regulations?

你如何解释出口规定的突然变化?

7. insurance premium 保险费

The risk is coverable at a premium of 2%.

The shares are being sold at a premium.

be at a premium 奇货可居,难以得到

Packing space is at a premium in most cities.

Chapter XI Insurance

I. Translate the following expressions.

A. From English into Chinese.
1. All Risks
2. Institute Cargo Clauses
3. Additional Risks
4. C.I.C.
5. be charged to your account
6. premium receipt

B. From Chinese into English.
1. 以CIF价格成交
2. 向中国人民保险公司投保
3. 承担额外的保费
4. 为这票货投保

II. Choose the best answer.

1. I'd like to have the insurance _____ for 130% of the invoice value.
   A. cover   B. covered   C. covering   D. to cover
2. We are pleased to confirm _____ the above goods against All Risks for $5,500.
   A. have arranged   B. having assured
   C. to have ensured   D. having insured
3. We thank you for your letter of March 25, requesting us to effect insurance on the captioned goods for your _____.
   A. cost   B. amount   C. account   D. expense
4. Since the premium varies with the extent of insurance, extra premium is borne by the buyer, _____ additional risks be covered.
   A. if   B. as   C. must   D. should
5. Insurance _____ will be added to invoice amount together with the freight charges.
   A. policies   B. premiums   C. money   D. amount

III. Please translate the following sentences into English.
1. 我们是按FOB价达成交易的，所以由你方去投保。
2. 对于按CIF价成交的货物，由我方按发票金额的110%投保一切险。
3. 因为这批货不是易碎品，不太可能在运输途中受损，所以平安险就够了。
4. 破碎险是一种特殊险别，要额外收保费。
5. 由于保险费率随保险范围而不同，因此如需增报其他险别，额外保费由买方负担。

Lesson 29 Asking for CIF Terms

From: bolsen@genway.com
To: jdeal@paemaesales.com
Date: 5 August, 2018 11:49
Subject: Asking for CIF Terms

Dear Scott,

We thank you for your Order No. 485 for 1×40' HQ of plush toys, which is placed on CFR basis.

In reply, we would like to inform you that most of our clients are placing their orders with us on CIF basis. This will save their time and simplify procedures. May we suggest that you would follow this practice?

For your information, we usually effect insurance with the People's Insurance Company of China. Our insurance company is a state-operated enterprise enjoying high prestige in settling claims promptly and equitably and has agents and surveyors in all main ports and regions of the world. Should any damage occur to the goods, you may file your claim with their agent at your end, who will take up the matter without delay.

We insure the goods against the usual risks and in the present case All Risks based on warehouse to warehouse clause. Should broader coverage be required, the extra premium is for the buyer's account.

If you have an open policy with your insurance company, we will advise you of the particulars of the shipment as soon as we ship the goods.

We hope the above will be helpful and welcome your further comments.

Best regards,
Amy

Chapter XI Insurance

1. **settle claims** 理赔

    settle（解决） the argument / difference / a problem / a question

    We need to get everything settled as soon as possible.

    我们需要尽快把一切都确定好。

    settle an account 结算，偿付

    settle down 安定下来

    settlement *n.* 解决，和解

    We hope to reach a settlement of the dispute amicably.

    我们希望能够友善地解决争端。

2. **file your claim with…** 向……提出索赔

    file / lodge / submit / raise a claim 提出索赔

    insurance claims 保险索赔

    Once you receive the shipment, you can put in a claim for the overcharge.

    你收到货后，可以为过多收费提出索赔。

    claim *v.* 宣称

    The terrorists claimed responsibility for the bombing.

    恐怖分子宣布对爆炸负责。

3. **agent** *n.* 代理

    sole / exclusive agent 独家代理

    general agent 总代理

    agency agreement 代理协议

4. **warehouse to warehouse clause** 仓至仓条款

    "仓至仓"条款所指的运输包括海上、陆上、内河和驳船运输的整个运输过程。海上货物运输保险合同中规定保险责任起止期的条款。保险期间自货物从保险单载明的起运港(地)发货人的仓库或储存处开始运输时生效，到货物运达保险单载明目的港(地)收发人的最后仓库或被保人用作分配、分派或非正常运输的其他储存处所为止。

5. **coverage** *n.* 覆盖范围；新闻报道

    Inadequate insurance coverage can lead to major financial loss.

    投保险别不足会导致重大的经济损失。

    Fortunately he has medical coverage.

很幸运他有医疗保险。
ABC gave the story extensive coverage in the evening news.
美国广播公司在晚间新闻中详细报道了此事。

6. **open policy** 预约保险单，即保险公司承保被保险人一定时期内所有进出口货物使用的保险单。

其他还有：

floating policy 流动保（险）单

voyage policy 航程保（险）单

specific policy 单独保（险）单，船名确定保单

7. **particulars** *n. pl.* 细节，详情
I gave him all the particulars he needed.
我给他提供了所有他要的细节内容。

in particular 尤其，特别

particular *adj.* 特定的
Several steps may be taken depending on the particular circumstances.
根据特定的形势采取一些措施。
The company is very particular about who it hires.
这家公司对聘用员工很苛求。

I. Translate the following expressions.

A. From English into Chinese.

1. on CIF basis
2. a state-operated enterprise
3. file a claim with
4. warehouse to warehouse clause
5. broader coverage
6. open policy

B. From Chinese into English.

1. 简化程序
2. 采取这种做法
3. 理赔
4. 通知您装运的细节

II. Complete the sentences with the patterns given below.

> to arrange insurance on your behalf, to insure…with…, to submit an insurance claim, to cover insurance, to compensate for, to issue an All-Risks policy, to insure…for, to cover…against

1. We usually (对这种货投保一切险) _____ _____ and TPND.
2. After damage has been incurred, the insured may (提出保险索赔) _____ _____ supported by a survey report with the insurer.
3. We can only (按发票金额的110%进行投保) _____ _____ according to the contract stipulations.
4. (这批货物由我们公司保险) _____ _____ and we have paid the loss on the strength of the policy conditions.
5. The seller will have to (赔偿买方的损失) _____ _____ which occurs in transit.
6. In accordance with your fax instructions, we have already today (代你方投保) _____ _____.
7. As agreed, we have (将此货按发票金额加10%投保) _____ _____ against All Risks.
8. Can the Simpson Insurance Company (为这些货签发全险保单) _____ _____.

III. Translate the following letter into Chinese.

> Dear Jane,
>
> We acknowledged receipt of your email yesterday, asking us to insure the goods against Order No. 304 for 130% of invoice.
>
> Firstly we have to clarify that we only make the insurance for 110% against All Risks as our usual practice, so the extra premium incurred is at the buyer's expense. Therefore, the 20% difference shall be borne by you.
>
> We will arrange the insurance immediately on receipt of your agreement.
>
> Best regards,
> James

Lesson 30

(A) Inquiring for Insurance Rate

From: bruce@toptextile.com
To: melisa@pingan.com.cn
Date: 29 April 2018 15:49
Subject: Quote Us the Lowest Rate Please

Dear Melisa,

Please quote us the lowest rate for floating policy on the goods mentioned below:

500 cartons of cotton goods, valued at US$26,500, going from Pusan, Korea, to Singapore by S.S. Breeze which is to set sail from Pusan on June 4. The goods are packed in strong cartons of international standard.

We'd like to cover insurance against ICC(A) & War Risk. Please send us the lowest insurance rate at the earliest. Thank you in advance.

Best Regards,
Bruce

(B) Offering Insurance Rate

From: melisa@pingan.com.cn
To: bruce@toptextile.com
Date: 30 April, 2018 9:37
Subject: Insurance Rate for Cotton Goods

Dear Bruce,

In response to your enquiry of yesterday, we wish to quote you the rate of Marine Insurance at 0.315%, ICC(A) including War Risk, on the shipment referred to in your last email.

This is an exceptionally low rate, because many of the insurance companies will hesitate to take the risk at any premium whatever, dreading the heavy average to which they are exposed on the East China Sea.

We trust you will give us the opportunity to handle your insurance business. The insurance policy will be ready in the next few days after we receive your favorable reply.

Best regards,
Melisa

1. **floating policy** 总保险单
   指用以承包多批次货运的一种持续性长期保险凭证，常译为"统保单"。是指保险单仅作笼统的规定，船舶的名称和其他事项将在以后申报中确定。

2. **ICC(A)** 协会货物条款A
   是以一切风险减除外责任的形式出现，因为这一险别中承保的责任范围最大，采用除列明风险和损失之外，一切风险损失都予承保的规定，最为简单明了。

3. **insurance rate** 保险费率
   The current insurance rate be $1.325 per 100.00 of insure value, which include 0.15 for war risk.
   现行保险费率：每100美元保险值交1.325美元，其中包括战争保险费率0.15。

The insurance rate for such kind of risk will vary according to the kind.
这类险别的保险费率将根据货物种类而定。

4. average *n.* 海损

海上运输中，由于自然灾害或意外事故引起的船舶或货物的任何损失，如船舶因触礁、搁浅、碰撞、沉没、火灾、风灾、爆炸等造成船舶或货物的物质损失及费用损失等，均属海损。

Particular Average (P/A) 单独海损

General Average (G/A) 共同海损

5. insurance policy 保单

保险人与被保险人订立保险合同的正式书面证明。保险单必须完整地记载保险合同双方当事人的权利义务及责任。

insurance certificate 保险凭证

保险凭证是保险人签发给投保人的，表明其已接受其投保的证明文件，是一种简化的保险单。保险凭证上不载明保单背面保险条款，其余内容与保单完全相同。

I. Translate the following expressions.

A. From English into Chinese.

1. floating policy
2. Particular Average
3. cover insurance against ICC(A) and War Risk
4. dread the heavy average
5. agency agreement
6. international standard

B. From Chinese into English.

1. 保单
2. 最低的保险费率
3. 0.315%的海运保费
4. 暴露于重大海损下

II. Choose the best answer.

1. Insurance is to be _____ by the buyer if a transaction is concluded on FOB or CFR basis.

   A. covered   B. done   C. made   D. taken

2. Since the premium varies with the extent of insurance, extra premium is for buyer's account, _____ additional risks be covered.

   A. if   B. as   C. must   D. should

3. Damage _____ the goods was caused by heavy rain _____ transit.
   A. of…in B. to…in C. for…during D. on…during

4. I regret to report the loss of the whole shipment _____ you under the above policy.
   A. insured with   B. to be insured with
   C. insuring for   D. being insured at

5. As requested, we have covered insurance _____ 2,500 TV sets _____ 110% above the invoice value _____ ICC(A) and War Risk.
   A. on…at...for   B. on…for...against
   C. with…at…for   D. with…at…against

III. Writing practice

Suppose that you work for Xiamen Electronic Appliances Company, write a reply letter to your client for the required Insurance Policy for invoice amount plus 10% for the goods of Contract No. JS749. Invent some details if necessary.

Skill Training

Exercise I. Please calculate the CIF value of this order according to the following information.

保险费=保险金额×保险费率

保险金额=发票到岸价(CIF 价)×发票加成率(一般是加成10%)= CIF 价×110%

在没有特别规定的情况下，一般是按照 CIF 价的110%，特殊情况下不超过CIF价120%。

Subject Matter Insured: 350 Cartons of plush toys under Order No. 485

Sum Insured: Cost of the goods: US$55,000

    Freight: US$1,000

      Insurance: 10% of the CIF value

To be covered against All Risks and War Risk

Rate of Premium: All Risks: 0.35%

        War Risk: 0.01%

Exercise II. Translate the following letter into English.

> 敬启者：
>
> 事由：我方第626号订单项下3000箱皮鞋
>
> 我们想请你方查阅我方订购3000箱皮鞋的第123号订单。这批货是按CFR订货的。
>
> 我们现在想把这批标题项下的货在你处投保。如果你方能代我方按发票金额的110%投保水渍险、偷窃、提货不着险、淡水雨淋险和战争险，我们将不胜感激。一俟收到你方的借记通知单和有关的保险单，我们立即把保险费付还你方。
>
> 期待早日收到你们的答复。
>
> 谨启
> ×××

Business Link

I. Risk & Coverage of Ocean Marine Cargo Insurance

Basic Insurance Coverage 基本险别

1) 平安险 Free from Particular Average
2) 水渍险 With Particular Average
3) 一切险 All Risks

II. Additional Risks 附加险

1) 偷窃提货不着险（Theft, Pilferage and Non-delivery, 简称TPND）
2) 淡水雨淋险（Fresh Water Rain Damage, 简称FWRD）
3) 短量险（Risk of Shortage）
4) 混杂、沾污险（Risk of Intermixture & Contamination）
5) 渗漏险（Risk of Leakage）
6) 碰损、破碎险（Risk of Clash & Breakage）
7) 串味险（Risk of Odor）
8) 受热、受潮险（Damage Caused by Heating & Sweating）
9) 钩损险（Hook Damage）
10) 包装破裂险（Loss for Damage by Breakage of Packing）
11) 锈损险（Risk of Rust）

III. Special Additional Risks 特殊附加险

1) 战争险 War Risk
2) 罢工险 Strike Risk
3) 交货不到险 Failure to Deliver Risk
4) 进口关税险 Import Duty Risk
5) 舱面货物险 On Deck Risk
6) 拒收险 Reject Risk
7) 黄曲霉素险 Aflatoxin Risk
8) 出口货物到中国香港（包括九龙在内）或中国澳门存仓火险责任扩展风险（Fire Risk Extension Clause for Storage of Cargo at Destination Hong Kong, including Kowloon, or Macao）

IV. Terms & Terminology

Risk of Packing Breakage	包装破裂险
Risk of Inherent Vice	内在缺陷险
Risk of Normal Loss (Natural Loss)	途耗或自然损耗险
Risk of Spontaneous Combustion	自燃险
Risk of Contingent Import Duty	进口关税险
Insurance against War Risk	战争险
Air Transportation Cargo War Risk	航空运输战争险
parcel post insurance	邮包运输保险
insurance law	保险法
insurance act	保险条例
insurance industry	保险业
insurance division	保险部
insurance treaty	保险合同
cover note	保险证明书
guarantee of insurance	保险担保书
premium rebate	保险费回扣
insurance claim	保险索赔
ceding, retrocession (for reinsurance)	分保
reinsurance	分保（再保险）
co-insurance company	共同保险公司
insurance document	保险单据
certificate of insurance	保险凭证

increasing coverage, extending coverage	加保
renewing coverage	续保
insurance commission	保险佣金
social insurance	社会保险
personal property insurance	个人财产保险
insurance of contents	家庭财产保险

Useful Sentences

1. For transactions concluded on CIF basis, we usually cover the insurance against All Risks for 110% of the full invoice value with the People's Insurance Company of China as per CIC of the 1st January, 1981.

2. The differences between CIF and CFR prices depends on the nature of the goods to be insured, the degree of coverage desired and the place of destination.

3. Your request for insurance to be covered for 150% of the invoice value can be met but the premium for the difference between 150% and 110% should be for your account.

4. We adopt the warehouse to warehouse clause which is commonly used in international insurance.

5. We cannot comply with your request for insuring your order for 130% of its invoice value.

6. This kind of additional risk is coverable at 2‰. This risk is coverable at a premium of 0.35%.

7. Insurance on the goods shall be covered by us for 110% of the CIF value, and any extra premium for additional coverage, if required, shall be borne by the buyers.

8. The cover shall be limited to sixty days upon discharge of the insured goods from the seagoing vessel at the final port of discharge.

9. Our underwriter has surveyors and agents in practically all the big cities in the world to handle claims. Should any damage occur to the goods a claim may be filed with the insurance agent at your end with the necessary documents.

10. If you have an open policy with your insurance company we do not object to your covering insurance at your end and in that case we will advise you of the particulars of the shipment as soon as we ship the goods.

11. Please quote your lowest rate for floating policy of $10,000 against WPA, general

merchandise, in wooden cases only per S.S. Queen from Shanghai to Liverpool.

12. We have noted that you require the insurance to be covered against Risk of Breakage. However, please be informed that our CIF prices include insurance to cover WPA only and if you wish to have the Risk of Breakage included in the coverage, you must bear the additional premium.

13. The insured should promptly submit an insurance claim to the insurer or its agent so as to provide the latter with ample time to pursue recovery from the relative party in fault.

14. The premium rates quoted to us do not meet our expectations. Therefore, we are unable to sign a general policy with your company at this time.

15. You're required to submit the following documents in presenting a claim to our agent: Original Policy or Certificate of Insurance, original or copy of B/L, Invoice and Packing List, Certificate of Loss or Damage, Survey Report and Statement of Claim.

Chapter XII
Complaints, Claims and Settlement

Objectives:
After learning this chapter, you will
1. understand basic terms related to complaints and claims;
2. learn the way of writing complaints and claims;
3. be familiar with the style of the complaint and claim letters;
4. identify the approach of writing complaint and claim letters.

Introduction

Generally speaking, complaints should not be necessary. In ideal business conditions, everything should be done so carefully, with details of offers and orders checked, packing supervised, handling of goods carried out expertly, that no mistakes are made and nothing is damaged.

Unfortunately, complaints or claims may sometimes arise in spite of our well-planned and careful work in the performance of a sales contract. As you know, nothing goes as well as we expected. Often, due to many unforeseen factors, errors occur and goods are mishandled; accidents happen. All these may result in subsequent complaints of different characters.

Regardless of characters of complaints, the making of complaints is an unpleasant business and needs to be well prepared and well documented. Otherwise, business would become unprofitable and pointless, and the future business relationship may be jeopardized.

A complaint or claim letter requests some sort of compensation for damaged merchandise, unsatisfactory quality, wrong delivery, or being overcharged. While many complaints can be made in person, some require formal business letters.

There are many ways in the settlement of an international trade dispute. Normally, amicable settlement or conciliation is the first choice because it saves time and cost and good business relations are maintained. If amicable settlement does not lead to a satisfactory result, the parties concerned may seek for arbitration in which the arbitration award shall be final and binding to both parties.

Writing Tips

When making a complaint, you should:

1) express the regret;

2) inform the receiver of the subject matter, such as order, contract number and date;

3) tell him directly why you are not satisfied;

4) give your suggestions and hope for an early reply.

If you receive a complaint, you should make an investigation. If the complaint is reasonable, just admit it readily and send a reply as follows:

1) Thank him for his complaint and admit a mistake is made at your end;

2) Promise that you will take actions to put it right;

3) Say you are sorry for the inconvenience caused;

4) Assure him that more care will be taken in the future;

If the complaint is not reasonable, tell him that it is not your responsibility and give your suggestions if possible.

Lesson 31 Complaint about Inferior Quality

From: joe@toptextile.com.es
To: eileenwang@public.xm.fj.cn
Date: 8 May, 2018 10:49
Subject: Cotton Prints under Order No. 110203 Must Be Delivered in Line with the Samples

Dear Eileen,

The consignment of the cotton prints we ordered on April 10 is NOT of the same quality as that of the samples.

The consignment arrived yesterday, but on checking the fabric with samples you sent us, we are surprised to find that they do not match each other. Their quality seems inferior to the samples, the shade being much lighter, in addition to the uneven colors of some pieces. So they can not meet our customers' requirement.

We have arranged for the production of the customized suits and planned to start as soon as the fabric arrives. However, we still have to postpone the original orders from our customers owing to the poor quality of the cotton prints you sent us. This is bringing us much inconvenience.

Would you take them back and replace them with the ones as we ordered? We allow you another 10 days to prepare them. If you cannot guarantee delivery for whatever reason before June 1, we should ask for a complete refund of the money and full compensation for all our losses.

Your prompt cooperation will be beneficial to both of us.

Best regards,
Joe

Chapter XII Complaints, Claims and Settlement

1. **complaint** *n.* 投诉

   The importer has filed a complaint with/against our company about poor packing of the goods.

   进口商对货物包装不当提出了投诉。

   complain *v.* 投诉

   Our users have complained to us about the damage of the goods.

   我们的用户向我们投诉货物损坏。

   They complained that our shipment was not up to the agreed specifications.

   他们投诉我们发的货没达到确定的规格。

2. **inferior to** 比……差

   Thank you for sending us the sample of inferior goods for examination.

   谢谢你发来次品的样品供我们检查。

   Synthetic fabric is inferior to cotton fabric.

   合成纤维织物不如棉织品好。

   inferior *n.* 级别（或地位）低的人

   The manager is friendly with his inferiors.

   经理对他的部属很友好。

3. **replace...with...** 以……代替……

   They later replaced the manager with a younger man.

   他们后来用一个较年轻的人接替了这个经理。

   Please omit from our order NO. 394 the following goods, and replace them with 10 pieces of the goods as per the attached sample.

   请取消我们第394号订单下的下列货物，用10件所附样品那样的产品来代替。

I. Translate the following expressions.

　　A. From English into Chinese.

　　　1. the shade being much lighter　　　2. match each other

　　　3. the customized suits　　　4. compensation for all our losses

B. From Chinese into English.

1. 比样品差   2. 颜色不均

3. 满足顾客的需求   4. 推迟订单

5. 退还全款   6. 公证报告

II. Choose the best answer.

1. Letters of complaint should be written with the care and tact _____ to harm future business relationship.
   A. in order not   B. in order   C. not in order   D. in order that not

2. After unpacking the case we found that the goods did not _____ with the original sample.
   A. measure   B. agree   C. come up   D. match

3. They will compensate you _____ the loss according to the provisions of insurance policy.
   A. on   B. with   C. for   D. /

4. We have replaced the broken china sets. _____, we offered you a 3% discount.
   A. And also   B. More also   C. In addition   D. In addition to

5. It was found upon examination that nearly 15% of the packages _____, which was obviously attributed to improper packing.
   A. was   B. broken
   C. had been broken   D. been already broken

6. We find that the quality of your shipment is not in conformity with the _____ specifications.
   A. agreed   B. is agreed   C. agreeing   D. to agree

III. Complete the following sentences in English.

1. (我们要求你方尽快装运破损物品的替代品) _____
   _____ While we will register our claim with the insurance company.

2. We trust that you will give special care to the packing of the goods _____
   _____ (以免货物在运输途中受损).

3. Upon examination, we found _____
   _____ (这批货没有达到样品的品质水平，不能达到顾客的要求).

4. Due to the bad quality of the consignment, _____
   _____ (我们要求全额退款，并赔偿我们的全部损失).

Chapter XII Complaints, Claims and Settlement

Lesson 32 Claim on Late Delivery

From: martin@genway.com.es
To: Jason@finefabirc.com
Date: 5 December, 2018 11:49
Subject: Our Order No. 50494

Dear Jason,

We regret to complain about late delivery of the captioned goods ordered on September 14th. We did not receive the goods till today though you guaranteed delivery in November. It was on the basis of this guarantee that we placed the order with you.

For some time we have been pressing you for the shipment of this order, and in our last email of 30 November we informed you that unless this order was already on the way, the consignment would arrive too late for the season and so be of no use to us.

Nevertheless, you have thought fit to send the goods, and now the only thing we can do to oblige you is either to take them on consignment and try to sell retail or to accept them for next season at an allowance, which we leave you to determine.

Unfortunately, we still have to lodge a claim for your delaying the shipment as contracted. There were similar deliveries on several occasions before and in recent months it has occurred more often. That is why we are compelled to say that business between us cannot be continued in conditions as these.

We feel it necessary to make our feeling clearly known. If the time of delivery our suppliers guaranteed cannot be relied on, it is impossible for us to give our end users a satisfactory explanation. We expect you will understand how we are placed.

Await your early reply.

Best regards,
Martin

1. claim *n./v.* 索赔

make/file/lodge/register/raise/put in/bring up a claim (against sb.) /(for/on sth.) 向……提出索赔

They submitted a claim on this shipment for US$5,000 on account of short weight.

由于这批货重量不足,我们索赔5000美元。

On the basis of Survey Report, we lodge our claim with / against / on you for US$10,000.

依据调查报告,我们向你索赔10,000美元。

accept/admit a claim 同意索赔　　entertain a claim 受理索赔

dismiss a claim 驳回索赔　　　　withdraw a claim 索赔

reject a claim 拒绝索赔　　　　　waive a claim 放弃索赔

2. oblige *v.* 感激,迫使,有义务做某事

We should be obliged if you would reply to us soon.

如您能尽快回复,我们将感激不尽。

We are obliged to close our Hong Kong office because of heavy loss.

由于损失惨重,我们被迫关闭香港办公室。

Please oblige me by turning down the radio.

劳您驾,请把收音机音量调低一些。

I felt obliged to tell her the truth.

我觉得有必要把真相告诉她。

3. take…on consignment 寄售

寄售(consignment)是一种委托代售的贸易方式,也是国际贸易中习惯采用的做法之一。它是指委托的(货主)先将货物运往寄售地,委托国外一个代销人(受委托人),按照寄售协议规定的条件,由代销人代替货主进行销售,货物出售后,由代销人向货主结算货款的一种贸易做法。

4. allowance *n.* 津贴,零用钱;允许;限额

at an allowance 打折

That store makes an allowance of 10% for cash payment.

那家商店给付现金的顾客打百分之十的折扣。

The child has a weekly allowance of five dollars.

这孩子每星期有五元零用钱。

Chapter XII Complaints, Claims and Settlement

His allowance for food is $100.

他拨出一百美元用于购买食物。

What is the baggage allowance of this airline?

这家航空公司的行李重量限额是多少?

5. compel *v.* 强迫

They often compelled us to work twelve or fourteen hours a day.

他们常常强迫我们每天工作十二或十四小时。

He was compelled by illness to give up his studies.

他因病被迫放弃学业。

I. Translate the following expressions.

A. From English into Chinese.

1. on the basis of this guarantee   2. captioned goods

3. waive a claim   4. short shipment

5. dismiss a claim   6. at an allowance

B. From Chinese into English.

1. 投诉某事   2. 将它们寄售

3. 因装运延误提出索赔   4. 被迫……

II. Choose the best answer.

1. Our customer has claimed _____ us _____ delayed delivery of the goods.

   A. with; with   B. for; about   C. with; for   D. for; with

2. We are sorry for our mistake in the number, _____ resulted _____ your receiving the wrong goods.

   A. that; of   B. this; from   C. which; in   D. it; as

3. We must insist on immediate delivery, _____ we shall be compelled to cancel the order in accordance with the contract stipulations.

   A. however   B. likewise   C. in other words   D. otherwise

4. We very much regret that we cannot accept your claim on the coffee sets from the batch _____ you complain.

   A. which   B. of which   C. about which   D. on which

5. We apologize for the underpayment of US$123.00 on your invoice No. 483-5499. This was _____ a misreading of the amount _____.
   A. due to; due
   B. owing to; owing
   C. due; owed
   D. owing to; due to

6. If the quality of the material delivered does not match _____ of the sample, we are ready to replace the unsold part of the batch.
   A. that
   B. with
   C. it
   D. those

7. We have made this allowance _____ we should like to do more business with you if possible.
   A. despite
   B. though
   C. because
   D. unless

III. Translate the following sentences into English.

1. 由于你方未能在所要求的时间内装运，我们就此取消订单，同时保留进一步追偿的权利。
2. 我们很遗憾不得不投诉你们的转运延误，准时装运对我们至关重要。
3. 此批货物品质极差，我方客户不愿提货，故请告知是否要我们将这批货退回，还是要我们把货物保存在我方仓库，留待你方处理？
4. 对于第493号销售合同项下的货物缺少5箱一事我们深表遗憾，按提单所载500箱货物确已全部装船，因此我们对此不负责任，建议你向保险公司提出索赔。

Chapter XII　Complaints, Claims and Settlement

Lesson 33　Settlement of Complaint

From: juliewang@ sales. zzqx.com.cn
To: steve_guan@Skyfood.com
Date: 29 April, 2018 15:49
Subject: About the Short Shipment of Order No. 0410-23

Dear Mr. Guan,

This is to acknowledge receipt of your email of 24 April, 2018, in which you informed us about the under-shipment of your candy bar order.

It was distressing to learn that seven cases of candy were left undelivered, but we have taken the matter up with management. I am sorry about this careless oversight on our side and sincerely apologize for the inconveniences and losses this unfortunate incident may have brought to you.

As per your request, a new shipment for seven cases left our dock this morning and is scheduled for afternoon delivery to you. It is expected to arrive on May 15th and we hope that you can hold on until that time.

I know how exasperating this must be for you, and to compensate for your loss, we would like to offer you two options: 20% off for this order (2018-0410-23) or $500—worth of credit to your account, which you can use anytime from now when you place an order with us.

You have been a valued customer of ours for a long time and we appreciate your affording us the opportunity to continue serving you. Please rest assured that this problem will not occur again.

Sincerely yours,
Julie

1. **acknowledge** *vt.* 告知收到；感谢

   We acknowledge your letter of June 18.

   我们已收到你方6月18号的来函。

   We acknowledge his helpful service with a present.

   我们送件礼物对他的服务表示感谢。

   acknowledgement *n.* 回执，表示收到的通知；感谢

   Your early acknowledgement will be highly appreciated.

   如你方早日答复，我们将十分感谢。

   We write this letter in acknowledge of your kind help.

   我们写这封信对你们的热情帮助表示感谢。

2. **credit to your account** 记入你方账户

   We have received your cheque, value RMB￥250,000 which we have passed to your credit on account.

   我们已收到贵方面额250,000元人民币支票一张，此款已转入贵方所赊贷方账户。

   credit note 贷方票据，也叫credit invoice 抵扣发票。（客户发现收到的货物的质量或数量有问题，就要求开出抵扣发票，在以后的业务中就凭借这个抵扣少付的货款。）

   debit note 借记单，借款通知书

3. **compensate** *v.* 补偿，赔偿

   compensate for 弥补

   She used her good looks to compensate for her lack of intelligence.

   她智力欠佳，权以美貌弥补。

   compensate sb. for sth. 赔偿，补偿

   Who will compensate for the losses? 谁将赔偿损失？

   compensation trade 补偿贸易

4. **a valued customer** 尊贵客户，重要客户

   Thank you for buying merchandise from us. You are a valued customer of ours. We appreciate your business and know that you want to keep your account current with us.

   感谢您购买我们的商品。您是我公司十分尊贵的客户，万分感谢您的惠顾并愿与我方进行业务往来。

Chapter XII Complaints, Claims and Settlement

 **Exercises**

I. Translate the following expressions.

A. From English into Chinese.

1. take the matter up
2. compensation trade
3. be scheduled for afternoon delivery
4. credit note
5. credit to your account
6. claim settlement

B. From Chinese into English.

1. 货物短装
2. 我方的疏忽
3. 借款通知
4. 赔偿你的损失

II. Fill in the following blanks with the words given below. Change the form where necessary.

| complain   claim   settle   compensate |

1. No _____ will be considered unless made immediately after the receipt of goods.
2. We are sure that the question in dispute will soon be _____.
3. The purpose of insurance is to provide _____ for those who suffer from loss.
4. After many years' roaming, he finally _____ down in the U.K.
5. The buyers _____ of the delay in shipment.
6. We reserve the right to put in a _____ against you for the shortage should the missing case not be found.
7. He enclosed a cheque in _____ of his account.
8. Our users have _____ to us about the damage of the goods.
9. We reserve the right to _____ compensation from you for any damage.
10. The quality of this Chinese product is _____ to be the best in the market.
11. The insurance company will undertake to _____ you for the losses according to the risks covered.
12. This helps us _____ for the inevitable high initial expenses of establishing a brand.

III. Writing practice.

- A long-time client has written to complain about the bad quality of your last shipment. You have been asked to write a letter to apologize and offer solutions.
- Write the email:
  ◇ Apologizing for the mistake on your side;
  ◇ Offering solutions to the problem;
  ◇ Showing your appreciation of their business;
  ◇ Promising that such problems will not happen again.

Skill Training

Exercise I. You have just received the complaint below. Decide upon an action that will correct the situation and write an adjustment letter to satisfy the customer.

Re: Claim for Our Loss

Dear Tom,

We have received your shipment of 500 electric calculators on our Order No. 453-90.

While appreciating your prompt shipment, we are surprised to find two cases labeled as C/No. 20 and 450 were broken with the result that 40 electric calculators contained were damaged to various degrees. We think the packing is not strong enough to protect the goods and the wooden materials should have been thicker.

We informed an authorized surveyor at once, who examined the goods in the presence of the shipping company's agents, and we are sure the enclosed surveyor's report will prove our view to be right.

Under such circumstances, we shall have to dispose of the damaged calculators at a greatly reduced price below 50% of their invoice cost. Therefore, we suggest you make us an allowance to make up for the loss according, say, $50 for each damaged calculator.

Looking forward to your comments.

Best regards,
Leo

Exercise II. Translate the following letter into Chinese.

A.B. SUB TRADING EST.

Sede legate: 51016 Viale November, 25

Luo egeaaggt delle scitture contalbii:

Tel: 12345678 Fax: 987654

Cateptial sociale interamente versato euro 60,000

N. REA: PA-168714

Date: 9 January, 2010

Inspection certificate

I state that the goods under proforma invoices W0803010, L/C NUMBER 41183196200, latest date of shipment before 31/01/2011 from FUZHOU PORT CHINA TO LEGHORN(LIVORNO) PORT ITALY as follows:

ORD	ART	NAME	CARTONS	PAIRS	AMOUNT
00024	FAIL	FAIL	3000	72000	$48,240.00
00025	FAIL	FAIL	200	4800	$3,264.00
00026	FAIL	FAIL	300	7200	$4,608.00
00027	FAIL	FAIL	300	7200	$4,608.00

are in conformity with the confirmation samples and are packed and labeled as per A.B.S.T orders. A.B.S.T reserves the right to claim any quality problem that cannot be seen before shipment.

A.B. SUB TRADING EST.

Encl.

P.S.

Business Link

Terms & Terminologies

short-weight	短重
short delivery	短交，缺交
short shipment	短装，装载不足
short-calculated	少算
short-delivered	短交，缺交
short-landed	短卸
short-shipped	短装
short-paid	少付
complaint	申诉方
defendant	被诉方
appeal	（解决争端）上诉
short unloaded	短卸
lost in transit	短失
survey report	公证报告
damage report	破损证书
marine protest	海难报告
E.& O.E. (Errors and Omissions Excepted)	
claim assessor	估损人
claim settling agent	理赔代理人
claim survey agent	理赔检验代理人
claim administration	索赔局
claim letter	索赔书
claim document	索赔证件
claim settlement	理赔
claim indemnity	索赔
claim department	索赔委员会

Chapter XII Complaints, Claims and Settlement

Useful Sentences

1. I am writing for a replacement of the dictionary included.
2. Would you please correct your shipment by sending the order No. by the first available vessel?
3. It would be highly appreciated if you could look into the personal computers, which should have reached our destination two weeks ago.
4. We feel it necessary to inform you that your last delivery of our order is not up to the usual standard.
5. Upon inspection, it was found that the total content had been short-delivered by cotons.
6. On comparing the goods received with the sample supplied, we were sorry to notice the great differences in the designs of the machines.
7. After having the boxes examined we found that they were not strong enough for long distance delivery.
8. It is regrettable to see that the chemical content of Item is not up to the percentage contracted.
9. There is a discrepancy in colors between the received materials and the samples.
10. While placing our order we emphasized that any delay in delivery would definitely add to the cost of the goods. That is why we have to raise a claim on refunds for the loss incurred.
11. The inspection report shows a report weight of 12 tons. And upon analysis, excessive moisture was found and that accounted for another 12 tons.
12. Your claim for shortage of weight amounts to US$1,000 in all.
13. We regret to learn that 3 cases out of the 10 shipped against your Order No. 100 arrived in a badly damaged condition. As the goods were packed with the greatest care, we can only presume that the cases have been roughly handled.
14. We thank you for sending us the sample of inferior goods for examination and we have passed it on to the manufacturers for inspection. Evidently, through an oversight some of the wrong goods were dispatched to you.
15. I'm afraid I have to insist that you approach the insurance company for the settlement, that is, if you have included this risk in your coverage.

Module V

Documents

Chapter XIII
Specimen of Documents

Objectives:
After learning this chapter, you will
1. be familiar with the documents;
2. be able to fill in the documents.

1. 发票

发票有多种形式：形式发票、商业发票、领事发票、样本发票、海关发票等。业务中最常用的是商业发票和海关发票。商业发票(Commercial Invoice)是表明所述货物质量、数量、单价、总额的单据。它是作为买卖双方交接货物和结算货款的主要单证，也是进出口报送关税必不可少的单证之一。

2. 汇票（Bill of Exchange; Draft）

在出口贸易中，通常使用的是随附单据的"跟单汇票"。

开具汇票的依据，也就是汇票的"出票条款"（drawn clause）。如属于信用证方式，应按照来证的规定文句填写。如信用证内没有规定具体文句，可在汇票上注明开证行名称、地点、信用证号码及开证日期。例如："凭××银行×××号×年×月×日×不可撤销信用证开立"（Drawn Under××Bank Irrevocable L/C NO.×××DATED××××）。如属于托收方式，汇票上应注明有关买卖合同的号码。

汇票到期日无论用after还是from，一律从第二天起算；而以运输单据日（有装运日记载的依记载，没有记载的依出单日）为依据计算交单日，用from的从当天起算。汇票中以运输单据日为基准日按规定天数计算汇票到期日的，不管用from还是after均从第二天起算。

COMMERCIAL INVOICE

1) SELLER SHANGHAI HERO IMP & EXP CORP. ROOM 4413, 47 JIANG NING RD SHANGHAI, CHINA	3) INVOICE NO. 96RE232	4) INVOICE DATE 5-Jan-97
	5) L/C NO. ELC-TFX-963749	6) DATE 11-Dec-96
	7) ISSUED BY EMIRATES BANK INTERNATIONAL	
2) BUYER AL ABRA HOME APPLIANCES TRADING EST P.O. BOX 21352 DUBAI, UAE	8) CONTRACT NO. 96RE232SC	9) DATE 15-Nov-96
	10) FROM SHANGHAI CHINA	11) TO DUBAI
	12) SHIPPED BY JASCO V34	13) PRICE TERM CFR DUBAI

14) MARKS	15) DESCRIPTION OF GOODS	16) QTY.	17) UNIT PRICE	18) AMOUNT
AL ABRA DUBAI TEL:65266634	PORTABLE TYPEWRITER ART.NO. TP200 ART. NO.TP900 ALL OTHER DETAILS AS PER INDENT NO.SSTE96/429/CN-10 OF SALEM SAUD TRADING EST, DUBAI UAE AND BENEFICIARY'S S/C NO.96GSS-003			CFR DUBAI
	TP200 TP900	1160 SET 1200 SET	US$35.94 US$32.19	US$41,690.40 US$38,628.00
				US$80,318.40

TOTAL AMOUNT IN WORDS: SAY USD EIGHTY THOUSAND THREE HUNDRED AND EIGHTEEN CENTS FORTY ONLY

TOTAL GROSS WEIGHT: 13870 KGS
TOTAL NUMBER OF PACKAGE: 590 CTNS

MANUFACTURER: SHANGHAI HERO CO.LTD ADDRESS: 550 KANGJIAN ROAD SHANGHAI CHINA
HS CODE: 8469.3900
WE CERTY THAT THE ORIGIN OF GOODS AND CONTENTS ARE TRUE AND CORRECT.

Chapter XIII　Specimen of Documents

BILL　OF　EXCHANGE

No. WIR16489

For　US$9,450.00　　　　　　　　　　　　SHANGHAI　　22-Feb-98
　　(amount in figure)　　　　　　　　　　　(place and date of issue)

At　30 DAYS'　　　　　　sight of this　FIRST　Bill of exchange(SECOND being unpaid)

pay to　BANK OF CHINA , SHANGHAI BRANCH　　　　　　　　　or order the sum of

SAY USD NINE THOUSAND FOUR HUNDRED AND FIFTY ONLY
　　　　　　　　　　　　　(amount in words)

Value received for　　　9000　PCS　　　of　SACK ON DISASTER
　　　　　　　　　　　　(quantity)　　　　　　　(name of commodity)

Drawn under　　INDUSTRIAL BANK OF KOREA, SEOUL

L/C No　M0480612SS00064　　　　dated　　18-Dec-97

To:　BOBO TRADING CO., LTD　　　　For and on behalf of
　　　　　　　　　　　　　　　SHANGHAI TECHNOLOGY IMP & EXP CORP. OF
　　　　　　　　　　　　　　　　　SCIENCE & EDUCATION

　　　　　　　　　　　　　　　　　　　　(Signature)

3. 原产地证书（Certificate of Origin）

这是一种证明货物原产地或制造地的证件。不用海关发票或领事发票的国家，通常要求提供产地证明，以便确定对货物应征收的税率。也有的国家要求以产地证来证明货物的来源。在我国，原产地证书可由中国出入境检验检疫局或贸促会签发。

ORIGINAL

1. Exporter (full name and address)	Certificate No.: 98432043
2. Consignee (full name, address, country)	**CERTIFICATE OF ORIGINS OF THE PEOPLE'S REPUBLIC OF CHINA**
3. Means of transport and route FROM: TO: 4. Destination port	5. For certifying authority use only

6. Marks and numbers of packages	7. Description of goods: numbers and kind of packages	8. S.H.S. Code	9. Quantity or weight	10. Number and date of invoices Invoice No.: Invoice Date:

11. Declaration by the exporter: The undersigned hereby declares that the above details and statements are correct; that all the goods were produced in China and that they comply with the Rules of origin of the People's Republic of China Place and date, signature and stamp of certifying authority	12. Certification: It is hereby certified that the declaration by the Exporter is correct. 中国国际贸易促进委员会 上海分会 China Council for the Promotion of International Trade (Shanghai) 19-Apr-98 章关静 SHANGHAI Place and date, signature and stamp of certifying authority

Chapter XIII Specimen of Documents

4. 保险单（Insurance Policy）

保险单是指保险人（即保险公司）与被保险人（即投保者，一般为进出口商）之间订立的保险合同的书面证明。当被保险货物遭受保险合同责任范围以内的损失时，保险单是被保险人向保险人提出索赔，以及保险人理赔的依据。

中 国 人 民 保 险 公 司
THE PEOPLE'S INSURANCE COMPANY OF CHINA
总公司设于北京　　　　一九四九年创立
Head office: BEIJING　　Established in 1949

保 险 单　　　　　　保险单号次
INSURANCE POLICY　　POLICY NO. PC97322214

中 国 人 民 保 险 公 司（以 下 简 称 本 公 司）
THIS POLICY OF INSURANCE WITNESSES THAT THE PEOPLE'S INSURANCE COMPANY OF CHINA(HEREINAFTER CALLED "THE COMPANY")

根　据
AT THE REQUEST OF　TO THE ORDER OF KREDIETBANK (NEDERLAND) N.V. ROTTERDAM
(以 下 简 称 被 保 险 人）的 要 求，由 被 保 险 人 向 本 公 司 缴 付 约
(HEREINAFTER CALLED "THE INSURED") AND IN CONSIDERATION OF THE AGREED PREMIUM PAID TO THE COMPANY BY THE
定 的 保 险，按 照 本 保 险 单 承 保 险 别 和 背 面 所 载 条 款 下 列
INSURED UNDERTAKES TO INSURE THE UNDERMENTIONED GOODS IN TRANSPORTATION SUBJECT TO THE CONDITIONS OF THIS POLICY
特 款 承 保 下 述 货 物 运 输 保 险，特 立 本 保 险 单
AS PER THE CLAUSES PRINTED OVERLEAF AND OTHER SPECIAL CLAUSES ATTACHED HEREON

标　记 MARKS & NOS	包装及数量 QUANTITY	保险货物项目 DESCRIPTION OF GOODS	保险金额 AMOUNT INSURED
As per Invoice No.: 97SL5232	432 CASES	PNEUMATIC RUBBER TIRES	US$249,718.00

总 保 险 金 额：　SAY USD TWO HUNDRED AND FORTY NINE THOUSAND SEVEN HUNDRED AND EIGHTEEN
TOTAL AMOUNT INSURED:　ONLY

保　费　　　　　　　费率　　　　　　　装 载 运 输 工 具
PREMIUM AS ARRANGED　RATE AS ARRANGED　PER CONVEYANCE SS.　FAILL　　V.188

开　航　日　期　　　　　　　　　　　　自　　　　　　　　　至
SLG. ON OR ABT. AS PER BILL OF LADING　　FROM SHANGHAI　　TO ROTTERDAM

承保险别：
CONDITIONS
　　　ALL RISKS AND WAR RISK AS PER CIC 1/1/1981

所 保 货 物，如 遇 出 险，本 公 司 凭 本 保 险 单 及 其 他 有 关 证 件 给 付 赔 款。
CLAIMS, IF ANY, PAYABLE ON SURRENDER OF THIS POLICY TOGETHER WITH OTHER RELEVANT DOCUMENTS
所 保 货 物，如 发 生 本 保 险 单 项 下 负 责 赔 偿 的 损 失 或 事 故，
IN THE EVENT OF ACCIDENT WHEREBY LOSS OR DAMAGE MAY RESULT IN A CLAIM UNDER THIS POLICY IMMEDIATE NOTICE
应 立 即 通 知 本 公 司 下 述 代 理 人 查 勘。
APPLYING FOR SURVEY MUST BE GIVEN TO THE COMPANY'S AGENT AS MENTIONED HEREUNDER:

SERIRES INSURANCE CO., LTD.
330 HANGDER ST. ROTTERDAM TEL:5337642
FAX:5337664

CLAIM PAYABLE AT TOTTERDAM IN THE SAME CURRENCY OF THIS　　中国人民保险公司上海分公司
CREDIT.　　　　　　　　　　　　　　　　　　　　　　　　　　THE PEOPLE'S INSURANCE CO. OF CHINA
赔　款　偿　付　地　点　　　　　　　　　　　　　　　　　　　　SHANGHAI BRANCH
CLAIM PAYABLE AT/IN　ROTTERDAM IN USD
日　期　　　　　　　　　　上海　　　　　　　　　　　　　　　何　静　芝
DATE　　17-Jun-97　　　　SHANGHAI　　　　　　　　　　　　General Manager

地址：中国上海中山东一路23号 TEL:3234305 3217466-44 Telex:33128 PICCS CN.
Address: 23 Zhongshan Dong Yi Lu Shanghai, China. Cable: 42001 Shanghai

5. 报关单（Customs Declaration Form）

出口方必须在装运前对出口货物进行报关，如果货物符合要求，海关官员就签署报关单对货物进行放行。

报关单有不同颜色，如白色报关单按一般贸易缮制，粉红色报关单用于加工贸易。

海关出口货物报关单

预录入编号： 　　　　　　　　　　海关编号：

出口口岸：	备案号：	出口日期：	申报日期：
经营单位：	运输方式：	运输工具名称：	提运单号：
发货单位：	贸易方式：	征免性质：	结汇方式：
许可证号：	运抵国：	指运港：	境内货源地：
批准文号：	成交方式：	运费：	保费：	杂费：
合同协议号：	件数：	包装种类：	毛重（公斤）：	净重（公斤）：
集装箱号：	随附单据：		生产厂家：

标记唛码及备注：

项号　商品编号　商品名称规格型号　数量及单位　最终目的国（地区）单价　总价　币制　征免

税费征收情况

录入员　录入单位 兹声明以上申报无讹并承担法律责任 报关员 单位地址　　　申报单位（签章） 邮编　电话　填制日期	海关审单批注及放行日期（签章）
	审单　　　审价
	征税　　　统计
	查验　　　放行

6. 提单（Bill of Lading）

提单是代表货物所有权的凭证，也是进出口业务中最重要的单据。因此，提单的各项内容（如提单的种类、收货人、货物的名称和件数、目的港、有关收取运费的记载、提单的份数等）一定要与信用证相符；但其中货物的描述只要与信用证的货物描述不抵触，可使用统称。

BILL OF LADING

1) SHIPPER SHANGHAI JIA YI TEXTILE IMP & EXP CO., LTD 50 LIN YUAN ROAD SHANGHAI CHINA	10) B/L NO. MA9722424
2) CONSIGNEE TO THE ORDER OF BURGAN BANK S.A.K. KUWAIT	**COSCO** 中国远洋运输（集团）总公司 **CHINA OCEAN SHIPPING (GROUP) CO.**
3) NOTIFY PARTY ABDULLA ZAMANI SONS CO FOR GEN TRAD & CPMT KUWAIT	

4) PLACE OF RECEIPT	5) OCEAN VESSEL SUSAN MAERSK	
6) VOYAGE NO. V. 23	7) PORT OF LOADING SHANGHAI	*ORIGINAL*
8) PORT OF DISCHARGE KUWAIT	9) PLACE OF DELIVERY	Combined Transport BILL OF LADING

11) MARKS	12) NOS. & KINDS OF PKGS.	13) DESCRIPTION OF GOODS	14) G.W.(kg)	15) MEAS(m3)
ZAMANI HM-97-A-1077 TEL 2427100 KUWAIT-ARABIA	225 CARTONS	GENT'S ARABIAN ROBE	4950.0kg	27.591M3

FREIGHT PAID

THE CARRYING VESSEL IS NOT AN ISRAELI OWNED VESSEL AND IS NOT SCHEDULED TO CALL AT ANY ISRAELI PORT ENROUTE TO ITS DESTINATION AND THE VESSEL IS NOT PROHIBITED TO ENTER ANY ARAB PORT FOR ANY REASON WHATSOEVER IN ACCORDANCE WITH IS BY UNITED ARAB SHIPPING COMPANY'S VESSELS SHIPMENT IS EFFECTED IN CONTAINER.

16) TOTAL NUMBER OF CONTAINERS OR PACKAGES(IN WORDS)	TOTAL TWO HUNDRED AND TWENTY FIVE CARTONS				
FREIGHT & CHARGES	REVENUE TONS	RATE	PER	PREPAID	COLLECT

PREPAID AT	PAYABLE AT	17) PLACE AND DATE OF ISSUE SHANGHAI 10-Nov-97
TOTAL PREPAID	18) NUMBER OF ORIGINAL B(S)L THREE(3)	21)
19) DATE 10-Nov-97	LOADING ON BOARD THE VESSEL 20) BY	

7. 商检证书（Inspection Certificate）

各种检验证书分别用以证明货物的品质、数量、重量和卫生条件等方面的状况。在我国，这类证书一般由国家出入境检验检疫局出具，如合同或信用证无特别规定，也可以根据不同情况，由进出口公司或生产企业出具。但应注意证书的名称及所列项目或检验结果，应与合同及信用证规定相同。出证日期迟于提单日期的商检证书无效。

出口商品检验申请单

报验日期： 报验号：
报验单位（盖章）： 联系人：
单位地址： 托收协议号： 电　话：

发货人	（中文）		装运日期	（约）　月　日
	（译文）		装运口岸	
受货人			包装情况	
商品名称 规　　格	（中文）		报验数量	
	（译文）		报验重量	毛
				净
HS编码		商品出口总值	US$	
预约工作日		商品收购总值	RMB	输往国别或地区
货物存放地		检验依据		
卫生注册/质量许可证号		合同　（　）		
合同、信用证对商检条款的特殊要求（详细填写）	报验人提供附件划√	发票　（　）		
		信用证（　）		
		磅码单（　）	标记及号码	
		厂验单（　）		
		商检预检结果单（　）		
		商检换证凭单　（　）		
		出口货物报关单（　）		
		出口货物合格单（　）		

续表

需商检证单	质量证	数量证	重量证	兽医证	卫生证	健康证	消毒证	换证凭单	纺织品标识单	放行

备注			检验费		

以下内容由商检局填写

检验方式（打√或补填）	商检自检（ ）	认可单位检验（ ）	口岸换证或放行（ ）	
商检施验项目（打√）	品质/规格（ ）	数量/重量（ ）	安全/卫生（ ）	包装（ ）

项目	经办人	月	日	时	项目	经办人	月	日	时	项目	经办人	月	日	时
受理报验					拟制证稿					制证				
检验处收单					复核					校对				
取样					检验处发单					发证				
检验					检务处收单					计费				

报验日期　年　月　日　　**领取出口商品检验证单凭条**　　报验号

报验单位		需商检证单	质量证	数量证	重量证	兽医证	卫生证	健康证	消毒证	放行证	换证单	标识单
品名及数量												

注意：1. 报验人凭此条领取出口商品检验证单。2. 申请人有责任与本局发证部门联系，及时领取证书。

8. 装箱单和重量单（Packing List and Weight Memo）

这两种单据是对商业发票的补充，便于国外买方在货物到达目的港时，供海关检查和进口商核对货物。装箱单又称码单，被出口企业用来说明商品包装的内在详细情况；重量单则列明每件货物的毛重、净重。

PACKING LIST

1) SELLER SHANGHAI HERO IMP & EXP CORP. ROOM 4413, 47 JIANG NING RD SHANGHAI, CHINA	3) INVOICE NO. 96RE232	4) INVOICE DATE 5-Jan-97
	5) FROM SHANGHAI CHINA	6) TO DUBAI
	7) TOTAL PACKAGES(IN WORDS) SAY FIVE HUNDRED AND NINETY CARTONS ONLY	

2) BUYER
AL ABRA HOME APPLIANCES TRADING EST
P.O. BOX 21352 DUBAI, UAE
	8) MARKS & NOS.
	  AL ABRA
	  DUBAI
	TEL:65266634	

9) C/NOS.	10) NOS. & KINDS OF PKGS.	11) ITEM	12) QTY.	13) G.W.	14) N.W.	15) MEAS(m3)
	PORTABLE TYPEWRITER ART.NO. TP200 ART. NO.TP900 ALL OTHER DETAILS AS PER INDENT NO.SSTE96/429/CN-10 OF SALEM SAUD TRADING EST, DUBAI UAE AND BENEFICIARY'S S/C NO.96GSS-003					
1-290	290 CTNS	TP200	1160 SET	6670.0kg	6090.0kg	27.840M3
291-590	300 CTNS	TP900	1200 SET	7200.0kg	6600.0kg	28.800M3
		TOTAL:	2360 Units	13870.0kg	12690.0kg	56.640M3

Skill Training

下列为2009国际商务单证操作题。

一、根据已知资料指出下列单据中错误的地方。

已知资料（一）：

SALES CONTRACT

Contract No.: NJT090218
Date: FEB. 18, 2009
Signed at: Nanjing, China

The Seller: NANJING JINLING TEXTILE CO., LTD.
Address: UNIT A 18/F，JINLING TOWER，NO. 118 JINLING ROAD, NANJING, CHINA
The Buyer: DEXICA SUPERMART S.A.
Address: BOULEVARD PACHECO 44, B-1000 BRUSSELS, BELGIUM

This Sales Contract is made by and between the Sellers and the Buyers, whereby the sellers agree to sell and buyers agree to buy the under-mentioned goods according to the terms and conditions stipulated below:

Commodity and specifications	Quantity	Unit Price	Amount
GIRLS GARMENTS	10800PCS	CIF BRUSSELS EUR5.00/PC	EUR54000.00

10% more or less in quantity and amount are acceptable.
Packing: IN CARTON   Shipping Mark: N/M
Time of Shipment: Within 30 days after receipt of L/C.
From NINGBO PORT CHINA to BRUSSELS, BELGIUM
Transshipment and Partial Shipment: Allowed.
Insurance: to be effected by the Seller for 110% of full invoice value covering all risks up to port of destination and war risks included with claim payable at destination.
Terms of Payment: By 100% Irrevocable Letter of Credit in favor of the Sellers to be available by sight draft to be opened and to reach China before APRIL 1, 2009 and to remain valid for negotiation in China until the 21 days after the foresaid Time of Shipment.

L/C must mention this contract number L/C advised by BANK OF CHINA JIANGSU BRANCH. All banking Charges outside China are for account of the Buyer.

The Seller	The Buyer
NANJING JINLING TEXTILE CO., LTD.	DEXICA SUPERMART S.A.
钟山	ALICE

已知资料（二）：

1. 装运信息：指定APL承运，装期2009-04-19；船名PRINCESS；航次V.018
2. 装箱资料：合计108箱，装入1×20'集装箱。
3. 商业发票号：NJT090218-09，签发日期2009年4月10日。
4. 信用证号：CMKK9180205

（1）一般原产地证（12分）

1. Exporter (full name address and country) DEXICA SUPERMART S.A. BOULEVARD PACHECO 44 B-1000 BRUSSELS, BELGIUM		Certificate No. CCPIT 091810528		
2. Consignee (full name, address and country) NANJING JINLING TEXTILE CO., LTD. UNIT A 18/F, JINLING TOWER, NO.118 JINLING ROAD, NANJING, CHINA		CERTIFICATE OF ORIGIN OF THE PEOPLE'S REPUBLIC OF CHINA		
3. Means of transport and route FROM NANJING PORT, CHINA TO BRUSSELS, BELGIUM BY AIR		5. For certifying authority use only		
4. Country/region of destination CHINA				
6. Marks and Numbers DEXICA S/C NJT090218	7. Number and kind of packages; description of goods LADIES GARMENTS PACKED IN (108) TWO HUNDRED AND EIGHT CARTONS ONLY. *****************************	8. H.S. code 6204430090	9. Quantity 10080 DOZEN	10. Number and date of invoices NJT090218 APR.9, 2009
11. Declaration by the exporter The undersigned hereby declares that the above details and statements are correct; that all the goods were produced in China and that they comply with the rules of origin of the People's Republic of China NANJING JINLING TEXTILE CO., LTD. ZHONG SHAN （出口商 申请章） NANJING APR.15, 2009 .... Place and date, signature and stamp of certifying authority		12. Certification It is hereby certified that the declaration by the exporter is correct. CHINA COUNCIL FOR THE PROMOTION OF INTERNATIONAL TRADE JIN LIAN CHENG （CCPIT 签证章） NANJING CHINA APR.16, 2009 .... Place and date, signature and stamp of certifying authority		

（2）保险单（12分）

货物运输保险单
CARGO TRANSPORTATION INSURANCE POLICY

发票号（INVOICE NO.） NJT090218-09　　　　保单号次　PYIE2006080
合同号（CONTRACT NO.） NJT090218　　　　POLICY NO.
信用证号（L/C NO.）：CCPIT 091810528
被保险人：Insured: NANJING JINLING TEXTILE LTD.

中国人民保险公司（以下简称"本公司"）根据被保险人的要求，由被保险人向本公司缴付约定的保险费，按照本保险单承保险别和背面所载条款与下列特款承保下述货物运输保险，特立本保险单。

THIS POLICY OF INSURANCE WITNESSES THAT THE PEOPLE'S INSURANCE COMPANY OF CHINA (HEREINAFTER CALLED "THE COMPANY") AT THE REQUEST OF THE INSURED AND IN CONSIDERATION OF THE AGREED PREMIUM PAID TO THE COMPANY BY THE INSURED, UNDERTAKES TO NISURE THE UNDERMENTIONED GOODS IN TRANSPORTATION SUBJECT TO THE CONDITIONS OF THIS POLICY AS PER THE CLAUSES PRINTED OVERLEAF AND OTHER SPECIL CLAUSES ATTACHED HEREON.

标记 MARKS&NOS	包装及数量 QUANTITY	保险货物项目 DESCRIPTION OF GOODS	保险金额 AMOUNT INSURED
DEXICA S/C NJT090218	10 800 DOZEN	LADIES GARMENTS	USD 54 000.00

总保险金额 TOTAL AMOUNT INSURED: <u>US DOLLARS FIFTY FOUR THOUSANDS ONLY</u>

保费　　　　　　　　启运日期　　　　　　　　　装载运输工具
<u>AS ARRANGED</u>　DATE OF COMMENCEMENT:　APR 09, 2009　PER CONVEYANCE: PRINCESS V.018
　　自　　　　　　　经　　　　　　　至
FROM: <u>NANJING PORT CHINA</u>　　VIA　——　　TO <u>BRUSSELS，BELGIUM</u>
　　承保险别：CONDITIONS: Covering F.P. A up to PORT OF DESTINATION.

所保货物，如发生保险单项下可能引起索赔的损失或损坏，应立即通知本公司下述代理人查勘。如有索赔，应向本公司提交保单正本（本保险单共有__3__份正本）及有关文件。如一份正本已用于索赔，其余正本自动失效。

IN THE EVENT OF LOSS OR DAMAGE WHICH MAY RESULT IN A CLAIM UNDER THIS POLICY, IMMEDIATE NOTICE MUST BE GIVEN TO THE COMPANY'S AGENT AS MENTIONED HEREUNDER. CLAIMS, IF ANY, ONE OF THE ORIGINAL POLICY WHICH HAS BEEN ISSUED IN__3__ORIGINAL (S) TOGETHER WITH THE RELEVENT DOCUMENTS SHALL BE SURRENDERED TO THE COMPANY. IF ONE OF THE ORIGINAL POLICY HAS BEEN ACCOMPLISHED. THE OTHERS TO BE VOID.

中国人民保险公司广州市分公司
THE PEOPLE'S INSURANCE COMPANY OF CHINA JIANGSU BRANCH

赔款偿付地点
CLAIM PAYABLE AT __Nanjing, CHINA__

出单日期 ISSUING DATE __APR.20,2009__

王天华
Authorized Signature

二、请根据银行来证及货物明细，缮制出口单据。（每小题8分，共40分）

  1. 货物明细   商品名称：Trolley Cases

货号	TS503214	TS503215	TS503216
产地		Dalian China	
商标		TAISHAN	
包装		1 pc in 1 PE bag: 3pcs/CTN	
箱子尺寸	53.5×37×79.5 cm 0.157 3 cbm	53.5×34.5×82 cm 0.151 cbm	48×32.5×78.5 cm 0.122 5 cbm
箱子尺寸（总）	57.886 4 cbm	57.833 cbm	58.8 cbm
净重/毛重（个）	4 KG/4.6 KG	3.5 KG/4 KG	3 KG/3.5 KG
净重/毛重（总）	4 416 KG/5 078.4 KG	4 021.5 KG/4 596 KG	4 320 KG/5 040 KG
数量	1 104 PCS	1 149 PCS	1 440 PCS
单价	USD6.50	USD6.00	USD5.80
金额	USD7 176	USD6 894	USD8 352
集装箱容量	Qty/40'FCL: 368 ctns	Qty/40'FCL:383 ctns	Qty/40'FCL: 480 ctns

    发票号码：TS10801005   发票日期：2008-8-5   授权签字人：张平

    装运船名：DONGFENG   航次：V.369   装船日期：2008-8-23

    运输标准：ORTAI
               TS10601005
               NEW YORK
               C/NO. 1-1231

    原产地标准："P"

2. 信用证相关内容

27: Sequence of Total: 1/1

40A: Form of Documentary Credit: IRREVOCABLE

20: Documentary Credit Number: N5632405TH11808

31C: Date of Issue: 080715

31D: Date and Place of Expiry: 080909 CHINA

51D: Applicant Bank: CITY NATIONAL BANK

133 MORNINGSIDE AVE NEW YORK, NY 10027 Tel:001-212-865-4763

50: Applicant: ORTAI CO., LTD.

    30 EAST 40th STREET, NEW YORK, NY 10016

    TEL: 001-212-992-9788 FAX: 001-212-992-9789

59: Beneficiary: DALIAN TAISHAN SUITCASE & BAG CO., LTD.

66 ZHONGSHAN ROAD DALIAN 116001, CHINA TEL: 0086-0411-84524789

32B: Currency Code Amount: USD 22 422.00

41D: Available With/By: ANY BANK IN CHINA BY NEGOTIATION

42C: Drafts at: SIGHT

42D: Drawee: ISSUING BANK

43P: Partial Shipments: NOT ALLOWED

43T: Transhipment: NOT ALLOWED

44E: Port Of Loading: DALIAN, CHINA

44F: Port Of Discharge: NEW YORK, U.S.A

44C: Latest Date of Shipment: 080825

45A: Description of Goods and/or Services:

  CIF NEWYORK TROLLEY CASES AS PER SC NO. TSSC0801005

46A: Documents Required

  +MANUALLY SIGNED COMMERCIAL INVOICE IN 2 COPYES INDICATING L/C NO. AND CONTRACT NO. CERTIFYING THE CONTENTS IN THIS INVOICE ARE TRUE AND CORRECT.

  +FULL SET OF ORIGINAL CLEAN ON BOARD MARINE BILLS OF LADING MADE OUT TO ORDER, ENDORSED IN BANK MARKED FREIGHT PREPAID AND NOYIFY APLICANT

  +PACKING LIST IN 2 COPYES ISSUED BY THE BENEFICIARY

  +ORIGINAL GSP FORM A CERTIFICATE OF ORIGN ON OFFICIAL FORM ISSUED BY A TRADE AUTHORITY OR GOVERNMENT BODY

  +INSURANCE POLICIES OR CERTIFICATES IN DUPLICATE, ENDORSED IN BANK FOR 110 PERCENT OF INVOICE VALUE COVERING ICC CLAUSES(A).

  +MANUFACTURER'S QUALITY CERTIFICATE CERTIFYING THE COMMODITY IS IN GOOD ORDER.

+BENEFICIARY'S CERTIFICATE CERTIFYING THAT ONE SET OF COPIES OF SHIPPING DOCUMENTS HAS BEEN SENT TO APPLICANT WITHIN 5 DAYS AFTER SHIPMENT.

47A: Additional Conditions

+UNLESS OTHERWISE EXPRESSLY STATED, ALL DOCUMENTS MUST BE IN ENGLISH.

+ANY PROCEEDS OF PRESENTATIONS UNDER THIS DC WILL BE SETTLED BY TELETRANSMISSION AND A CHARGE OF USD50.00 (OR CURRENCY EQUIVALENT) WILL BE DEDUCTED.

49: Confirmation Instructions: WITHOUT

57D: Advise Through Bank: BANK OF CHINA DALIAN BRANCH

72: Sender to Receiver Information:

DOCUMENTS TO BE DESPATCHED BY COURIER SERVICE IN ONE LOT TO CITY NATIONAL BANK

3. 制单

（1）质量证明（8分）

DALIAN TAISHAN SUITCASE & BAG CO., LTD.

66 ZHONGSHAN ROAD DALIAN 116001, CHINA

TEL: 0086-0411-84524789

（2）商业发票（8分）

Issuer	商业发票 COMMERCIAL INVOICE	
TO	Invoice No.	Date
Transport Details	S/C NO.	L/C NO.

Marks and Numbers	Description of Goods	Quantity	Unit Price	Amount

TOTAL VALUE IN WORDS:

（3）装箱单（8分）

Issuer			装箱单 PACKING LIST		
TO			Invoice No.		Date
			S/C NO.		L/C NO.
Marks and Numbers	C/NOS.	Number and Kind of Packages; Description of Goods	Quantity	G. W. (KGS)	N. W. (KGS)	MEAS. (CBM)
Total						

TOTAL PACKAGES IN WORDS:

（4）普惠制产地证（8分）

1. Goods consigned from (Exporter's full name and address, country)	Reference No. T200510819 GENERALIZED SYSTEM OF PREFERENCES CERTIFICATE OF ORIGIN (Combined declaration and certificate) FORM A Issued in _____ (Country) See Notes Overleaf				
2. Goods consigned to (Consignee's full name, address, country)					
3. Means of transport and route (as far as known)	4. For certifying authority use only				
5. Item number	6. Marks and numbers of packages	7. Number and kind of packages; Description of goods	8. Origin criterion (see notes overleaf)	9. Gross weight or other quantity	10. Number and date of invoices
11. Certification It is hereby certified that the declaration by the exporter is correct. **CIQ** -- Place and date, signature and stamp of certifying authority	12. Declaration by the exporter The undersigned hereby declares that the above details and statements are correct, that all the goods were produced in _____ and that they comply with the origin requirements specified for those goods in the Generalized System of Preferences for goods exported to _____ (importing country) -- Place and date, signature and stamp of authorized signatory				

(5) 受益人证明（8分）

DALIAN TAISHAN SUITCASE & BAG CO., LTD.
66 ZHONGSHAN ROAD DALIAN 116001, CHINA
TEL:0086-0411-84524789

Appendix I
国际机构

ABAC, APEC Business Advisory Council APEC 工商咨询理事会

ADB, Asian Development Bank 亚洲开发银行

APEC, Asia-Pacific Economic Cooperation 亚太经济合作组织

ASEAN, Association of South-East Asian Nations 东南亚国家联盟

BIS, Bank for International Settlements 国际清算银行

ETSI, European Telecommunications Standards Institute 欧洲电信标准协会

EU, European Union 欧盟

FAO, Food and Agriculture Organization of the United Nations 联合国粮食及农业组织

ICC, International Chamber of Commerce 国际商会

ILO, International Labour Organization 国际劳工组织

IMF, International Monetary Fund 国际货币基金组织

ISO, International Organization for Standardization 国际标准化组织

ITCB, International Textiles and Clothing Bureau 国际纺织品与服装局

JCCT, China-US Joint Commission on Commerce and Trade 中美商贸联合委员会

NAFTA, North American Free Trade Area 北美自由贸易区

OECD, Organization for Economic Cooperation and Development 经济合作与发展组织

UNCTAD, United Nations Conference on Trade and Development 联合国贸易和发展会议

WCO, World Customs Organization 世界海关组织

WIPO, World Intellectual Property Organization 世界知识产权组织

WTO, World Trade Organization 世界贸易组织

Chinese Association for International Understanding 中国国际交流协会

China International Economic Consultants 国际经济咨询有限公司

China Import & Export Fair 中国进出口商品交易会，即广交会

CCPIT, China Council for the Promotion of International Trade 中国国际贸易促进委员会

Appendix II
海外展会

2006 年国际展会列表

国际展会名称	时间	地点
2006 年美国奥兰多国际建筑行业展览会 The International Builders' Show	2006.01.11-14	美国 奥兰多
2006 年美国奥兰多国际石材展 Coverings	2006.04.04-07	
2006 年加州国际礼品展 California Gift Show	2006.07.28-31	美国 洛杉矶
2006 年美国国际消费电子展 CES	2006.01.05-08	美国 拉斯维加斯
2006 年拉斯维加斯世界鞋业协会展 The World Shoe Association Show	2006.02.10-13	
2006 年春季拉斯维加国际服装展览会 MAGIC Show	2006.02.21-24	
2006 年国际安全防护用品展 ISC West	2006.04.05-07	
2006 年美国国际五金展 National Hardware Show	2006.05.09-11	
2006 年拉斯维加斯国际家具展 Las Vegas Market	2006.07.25-28	
2006 年美国拉斯维加斯贸易展览会 ASD/AMD	2006.08.13-17	
2006 年秋季拉斯维加斯国际服装展览会 MAGIC Show	2006.08.28-31	
2006 年美国拉斯维加斯汽配展 AAPEX	2006.10.31-11.03	
2006 年纽约国际文具博览会 National Stationery Show	2006.05.21-05.24	美国 纽约
2006 国际酒店餐饮博览会 The International Hotel/Motel and Restaurant Show	2006.12.12-14	
2006 年芝加哥国际家居和家庭用品展 International Home & Housewares Show	2006.03.12-14	美国 芝加哥
2006 年国际塑料展览会 The Plastics Exposition and Conference NPE	2006.06.12-14	
2006 年国际制造技术博览会 International Manufacturing Technology Show (IMTS)	2006.09.06-13	
2006 年意大利米兰马契夫春季博览会 MACEF-Gifts and Houseware Fair	2006.01	意大利 米兰
2006 年意大利博洛尼亚国际建筑展览会 SAIE-International Building Trade Fair	2006.10	意大利 博洛尼亚
2006 年春季德国杜塞尔多夫国际服装展 CPD Woman_Man	2006.01.08-10	德国 杜塞尔多夫
2006 年德国杜塞尔多夫鞋展 GDS	2006.09	

续表

国际展会名称	时间	地点
2006年德国法兰克福国际礼品及办公用品博览会 Paperworld	2006.01.25-29	德国 法兰克福
2006春季法兰克福国际家用纺织品展 Heimtextil	2006.01.11-14	
2006年春季德国法兰克福国际消费品博览会 Ambiente	2006.02.10-14	
2006阿赫玛美洲展（国际化学工程、环境保护和生物技术展览暨会议）ACHEMA	2006.05.15-19	
2006年秋季德国法兰克福国际消费品博览会 Tendence	2006.09	
2006年德国汉诺威国际信息及通信技术博览会 Cebit	2006.03.09-15	德国 汉诺威
2006年科隆家具展 IMM Cologne	2006.01.16-22	德国 科隆
2006年科隆国际五金展 Practical World	2006.03.05-08	
2006年德国慕尼黑夏季国际体育用品及运动时装贸易博览会 Ispo summer	2006.07.16-18	德国 慕尼黑
2006年德国慕尼黑国际电子展 Electronica	2006.11.14-17	
2006年德国纽伦堡国际玩具博览会 Spielwarenmesse	2006.02.02-07	德国 纽伦堡
2006年法国国际食品和饮料展 Sial	2006.10.22-26	法国 巴黎
2006年春季广交会 China Export Commodities Fair	2006.04.15-30	中国 广州
2006年秋季广交会 China Export Commodities Fair	2006.10.15-30	
Taitronics-Taipei International Electronics Autumn Show 台北秋季国际电子展	2006.10.09-13	中国 台北
2006年香港礼品工艺展 Hong Kong Gifts & Premium Fair	2006.04.28-05.01	中国 香港
2006年香港国际玩具礼品展 Hong Kong International Toys & Gifts Show	2006.10	
2006年香港秋季亚太区皮革展时装产品展 APLF-Fashion Access	2006.10.04-06	
2006年西班牙国际食品展 Alimentaria	2006.03.06-10	西班牙 巴塞罗那

Appendix III
世界各大船公司名录

1. AMERICAN PRESIDENT LINES CO., LTD.：简写 APL，中文名"美国总统轮船有限公司"，中文简称"美国总统"，美国船公司。
2. CHINA SHIPPING CONTAINER LINES CO., LTD.：简写 CSCL，中文名"中海集装箱运输股份有限公司"，中文简称"中海集运"，中国船公司。
3. CMA CGM SHIPPING CO., LTD.：简写 CMA，中文名"达飞轮船有限公司"，中文简称"达飞"，法国船公司。
4. COSCO LOGISTICS CO., LTD.：简写 COSCO，中文名"中国远洋物流有限公司"，中文简称"中远"，中国船公司。
5. EVERGREEN MARINE CORPORATION：简写 EMC，中文名"长荣海运股份有限公司"，中文简称"长荣"，中国台湾船公司。
6. HANJIN SHIPPING：简写 HANJIN，中文名"韩进海运"，中文简称"韩进"，韩国船公司。
7. MAERSK SHIPPING CO., LTD.：简写 MAERSK，中文名"马士基航运有限公司"，中文简称"马士基"，丹麦船公司。
8. MEDITERRANEAN SHIPPING COMPANY：简写MSC，中文名"地中海航运公司"，瑞士船公司。
9. NIPPON YUSEN KAISHA LINE CO., LTD.：简写 NYK，中文名"日本邮船有限公司"，中文简称"日本邮船"，日本船公司。
10. ORIENT OVERSEAS CONTAINER LINE：简写 OOCL，中文名"东方海外货柜航运公司"，简称"东方海外"，中国香港船公司。
11. SINOTRANS LIMITED：简写 SINOTRANS，中文名"中国外运股份有限公司"，中文简称"中国外运"，中国船公司。

参考书目

董晓波主编:《国际贸易英语函电》,北京:清华大学出版社,2010年。
冯祥春、隋思忠主编:《外经贸函电核心英语》,北京:中国商务出版社,2005年。
傅龙海主编:《国际贸易实务》,北京:对外经济贸易大学出版社,2009年。
黄宪西、闫兴伯主编:《商务英语函电》,北京:高等教育出版社,2002年。
梁金水:《外贸英语函电实战》,北京:中国海关出版社,2010年。
全国国际商务专业人员职业资格考试用书编委会编:《国际商务英语》,北京:中国商务出版社,2007年。
王乃彦主编:《对外经贸英语函电(教学与自学参考书)》,北京:对外经济贸易大学出版社,2002年。
吴宝康主编:《国际商务英语信函及写作》,上海:复旦大学出版社,2010年。
谢金领、徐以敬主编:《新编国际商务英语函电》,太原:山西经济出版社,1999年。
徐美荣主编:《外贸英语函电(第二版)》,北京:对外经济贸易大学出版社,2007年。
尹小莹、杨润辉编著:《外贸英语函电——商务英语应用文写作(第4版)(学生用书)》,西安:西安交通大学出版社,2008年。
中国国际贸易学会商务专业培训考试办公室编:《外贸跟单理论与实务(2011年版)》,北京:中国商务出版社,2011年。
中国国际贸易学会商务专业培训考试办公室编:《外贸业务员英语(2008年版)》,北京:中国商务出版社,2008年。
周树玲主编:《外贸跟单英语》,北京:对外经济贸易大学出版社,2008年。
诸葛霖、王燕希编著:《外贸英文书信(第三版)》,北京:对外经济贸易大学出版社,2007年。

国际商务英语函电（第四版）

尊敬的老师：

您好！

为了方便您更好地使用本教材，获得最佳教学效果，我们特向使用该书作为教材的教师赠送本教材配套电子资料。如有需要，请完整填写"教师联系表"并加盖所在单位系（院）公章，免费向出版社索取。

北京大学出版社

教 师 联 系 表

教材名称	国际商务英语函电（第四版）		
姓名：	性别：	职务：	职称：
E-mail：	联系电话：	邮政编码：	
供职学校：		所在院系：	（章）
学校地址：			
教学科目与年级：		班级人数：	
通信地址：			

填写完毕后，请将此表邮寄给我们，我们将为您免费寄送本教材配套资料，谢谢！

北京市海淀区成府路205号
北京大学出版社外语编辑部　初艳红　　　外语编辑部电话：010-62759634
邮政编码：100871　　　　　　　　　　　　邮　购　部　电　话：010-62752015
电子邮箱：alicechu2008@126.com　　　　市场营销部电话：010-62750672